# MANIFEST DESTINY

CHRIS DINGESS ⟶ WRITER

MATTHEW ROBERTS ⟶ PENCILLER
& INKER PAGES 23-32

TONY AKINS ⟶ INKER

OWEN GIENI ⟶ COLORIST

PAT BROSSEAU ⟶ LETTERER

ARIELLE BASICH ⟶ ASSISTANT EDITOR

SEAN MACKIEWICZ ⟶ EDITOR

**MATTHEW ROBERTS & OWEN GIENI**
COVER ART

**IMAGE COMICS, INC.**
Robert Kirkman – Chief Operating Officer
Erik Larsen – Chief Financial Officer
Todd McFarlane – President
Marc Silvestri – Chief Executive Officer
Jim Valentino – Vice President

Eric Stephenson – Publisher
Corey Murphy – Director of Sales
Jeff Boison – Director of Publishing Planning & Book Trade Sales
Chris Ross – Director of Digital Sales
Jeff Stang – Director of Specialty Sales
Kat Salazar – Director of PR & Marketing
Branwyn Bigglestone – Controller
Kall Dugan – Senior Accounting Manager
Sue Korpela – Accounting & HR Manager
Drew Gill – Art Director
Heather Doornink – Production Director
Leigh Thomas – Print Manager
Tricia Ramos – Traffic Manager
Briah Skelly – Publicist
Aly Hoffman – Events & Conventions Coordinator
Sasha Head – Sales & Marketing Production Designer
David Brothers – Branding Manager
Melissa Gifford – Content Manager
Drew Fitzgerald – Publicity Assistant
Vincent Kukua – Production Artist
Erika Schnatz – Production Artist
Ryan Brewer – Production Artist
Shanna Matuszak – Production Artist
Carey Hall – Production Artist
Esther Kim – Direct Market Sales Representative
Emilio Bautista – Digital Sales Representative
Leanna Caunter – Accounting Analyst
Chloe Ramos-Peterson – Library Market Sales Representative
Marla Eizik – Administrative Assistant
IMAGECOMICS.COM

For SKYBOUND ENTERTAINMENT

Robert Kirkman – Chairman
David Alpert – CEO
Sean Mackiewicz – SVP, Editor-in-Chief
Shawn Kirkham – SVP, Business Development
Brian Huntington – Online Editorial Director
June Alian – Publicity Director
Andres Juarez – Art Director
Jon Moisan – Editor
Arielle Basich – Assistant Editor
Carina Taylor – Production Artist
Paul Shin – Business Development Assistant
Johnny O'Dell – Online Editorial Assistant
Sally Jacka – Online Editorial Assistant
Dan Petersen – Director of Operations & Events
Nick Palmer – Operations Coordinator

International Inquiries: ap@sequentialrights.com
Licensing Inquiries: contact@skybound.com

www.skybound.com

 MANIFEST DESTINY
CREATED BY
CHRIS DINGESS

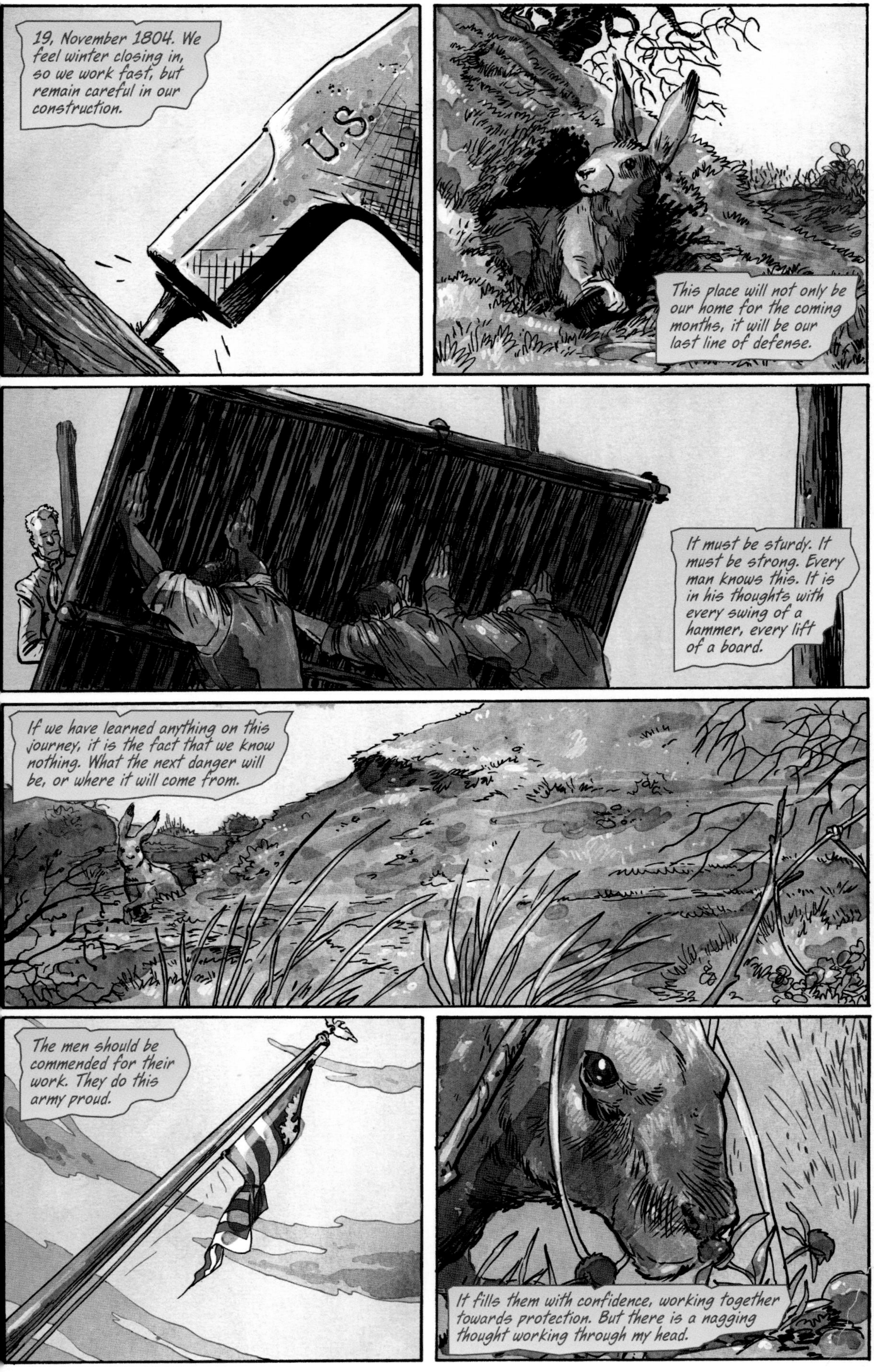
19, November 1804. We feel winter closing in, so we work fast, but remain careful in our construction.
U.S.
This place will not only be our home for the coming months, it will be our last line of defense.
It must be sturdy. It must be strong. Every man knows this. It is in his thoughts with every swing of a hammer, every lift of a board.
If we have learned anything on this journey, it is the fact that we know nothing. What the next danger will be, or where it will come from.
The men should be commended for their work. They do this army proud.
It fills them with confidence, working together towards protection. But there is a nagging thought working through my head.

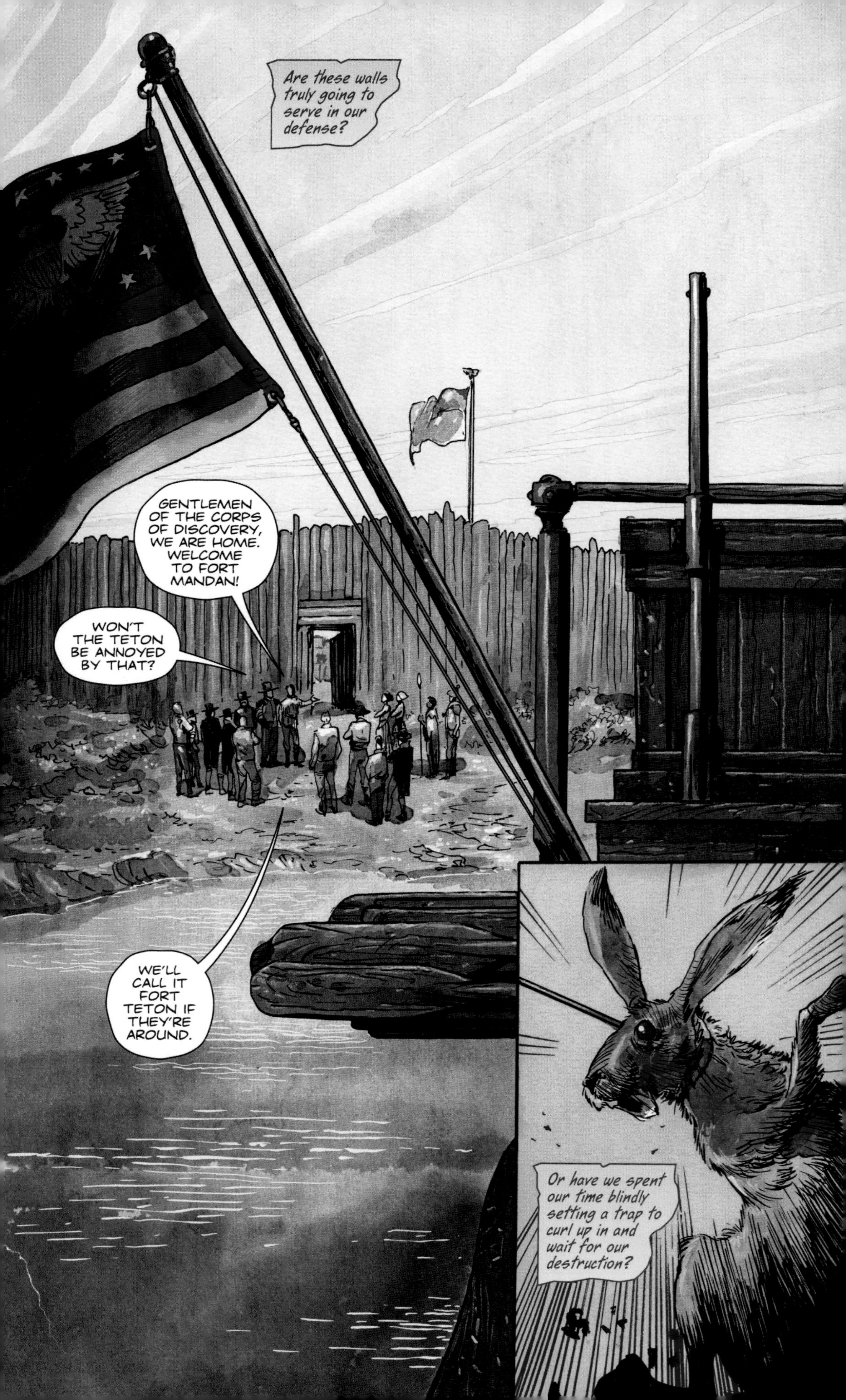
Are these walls truly going to serve in our defense?
GENTLEMEN OF THE CORPS OF DISCOVERY, WE ARE HOME. WELCOME TO FORT MANDAN!
WON'T THE TETON BE ANNOYED BY THAT?
WE'LL CALL IT FORT TETON IF THEY'RE AROUND.
Or have we spent our time blindly setting a trap to curl up in and wait for our destruction?

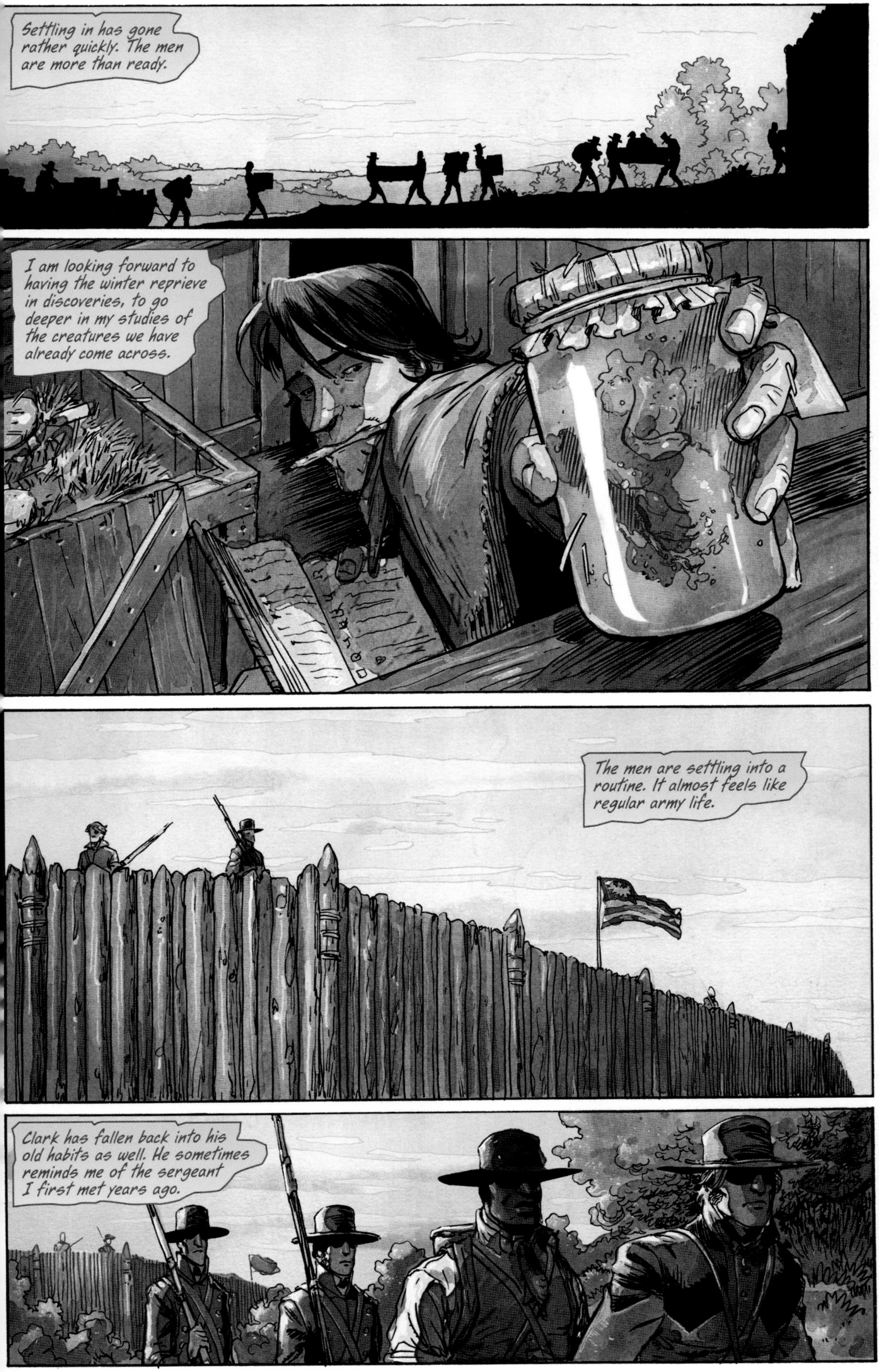
Settling in has gone rather quickly. The men are more than ready.
I am looking forward to having the winter reprieve in discoveries, to go deeper in my studies of the creatures we have already come across.
The men are settling into a routine. It almost feels like regular army life.
Clark has fallen back into his old habits as well. He sometimes reminds me of the sergeant I first met years ago.

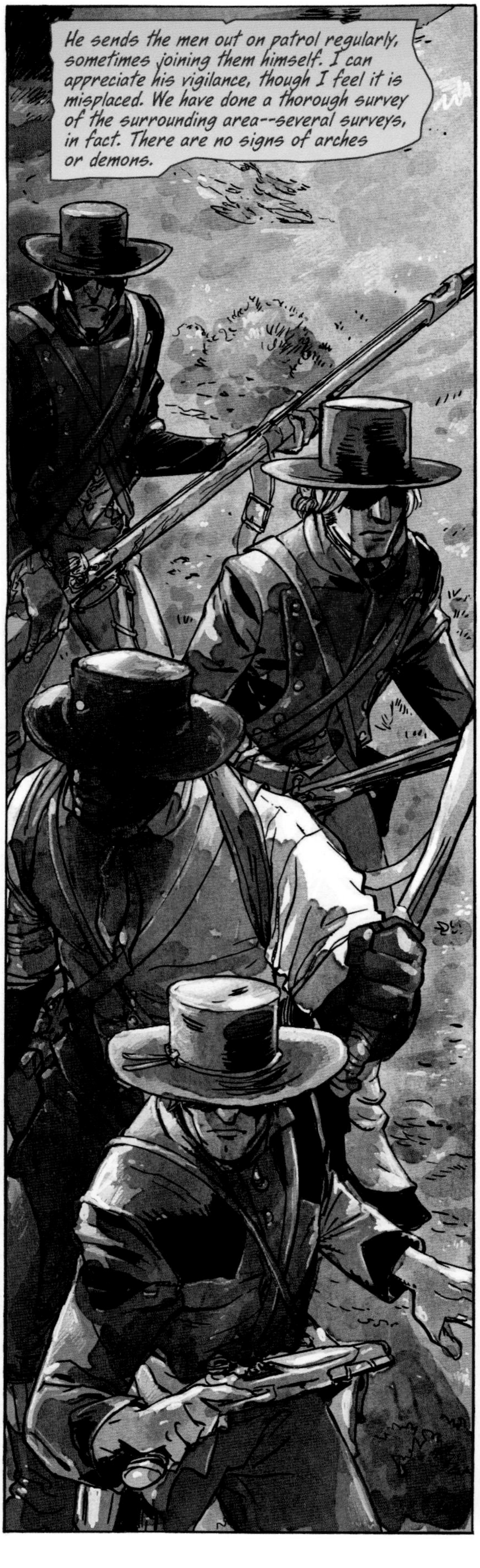
He sends the men out on patrol regularly, sometimes joining them himself. I can appreciate his vigilance, though I feel it is misplaced. We have done a thorough survey of the surrounding area--several surveys, in fact. There are no signs of arches or demons.

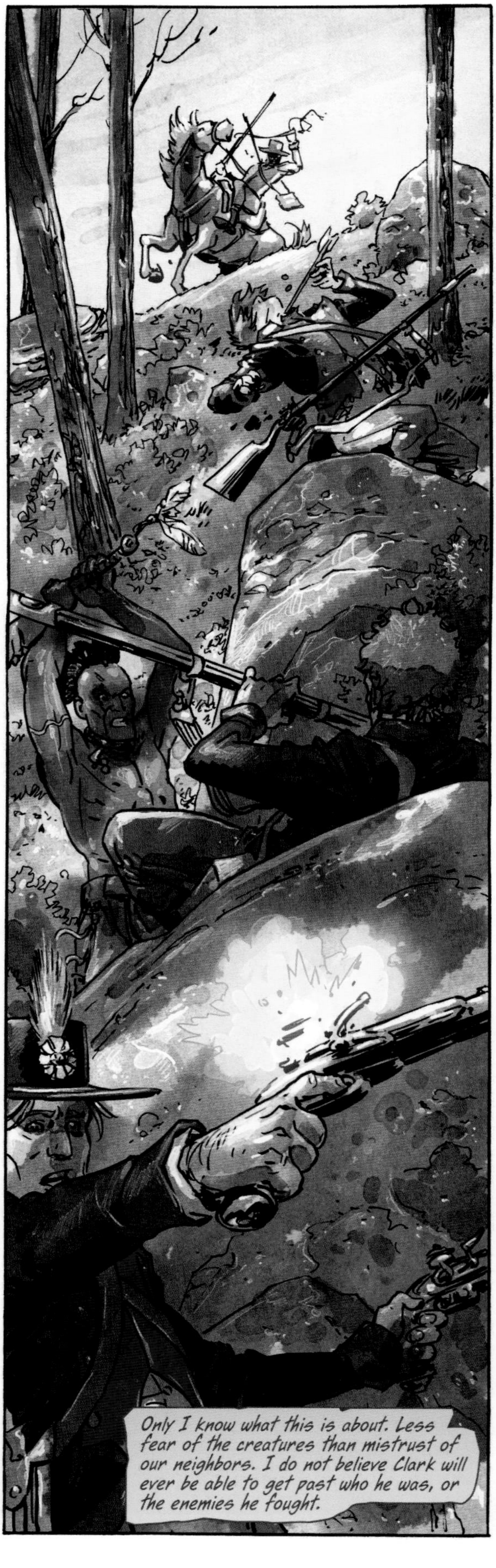
Only I know what this is about. Less fear of the creatures than mistrust of our neighbors. I do not believe Clark will ever be able to get past who he was, or the enemies he fought.

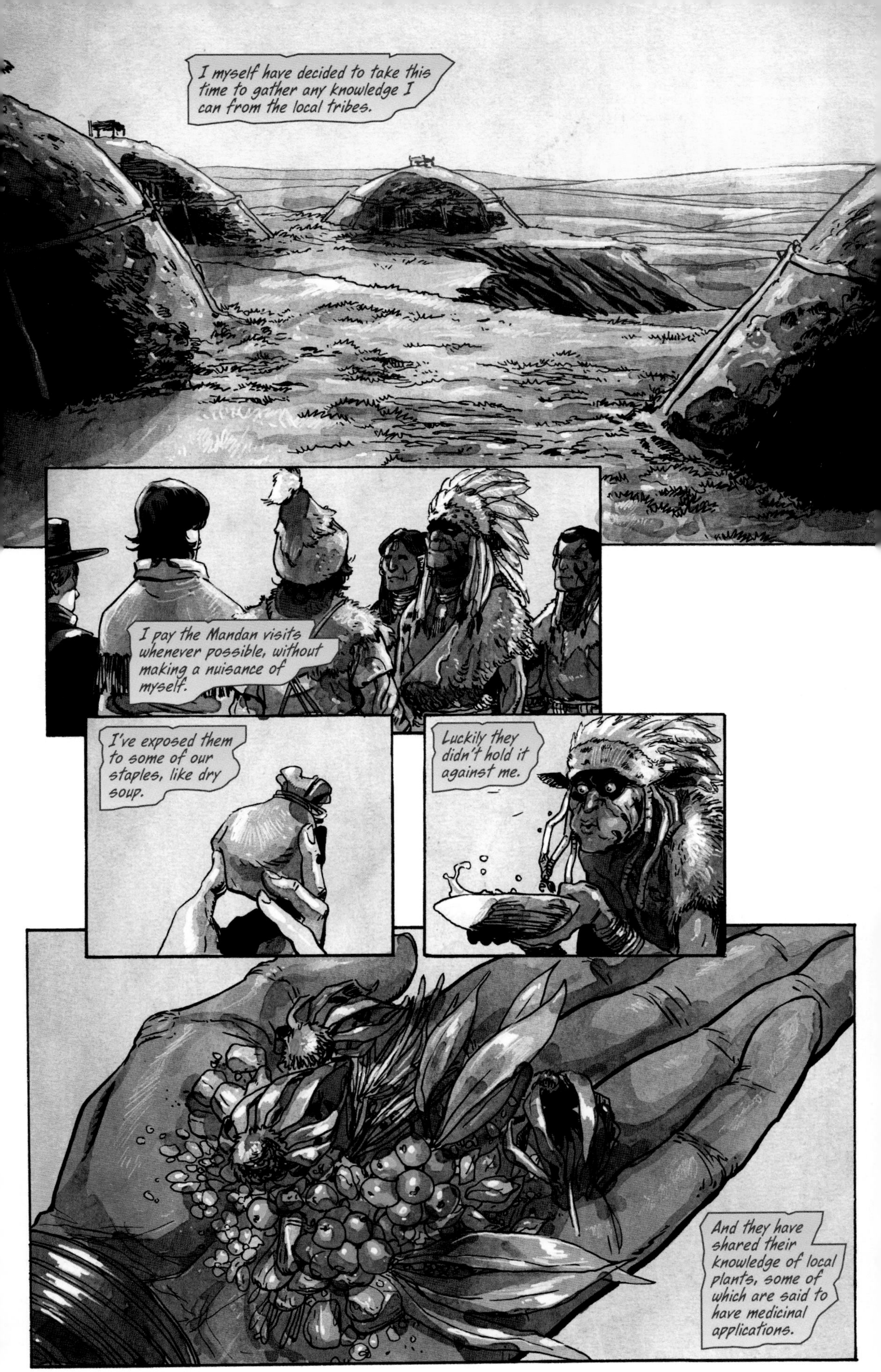
I myself have decided to take this time to gather any knowledge I can from the local tribes.
I pay the Mandan visits whenever possible, without making a nuisance of myself.
I've exposed them to some of our staples, like dry soup.
Luckily they didn't hold it against me.
And they have shared their knowledge of local plants, some of which are said to have medicinal applications.

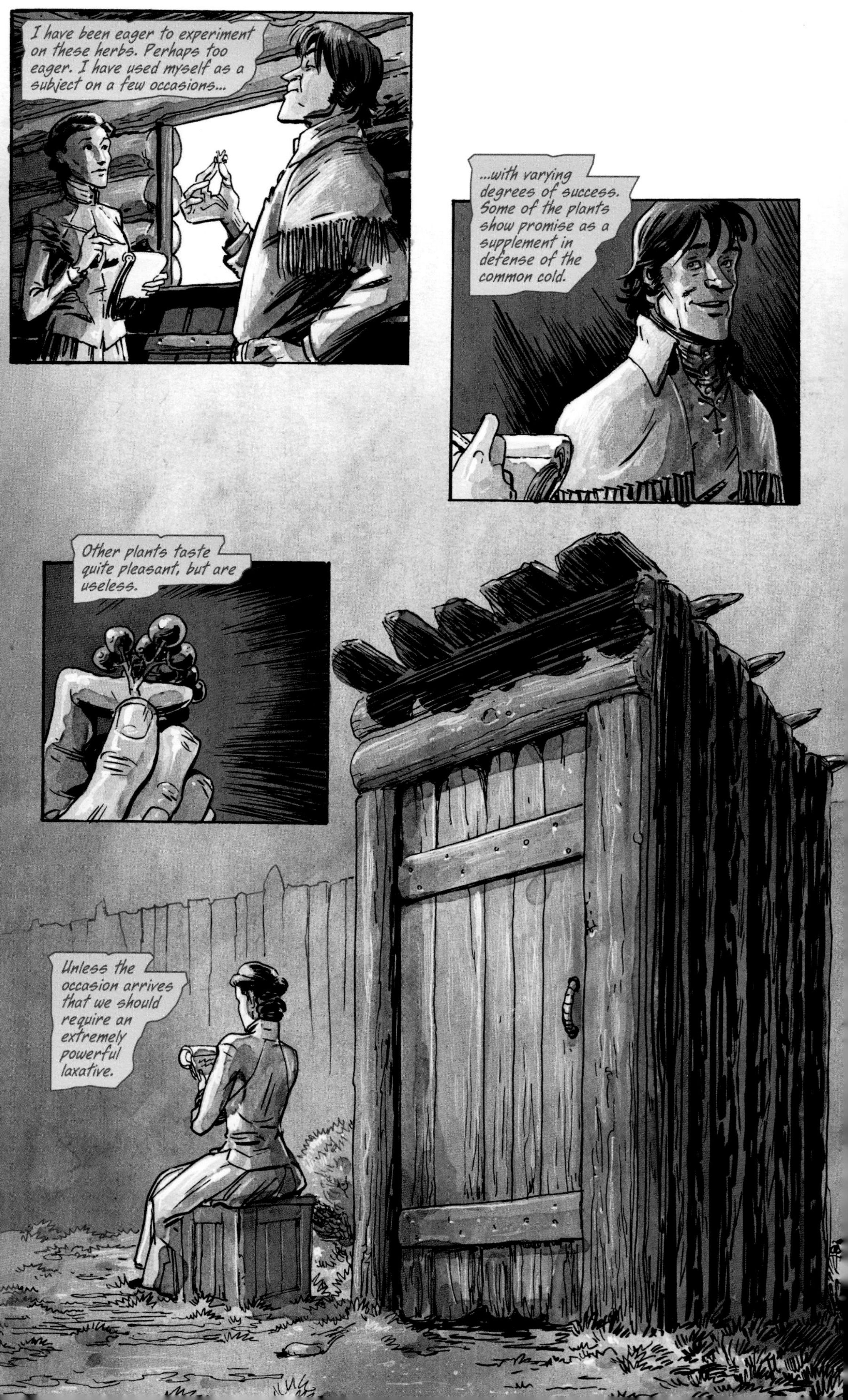
I have been eager to experiment on these herbs. Perhaps too eager. I have used myself as a subject on a few occasions...
...with varying degrees of success. Some of the plants show promise as a supplement in defense of the common cold.
Other plants taste quite pleasant, but are useless.
Unless the occasion arrives that we should require an extremely powerful laxative.

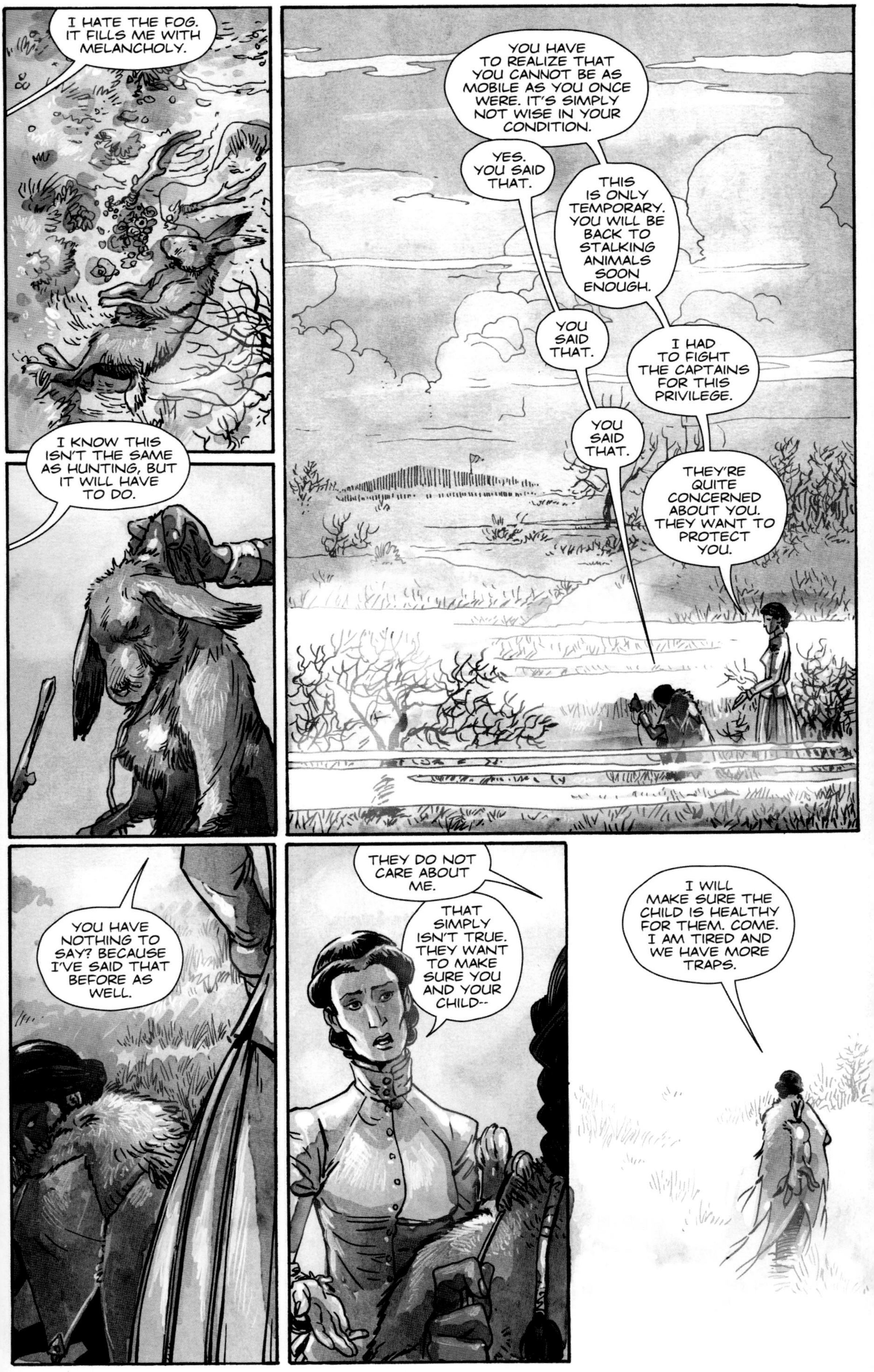
I HATE THE FOG. IT FILLS ME WITH MELANCHOLY.
I KNOW THIS ISN'T THE SAME AS HUNTING, BUT IT WILL HAVE TO DO.
YOU HAVE TO REALIZE THAT YOU CANNOT BE AS MOBILE AS YOU ONCE WERE. IT'S SIMPLY NOT WISE IN YOUR CONDITION.
YES. YOU SAID THAT.
THIS IS ONLY TEMPORARY. YOU WILL BE BACK TO STALKING ANIMALS SOON ENOUGH.
YOU SAID THAT.
I HAD TO FIGHT THE CAPTAINS FOR THIS PRIVILEGE.
YOU SAID THAT.
THEY'RE QUITE CONCERNED ABOUT YOU. THEY WANT TO PROTECT YOU.
YOU HAVE NOTHING TO SAY? BECAUSE I'VE SAID THAT BEFORE AS WELL.
THEY DO NOT CARE ABOUT ME.
THAT SIMPLY ISN'T TRUE. THEY WANT TO MAKE SURE YOU AND YOUR CHILD--
I WILL MAKE SURE THE CHILD IS HEALTHY FOR THEM. COME. I AM TIRED AND WE HAVE MORE TRAPS.

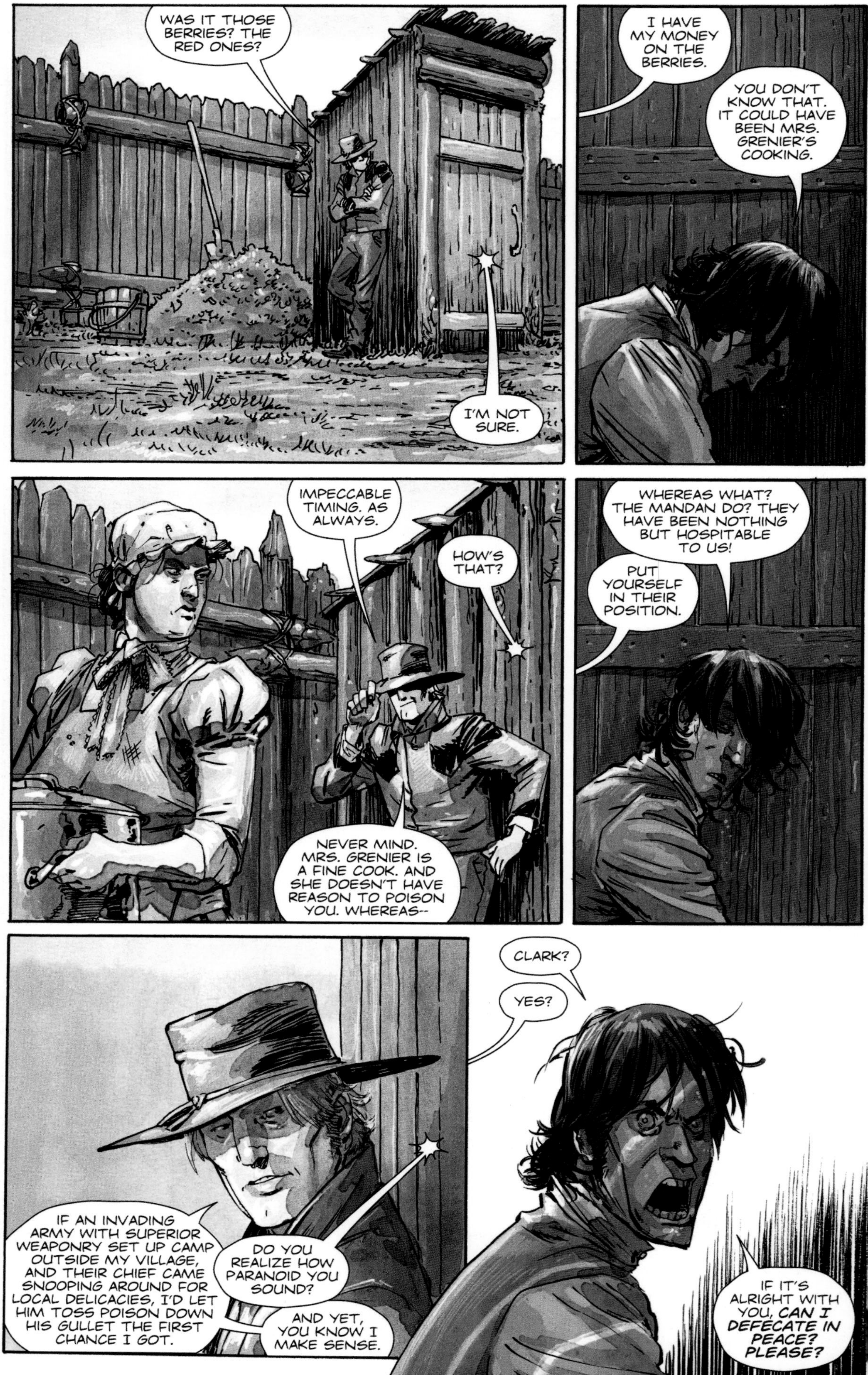

WAS IT THOSE BERRIES? THE RED ONES?
I'M NOT SURE.
I HAVE MY MONEY ON THE BERRIES.
YOU DON'T KNOW THAT. IT COULD HAVE BEEN MRS. GRENIER'S COOKING.
IMPECCABLE TIMING. AS ALWAYS.
HOW'S THAT?
NEVER MIND. MRS. GRENIER IS A FINE COOK. AND SHE DOESN'T HAVE REASON TO POISON YOU. WHEREAS--
WHEREAS WHAT? THE MANDAN DO? THEY HAVE BEEN NOTHING BUT HOSPITABLE TO US!
PUT YOURSELF IN THEIR POSITION.
IF AN INVADING ARMY WITH SUPERIOR WEAPONRY SET UP CAMP OUTSIDE MY VILLAGE, AND THEIR CHIEF CAME SNOOPING AROUND FOR LOCAL DELICACIES, I'D LET HIM TOSS POISON DOWN HIS GULLET THE FIRST CHANCE I GOT.
DO YOU REALIZE HOW PARANOID YOU SOUND?
AND YET, YOU KNOW I MAKE SENSE.
CLARK?
YES?
IF IT'S ALRIGHT WITH YOU, CAN I DEFECATE IN PEACE? PLEASE?

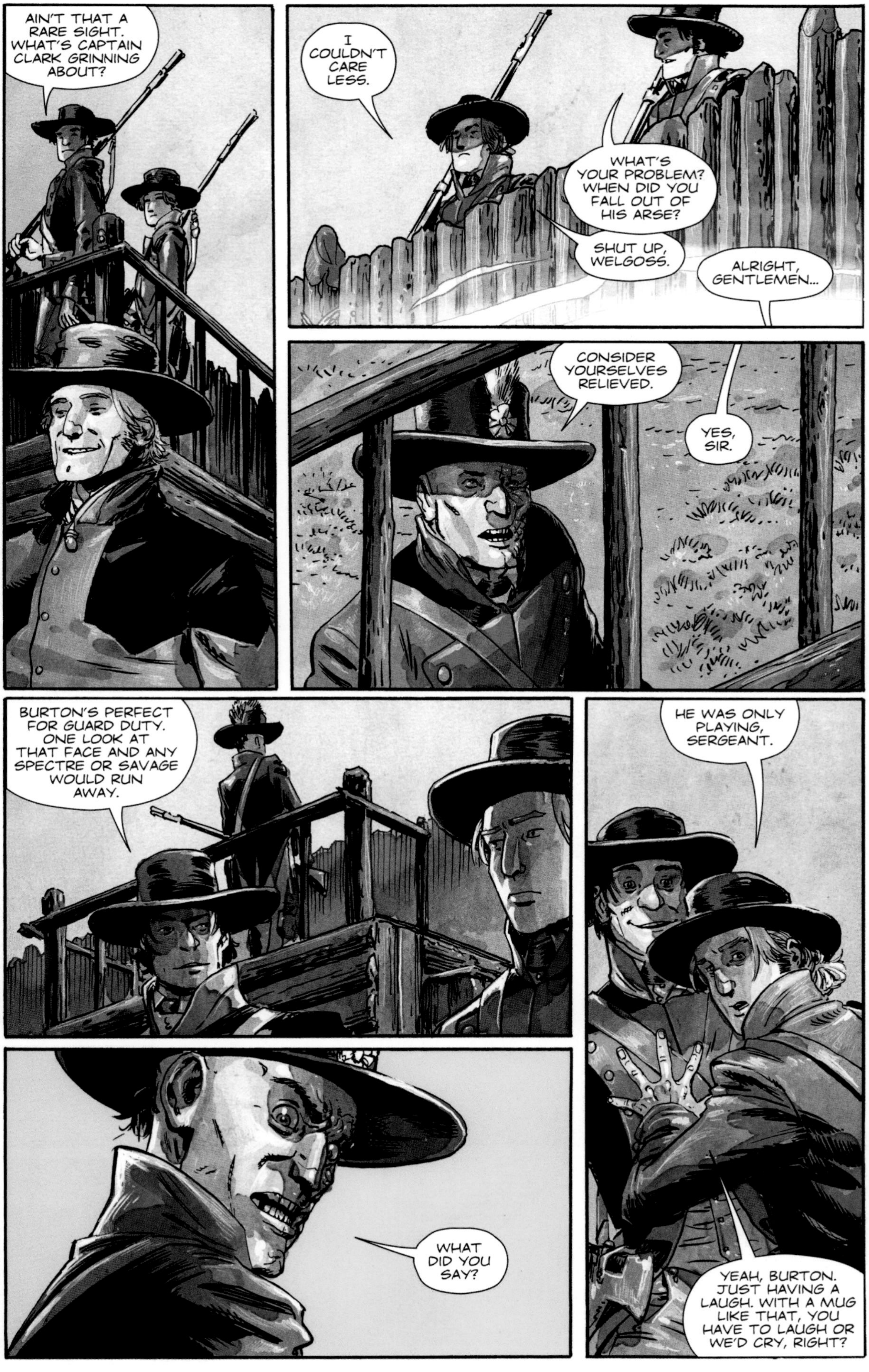
AIN'T THAT A RARE SIGHT. WHAT'S CAPTAIN CLARK GRINNING ABOUT?
I COULDN'T CARE LESS.
WHAT'S YOUR PROBLEM? WHEN DID YOU FALL OUT OF HIS ARSE?
SHUT UP, WELGOSS.
ALRIGHT, GENTLEMEN...
CONSIDER YOURSELVES RELIEVED.
YES, SIR.
BURTON'S PERFECT FOR GUARD DUTY. ONE LOOK AT THAT FACE AND ANY SPECTRE OR SAVAGE WOULD RUN AWAY.
WHAT DID YOU SAY?
HE WAS ONLY PLAYING, SERGEANT.
YEAH, BURTON. JUST HAVING A LAUGH. WITH A MUG LIKE THAT, YOU HAVE TO LAUGH OR WE'D CRY, RIGHT?

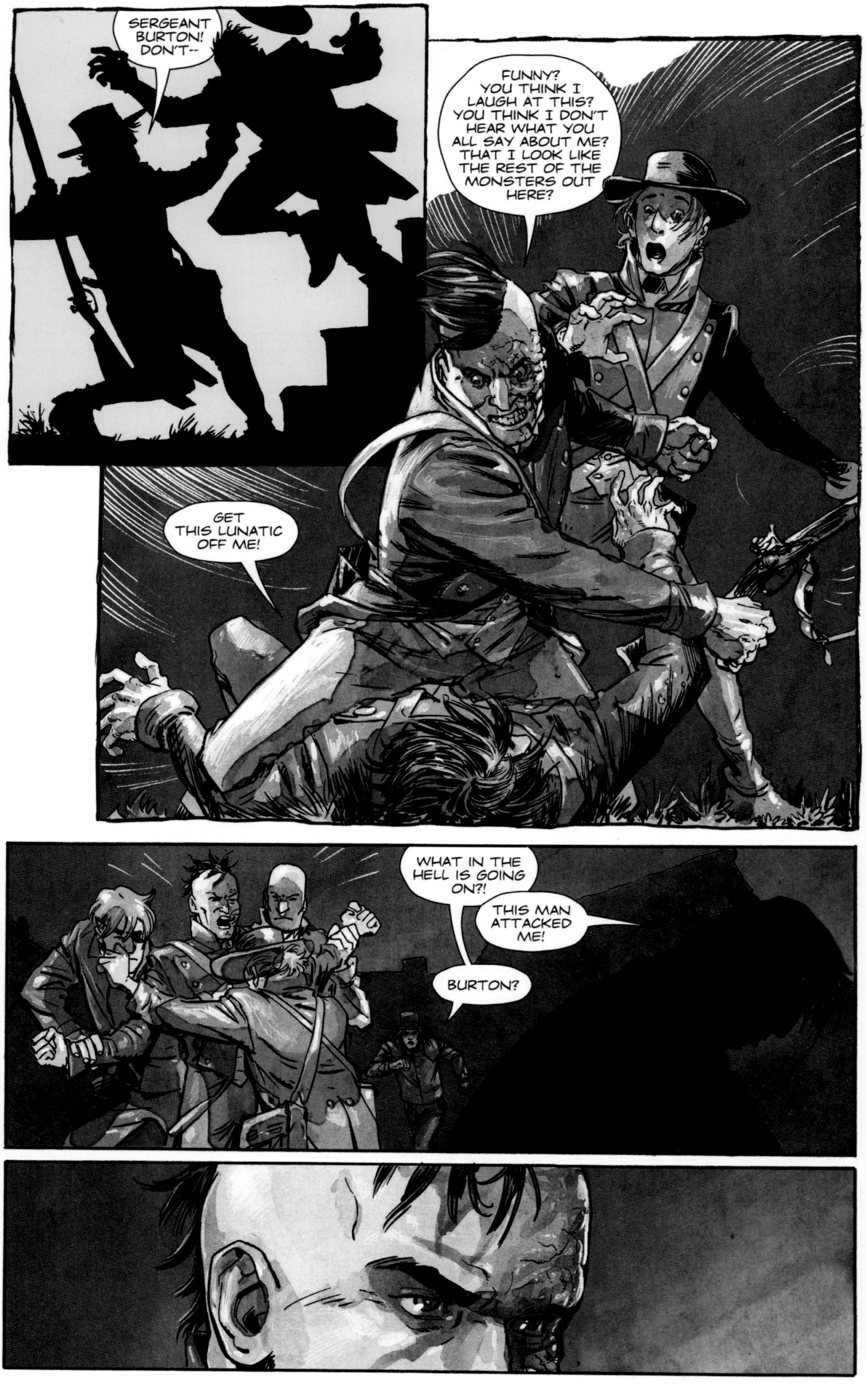
SERGEANT BURTON! DON'T--
FUNNY? YOU THINK I LAUGH AT THIS? YOU THINK I DON'T HEAR WHAT YOU ALL SAY ABOUT ME? THAT I LOOK LIKE THE REST OF THE MONSTERS OUT HERE?
GET THIS LUNATIC OFF ME!
WHAT IN THE HELL IS GOING ON?!
THIS MAN ATTACKED ME!
BURTON?

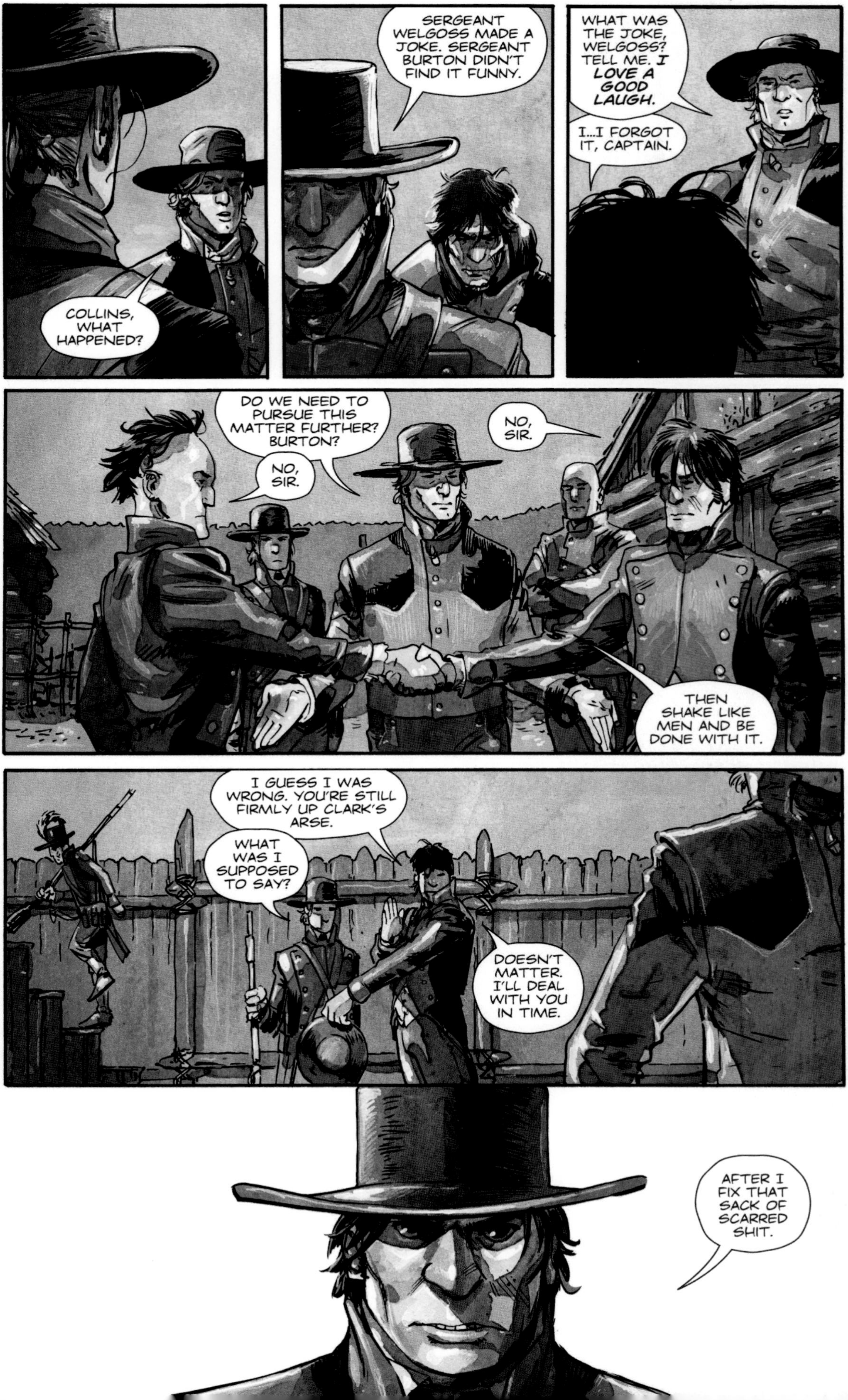
COLLINS, WHAT HAPPENED?
SERGEANT WELGOSS MADE A JOKE. SERGEANT BURTON DIDN'T FIND IT FUNNY.
WHAT WAS THE JOKE, WELGOSS? TELL ME. I LOVE A GOOD LAUGH.
I...I FORGOT IT, CAPTAIN.
DO WE NEED TO PURSUE THIS MATTER FURTHER? BURTON?
NO, SIR.
NO, SIR.
THEN SHAKE LIKE MEN AND BE DONE WITH IT.
I GUESS I WAS WRONG. YOU'RE STILL FIRMLY UP CLARK'S ARSE.
WHAT WAS I SUPPOSED TO SAY?
DOESN'T MATTER. I'LL DEAL WITH YOU IN TIME.
AFTER I FIX THAT SACK OF SCARRED SHIT.

YOU'RE NOT EATING, CAPTAIN?

I THINK I'LL REFRAIN THIS EVENING. WHAT'S MRS. GRENIER SERVING?

RABBIT STEW. QUITE GOOD.

FRESH RABBIT. CAUGHT BY MY PATIENT.

HOW LONG ARE YOU GOING TO LET THAT GO ON?

YES. WHAT IF SHE GOES INTO LABOR OUT THERE?

SHE IS FINE. I'VE TAKEN MOST OF HER ACTIVITIES AWAY. HER SPIRITS ARE ALREADY LOW. I HATE TO TAKE THIS FROM HER.

WE JUST WANT HER TO BE SAFE. ONE OF US COULD TRY TO TALK SOME SENSE INTO HER.

THAT'S THE LAST THING SHE WANTS.

HOW DO YOU MEAN?

SHE DOESN'T TRUST YOU.

WHAT DID SHE SAY?

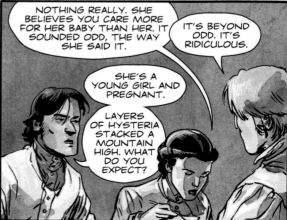

NOTHING REALLY. SHE BELIEVES YOU CARE MORE FOR HER BABY THAN HER. IT SOUNDED ODD, THE WAY SHE SAID IT.

IT'S BEYOND ODD. IT'S RIDICULOUS.

SHE'S A YOUNG GIRL AND PREGNANT.

LAYERS OF HYSTERIA STACKED A MOUNTAIN HIGH. WHAT DO YOU EXPECT?

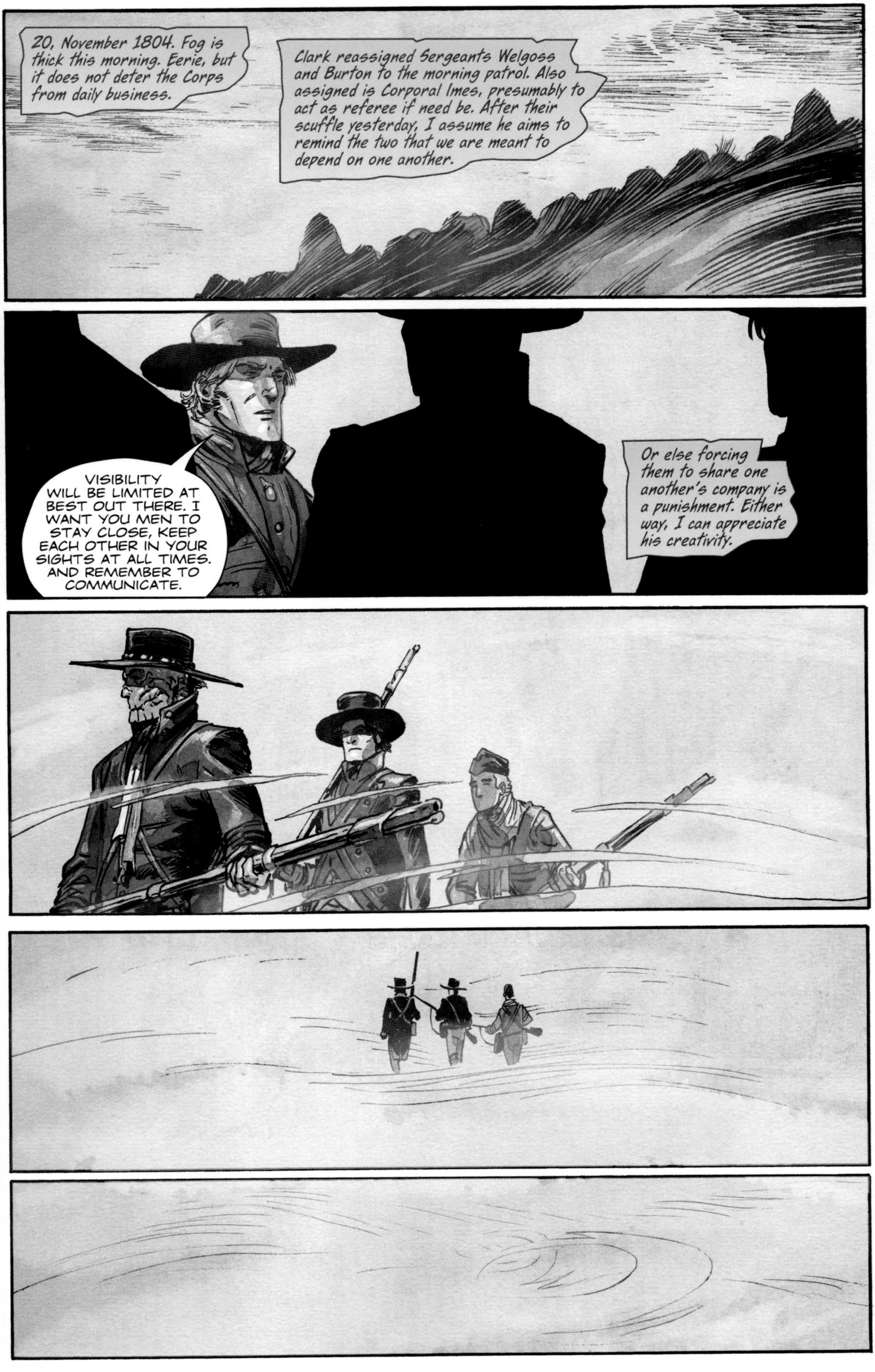
20, November 1804. Fog is thick this morning. Eerie, but it does not deter the Corps from daily business.
Clark reassigned Sergeants Welgoss and Burton to the morning patrol. Also assigned is Corporal Imes, presumably to act as referee if need be. After their scuffle yesterday, I assume he aims to remind the two that we are meant to depend on one another.
VISIBILITY WILL BE LIMITED AT BEST OUT THERE. I WANT YOU MEN TO STAY CLOSE, KEEP EACH OTHER IN YOUR SIGHTS AT ALL TIMES. AND REMEMBER TO COMMUNICATE.
Or else forcing them to share one another's company is a punishment. Either way, I can appreciate his creativity.

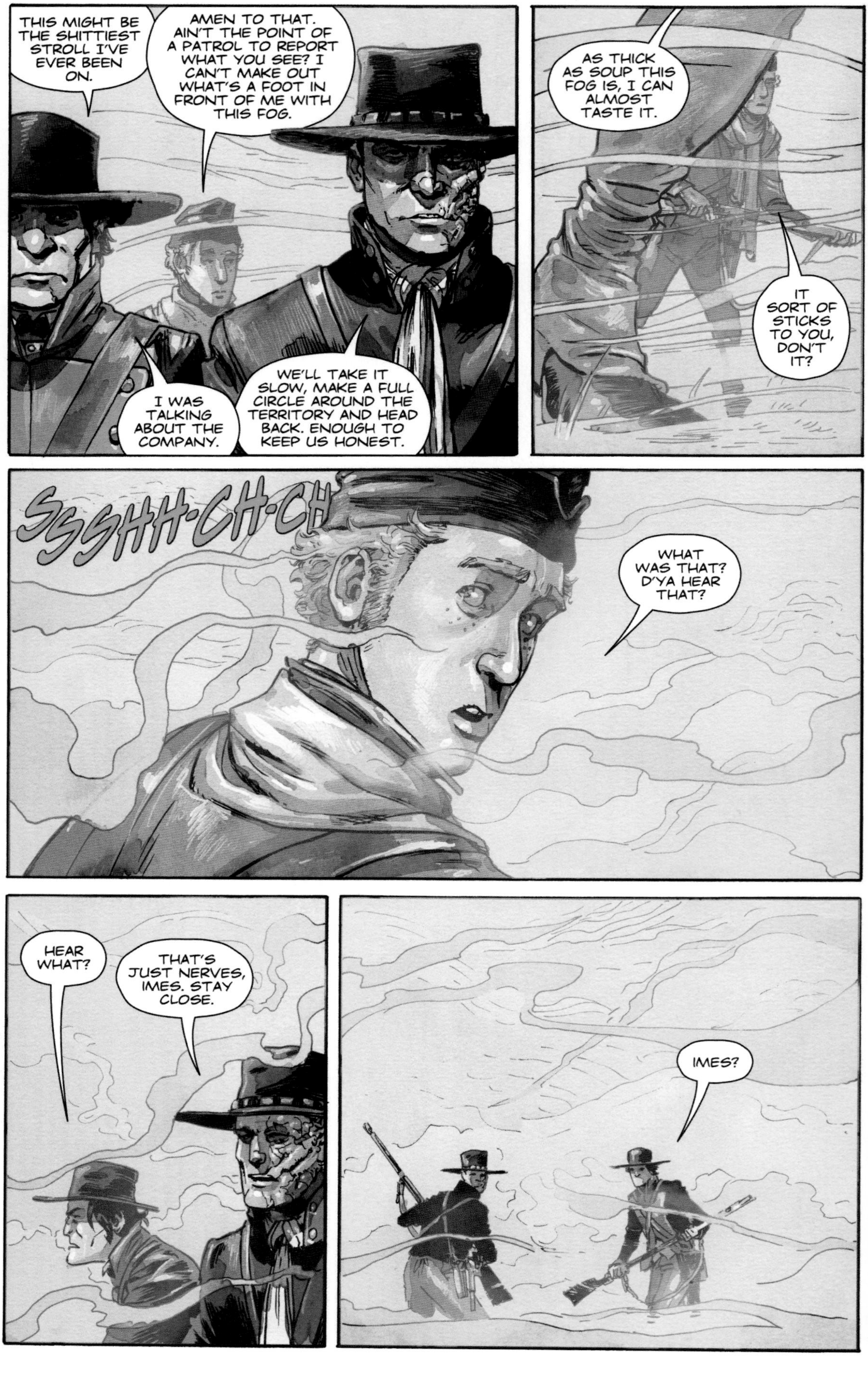
THIS MIGHT BE THE SHITTIEST STROLL I'VE EVER BEEN ON.
AMEN TO THAT. AIN'T THE POINT OF A PATROL TO REPORT WHAT YOU SEE? I CAN'T MAKE OUT WHAT'S A FOOT IN FRONT OF ME WITH THIS FOG.
I WAS TALKING ABOUT THE COMPANY.
WE'LL TAKE IT SLOW, MAKE A FULL CIRCLE AROUND THE TERRITORY AND HEAD BACK. ENOUGH TO KEEP US HONEST.
AS THICK AS SOUP THIS FOG IS, I CAN ALMOST TASTE IT.
IT SORT OF STICKS TO YOU, DON'T IT?
SSSHH-CH-CH
WHAT WAS THAT? D'YA HEAR THAT?
HEAR WHAT?
THAT'S JUST NERVES, IMES. STAY CLOSE.
IMES?

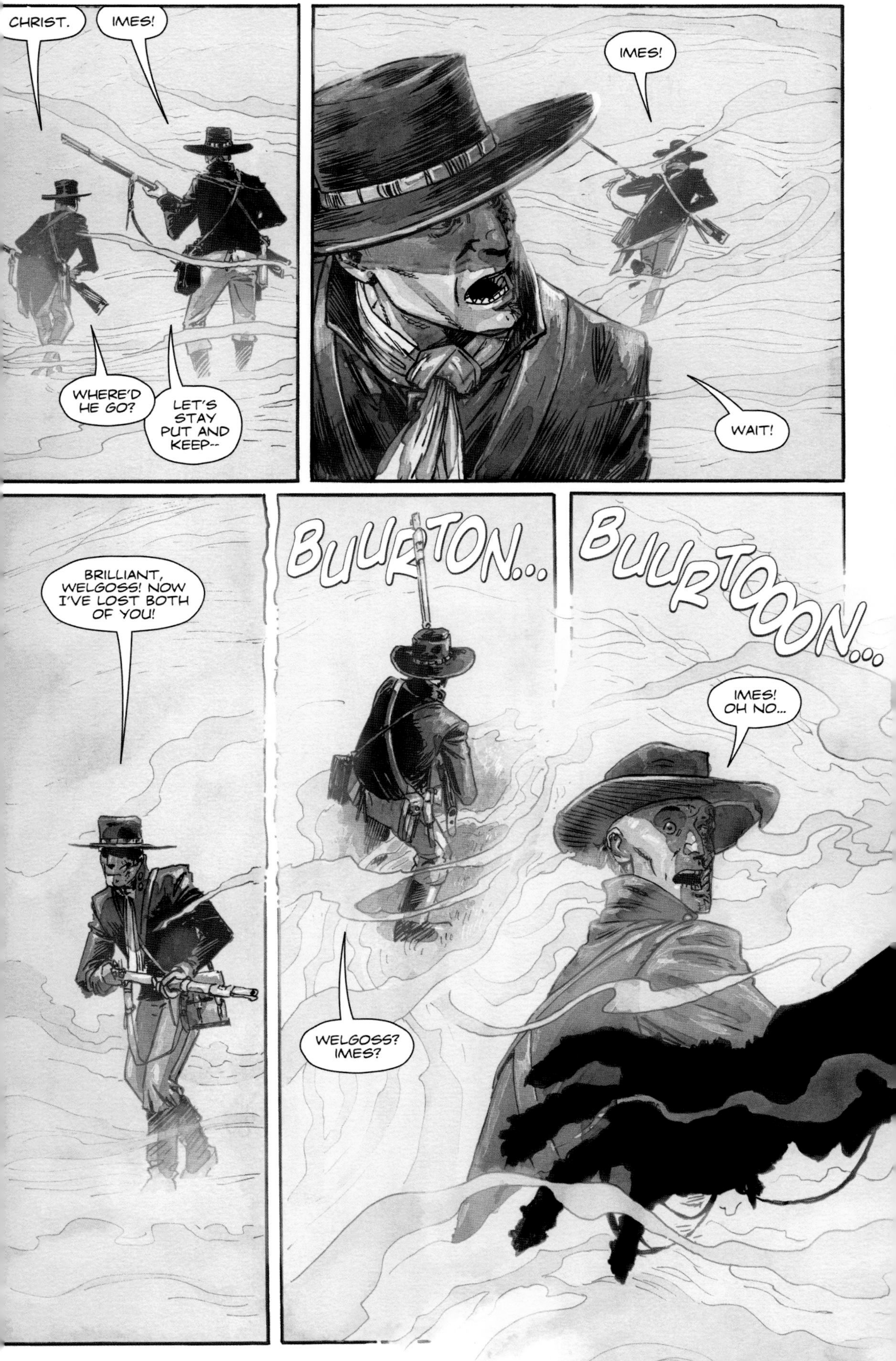
CHRIST.
IMES!
WHERE'D HE GO?
LET'S STAY PUT AND KEEP--
IMES!
WAIT!
BRILLIANT, WELGOSS! NOW I'VE LOST BOTH OF YOU!
BUURTON...
WELGOSS? IMES?
BUURTOOON...
IMES! OH NO...

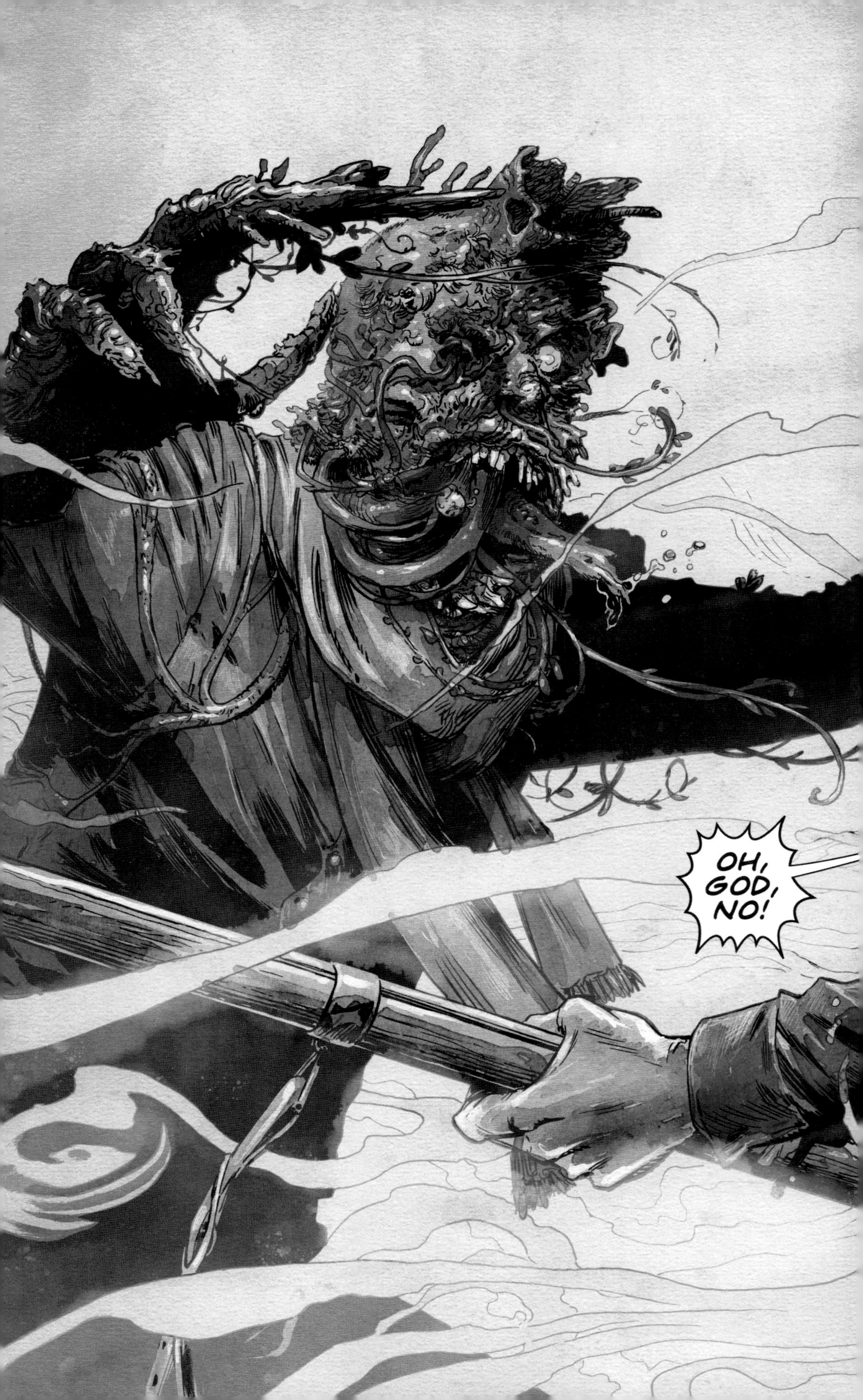
OH, GOD, NO!

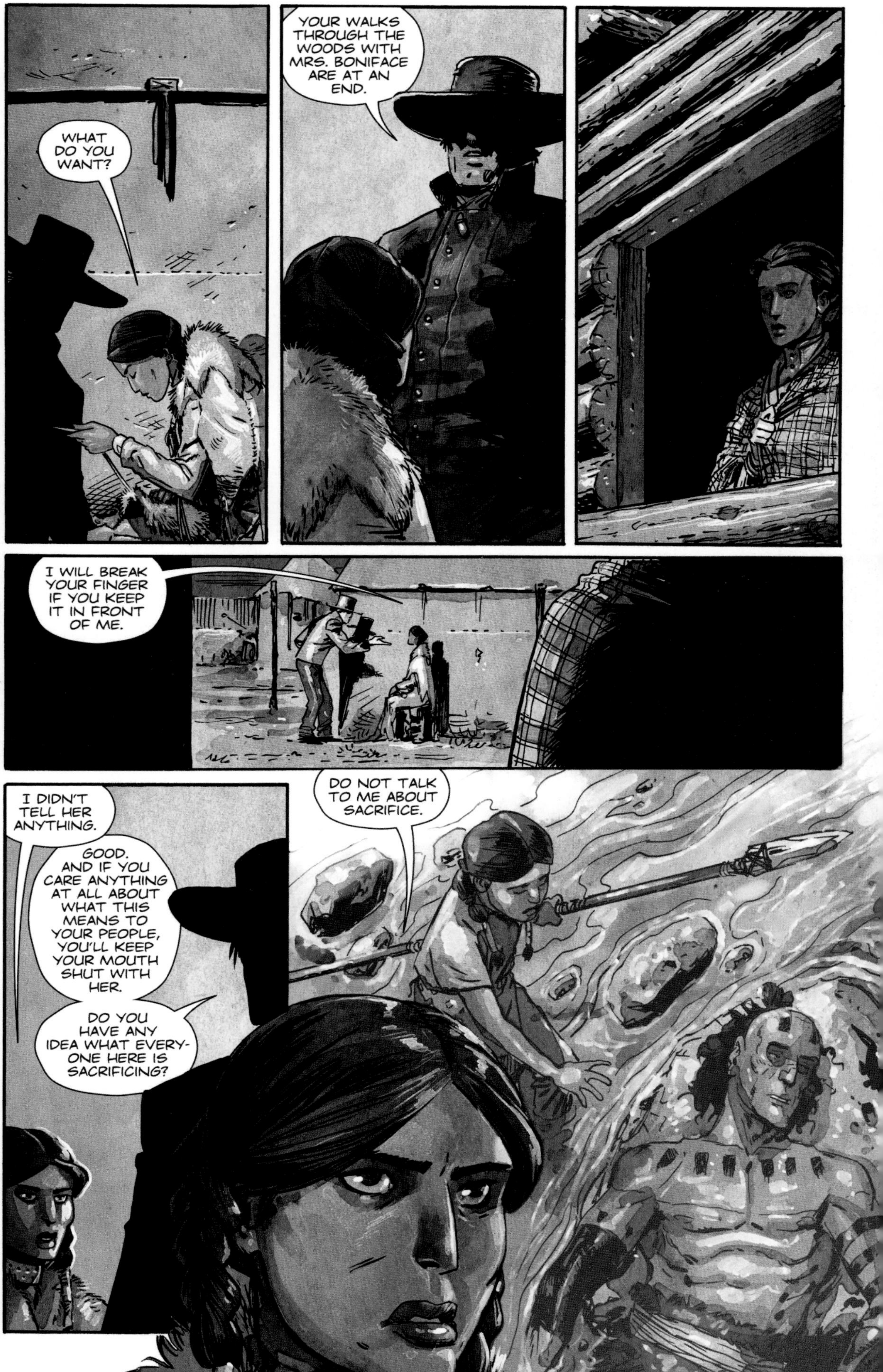
WHAT DO YOU WANT?
YOUR WALKS THROUGH THE WOODS WITH MRS. BONIFACE ARE AT AN END.
I WILL BREAK YOUR FINGER IF YOU KEEP IT IN FRONT OF ME.
I DIDN'T TELL HER ANYTHING.
GOOD. AND IF YOU CARE ANYTHING AT ALL ABOUT WHAT THIS MEANS TO YOUR PEOPLE, YOU'LL KEEP YOUR MOUTH SHUT WITH HER.
DO YOU HAVE ANY IDEA WHAT EVERY-ONE HERE IS SACRIFICING?
DO NOT TALK TO ME ABOUT SACRIFICE.

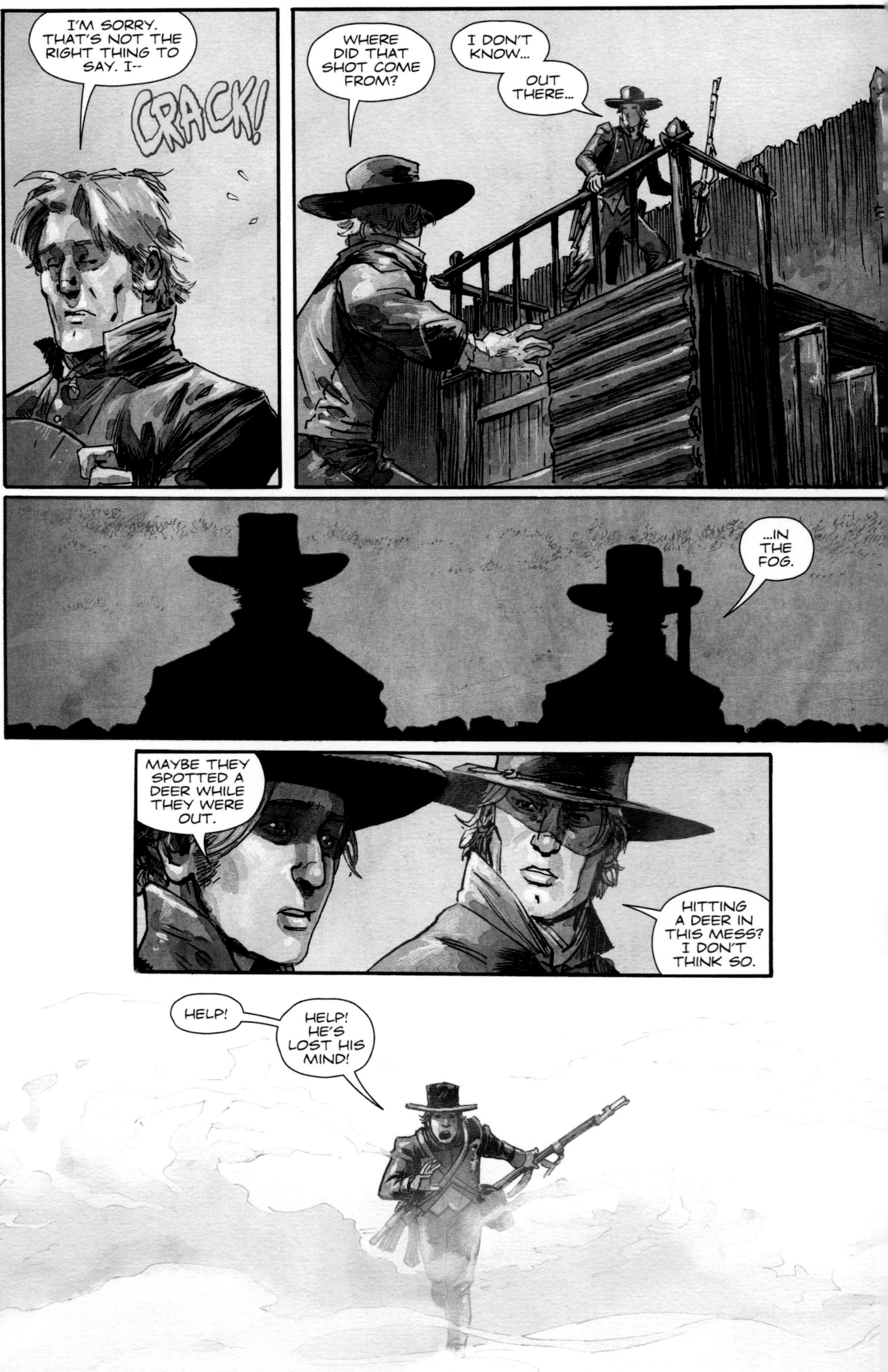
I'M SORRY. THAT'S NOT THE RIGHT THING TO SAY. I--
CRACK!
WHERE DID THAT SHOT COME FROM?
I DON'T KNOW...
OUT THERE...
...IN THE FOG.
MAYBE THEY SPOTTED A DEER WHILE THEY WERE OUT.
HITTING A DEER IN THIS MESS? I DON'T THINK SO.
HELP!
HELP! HE'S LOST HIS MIND!

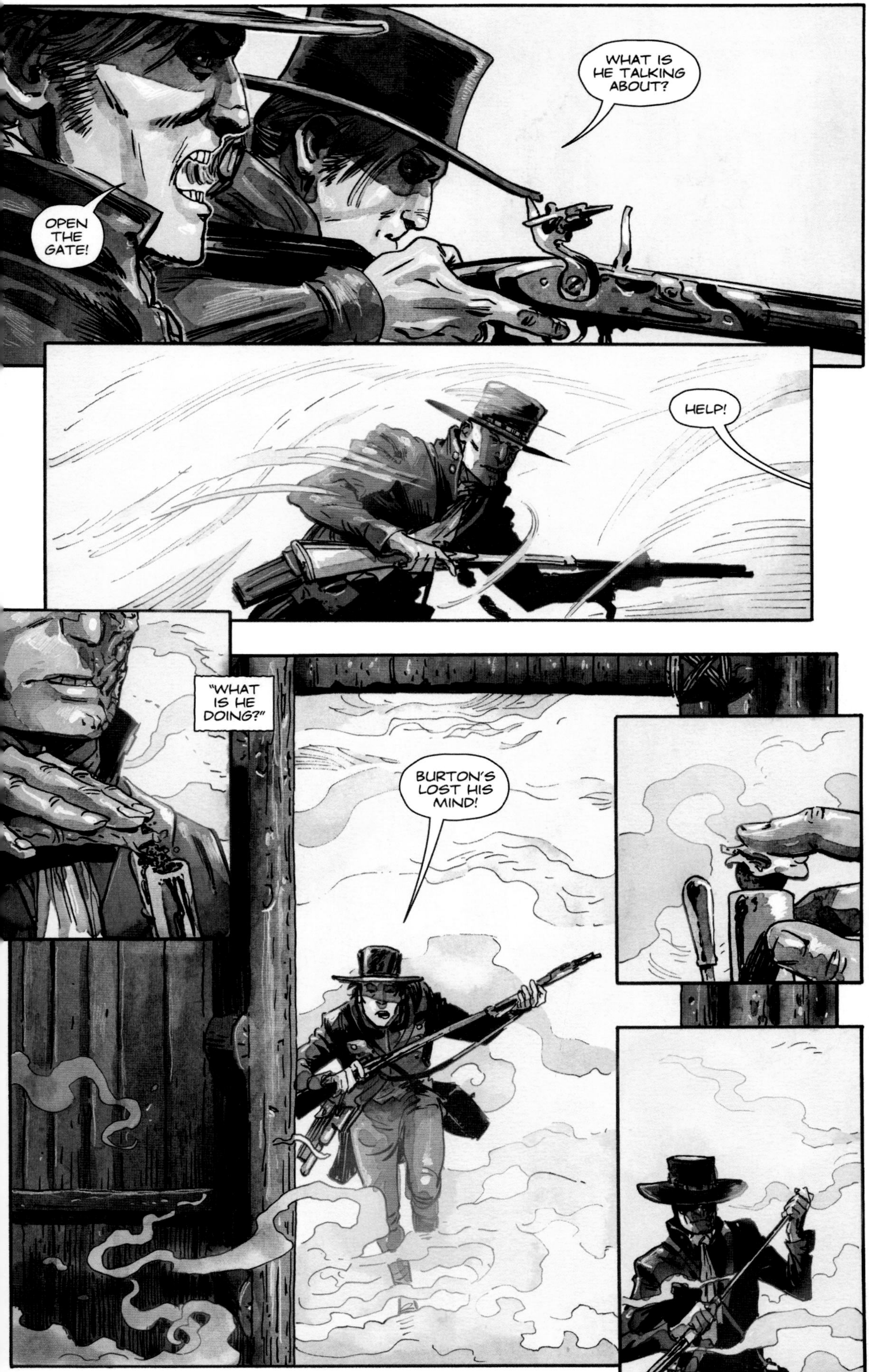
OPEN THE GATE!
WHAT IS HE TALKING ABOUT?
HELP!
"WHAT IS HE DOING?"
BURTON'S LOST HIS MIND!

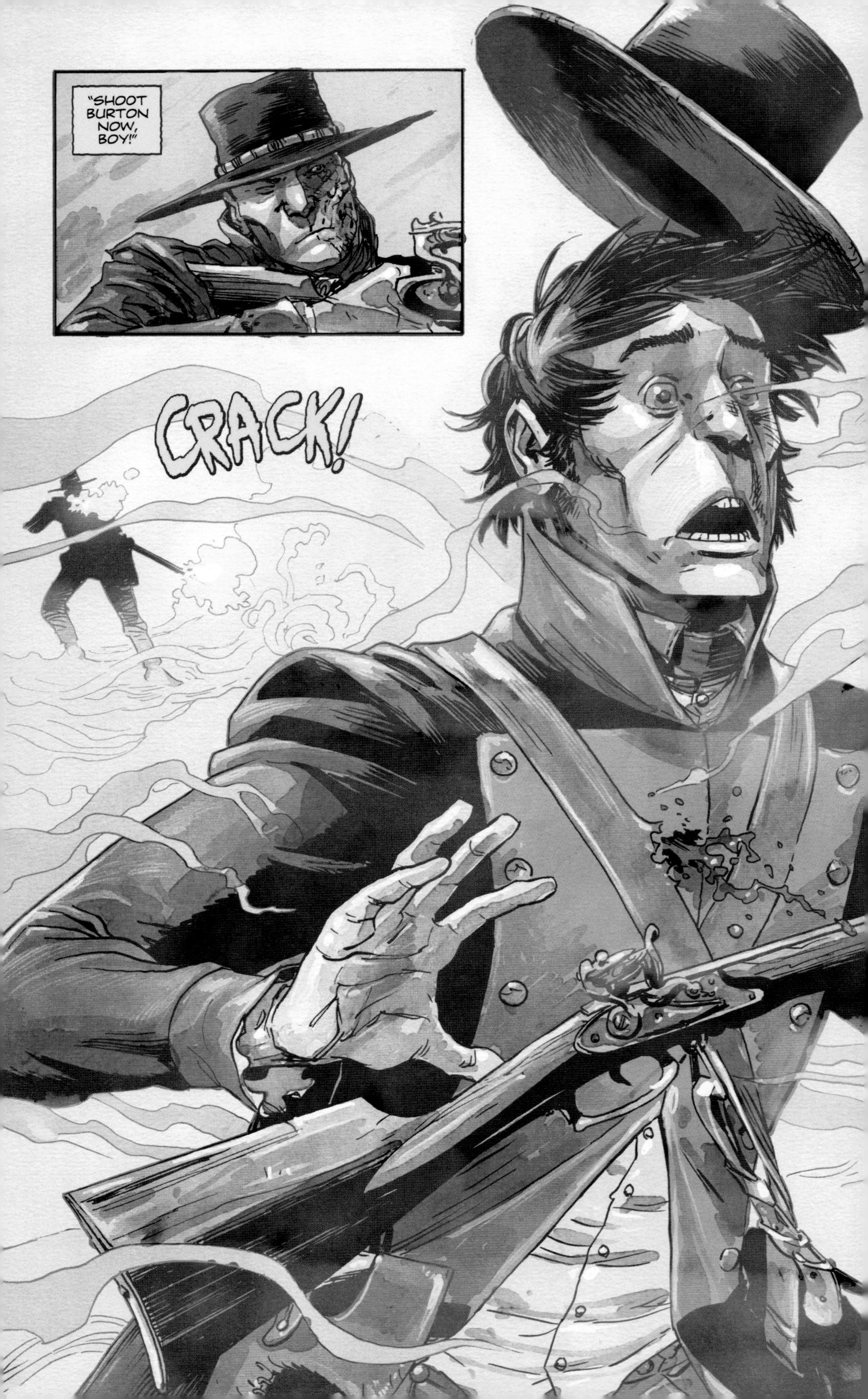
"SHOOT BURTON NOW, BOY!"
CRACK!

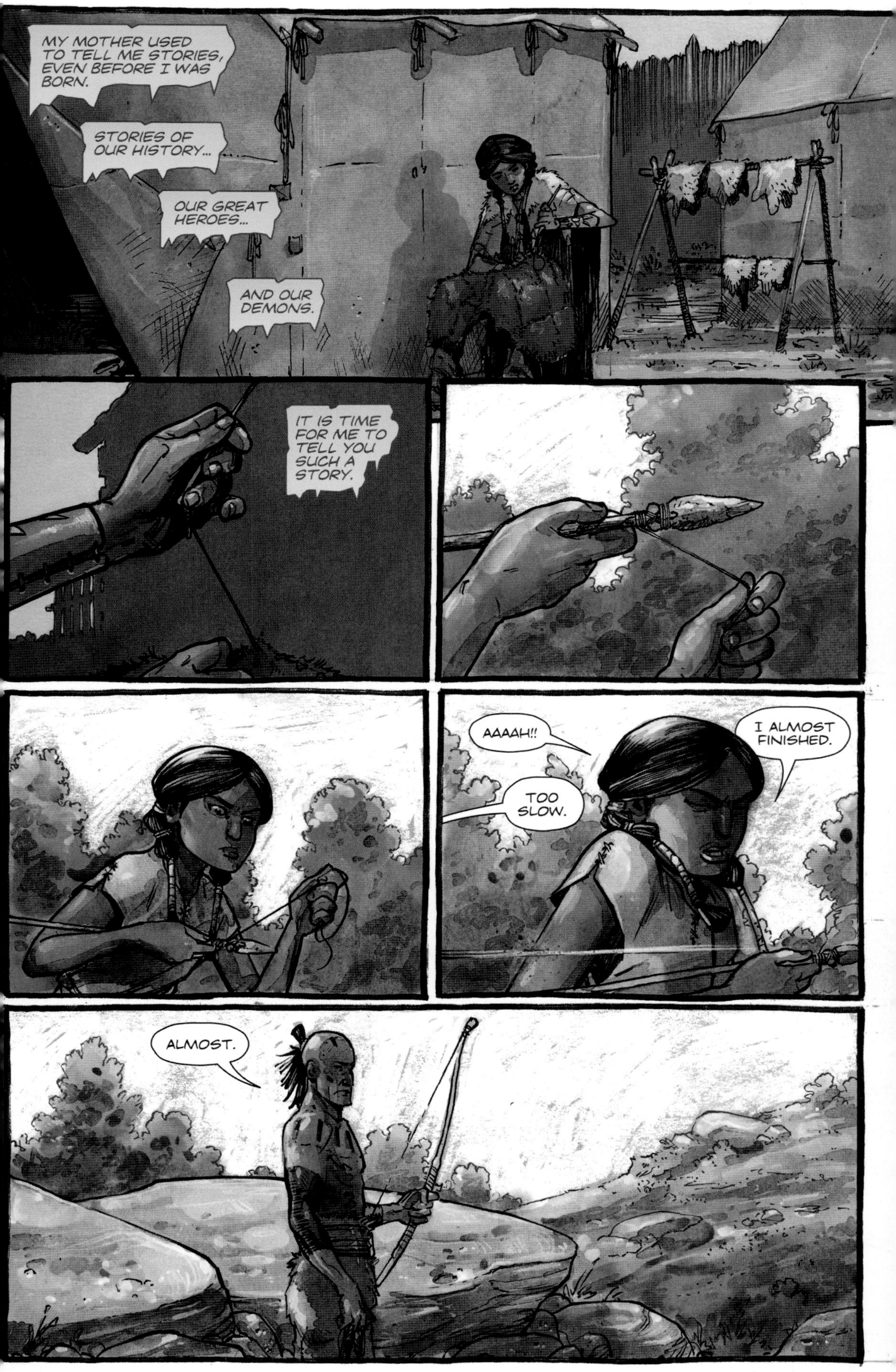
MY MOTHER USED TO TELL ME STORIES, EVEN BEFORE I WAS BORN.
STORIES OF OUR HISTORY...
OUR GREAT HEROES...
AND OUR DEMONS.
IT IS TIME FOR ME TO TELL YOU SUCH A STORY.
AAAAH!!
I ALMOST FINISHED.
TOO SLOW.
ALMOST.

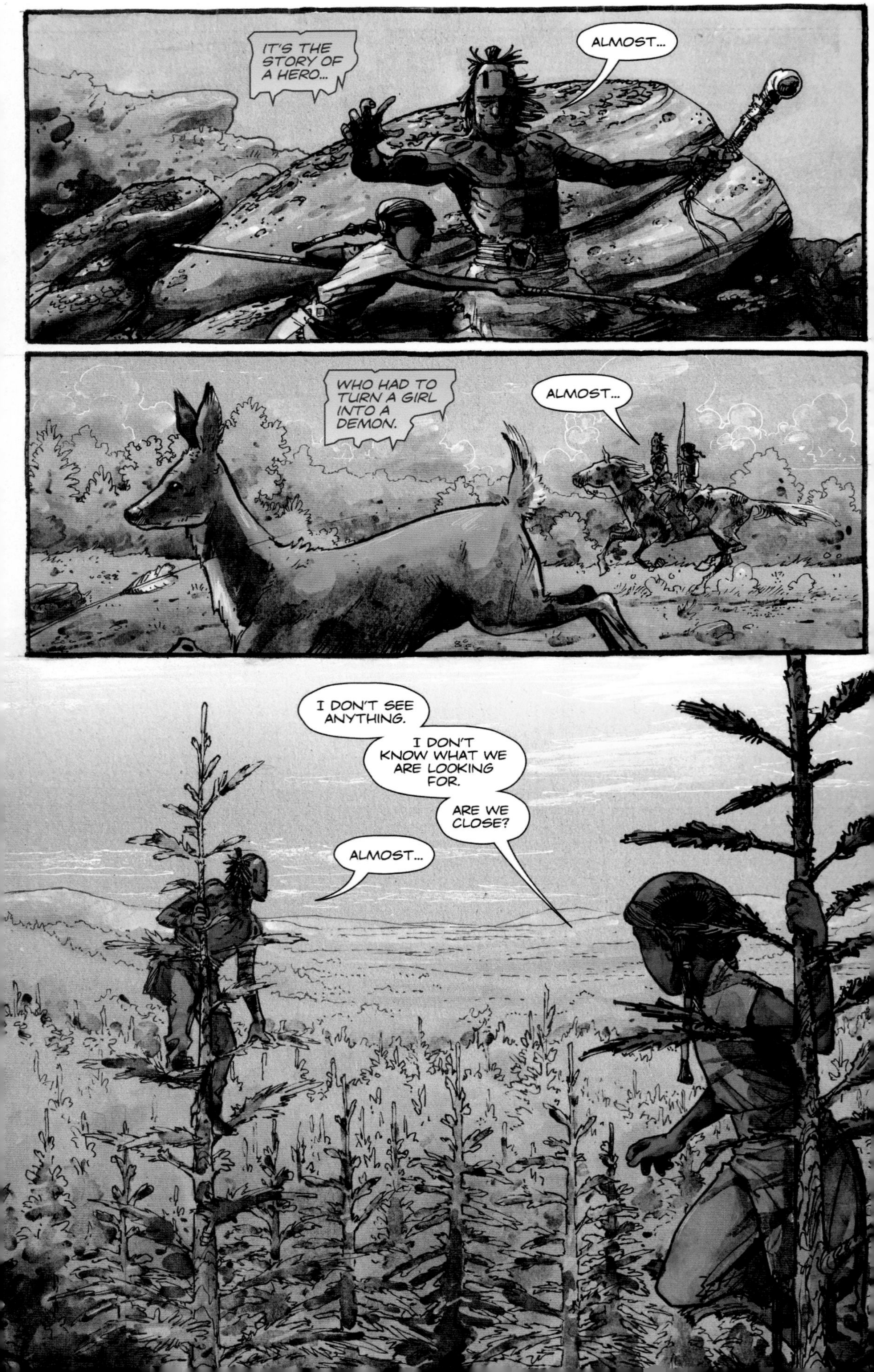
IT'S THE STORY OF A HERO...
ALMOST...
WHO HAD TO TURN A GIRL INTO A DEMON.
ALMOST...
I DON'T SEE ANYTHING.
I DON'T KNOW WHAT WE ARE LOOKING FOR.
ARE WE CLOSE?
ALMOST...

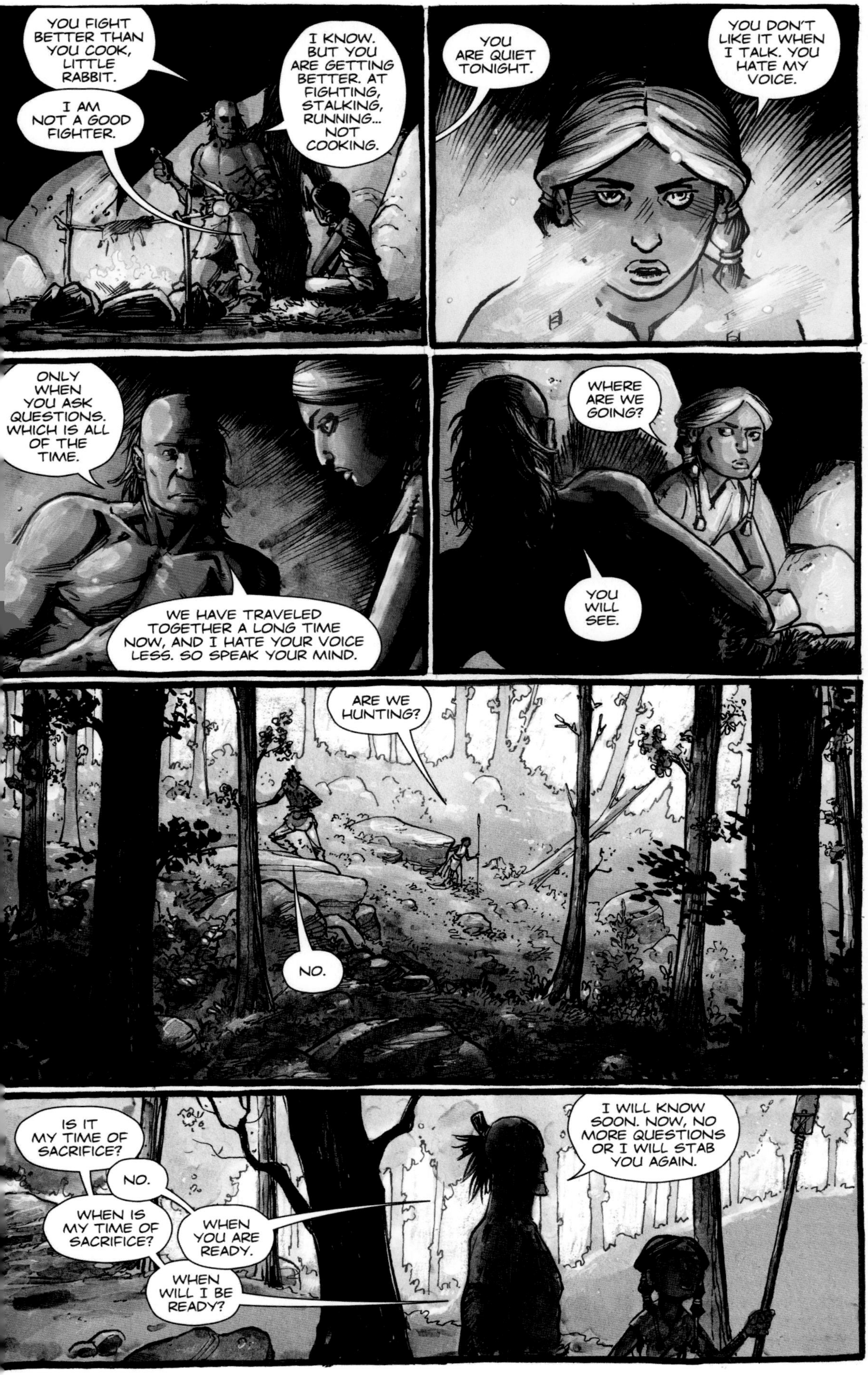
YOU FIGHT BETTER THAN YOU COOK, LITTLE RABBIT.
I AM NOT A GOOD FIGHTER.
I KNOW. BUT YOU ARE GETTING BETTER. AT FIGHTING, STALKING, RUNNING... NOT COOKING.
YOU ARE QUIET TONIGHT.
YOU DON'T LIKE IT WHEN I TALK. YOU HATE MY VOICE.
ONLY WHEN YOU ASK QUESTIONS. WHICH IS ALL OF THE TIME.
WE HAVE TRAVELED TOGETHER A LONG TIME NOW, AND I HATE YOUR VOICE LESS. SO SPEAK YOUR MIND.
WHERE ARE WE GOING?
YOU WILL SEE.
ARE WE HUNTING?
NO.
IS IT MY TIME OF SACRIFICE?
NO.
WHEN IS MY TIME OF SACRIFICE?
WHEN YOU ARE READY.
WHEN WILL I BE READY?
I WILL KNOW SOON. NOW, NO MORE QUESTIONS OR I WILL STAB YOU AGAIN.

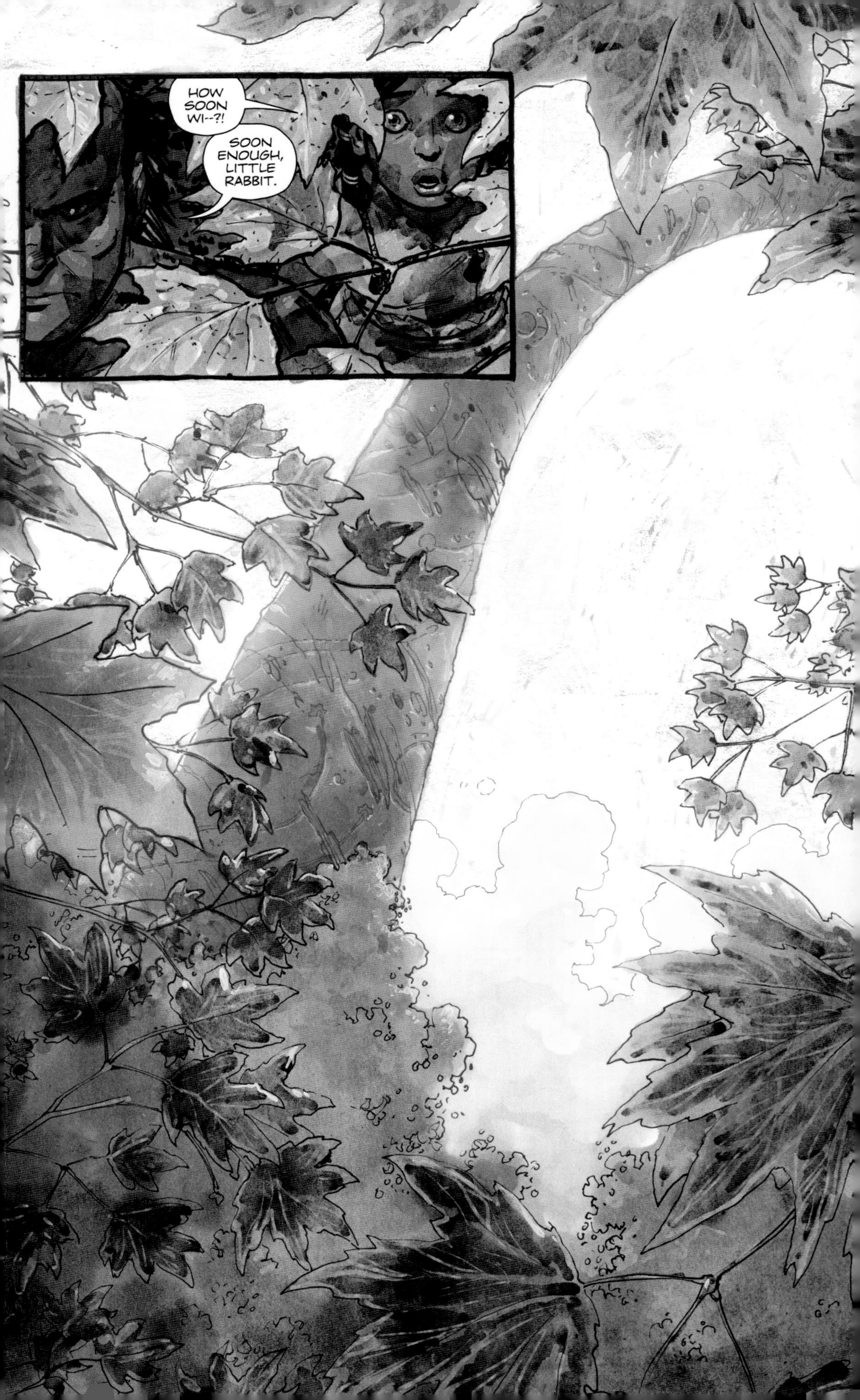
HOW SOON WI--?!
SOON ENOUGH, LITTLE RABBIT.

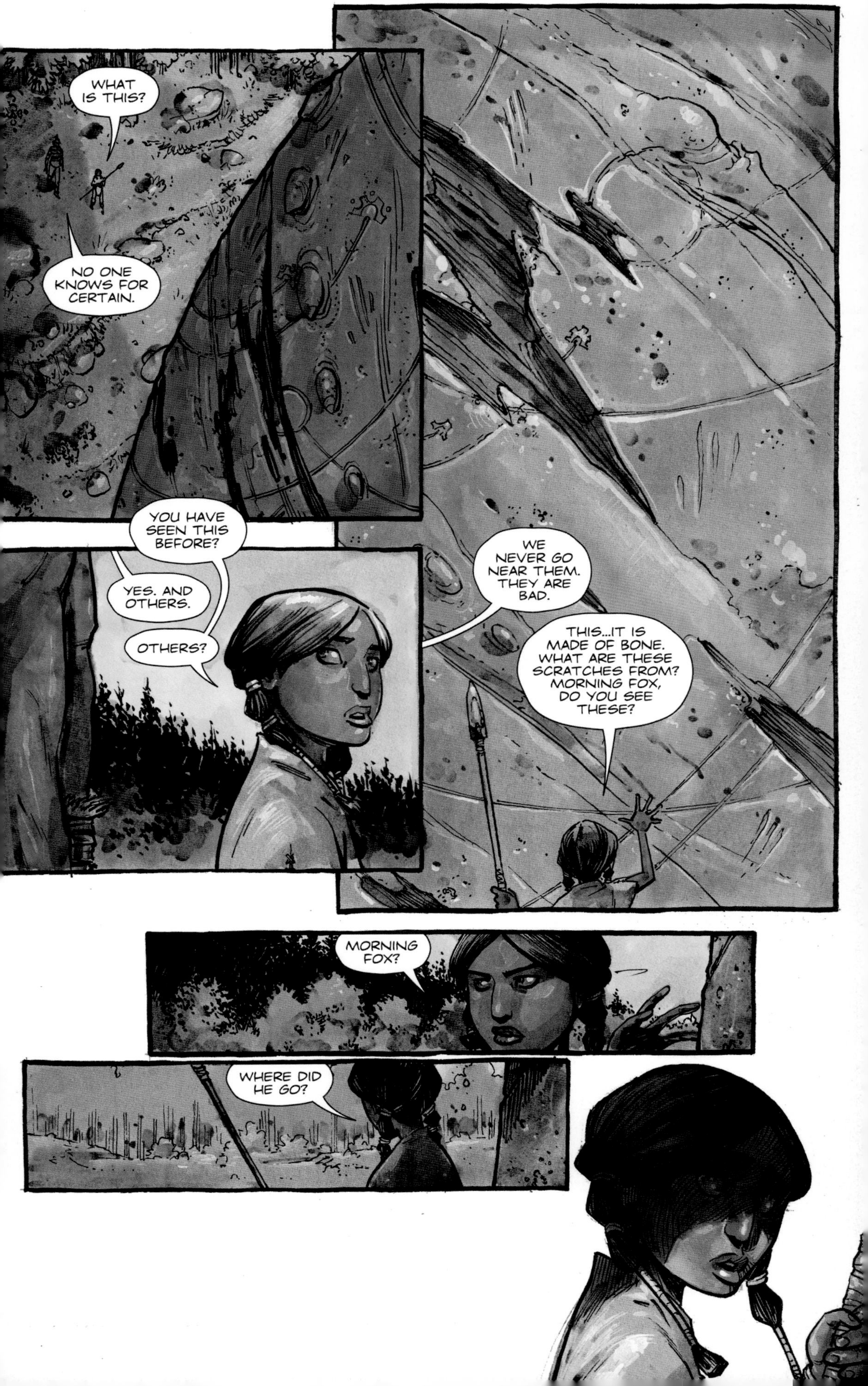
WHAT IS THIS?
NO ONE KNOWS FOR CERTAIN.
YOU HAVE SEEN THIS BEFORE?
YES. AND OTHERS.
OTHERS?
WE NEVER GO NEAR THEM. THEY ARE BAD.
THIS...IT IS MADE OF BONE. WHAT ARE THESE SCRATCHES FROM? MORNING FOX, DO YOU SEE THESE?
MORNING FOX?
WHERE DID HE GO?

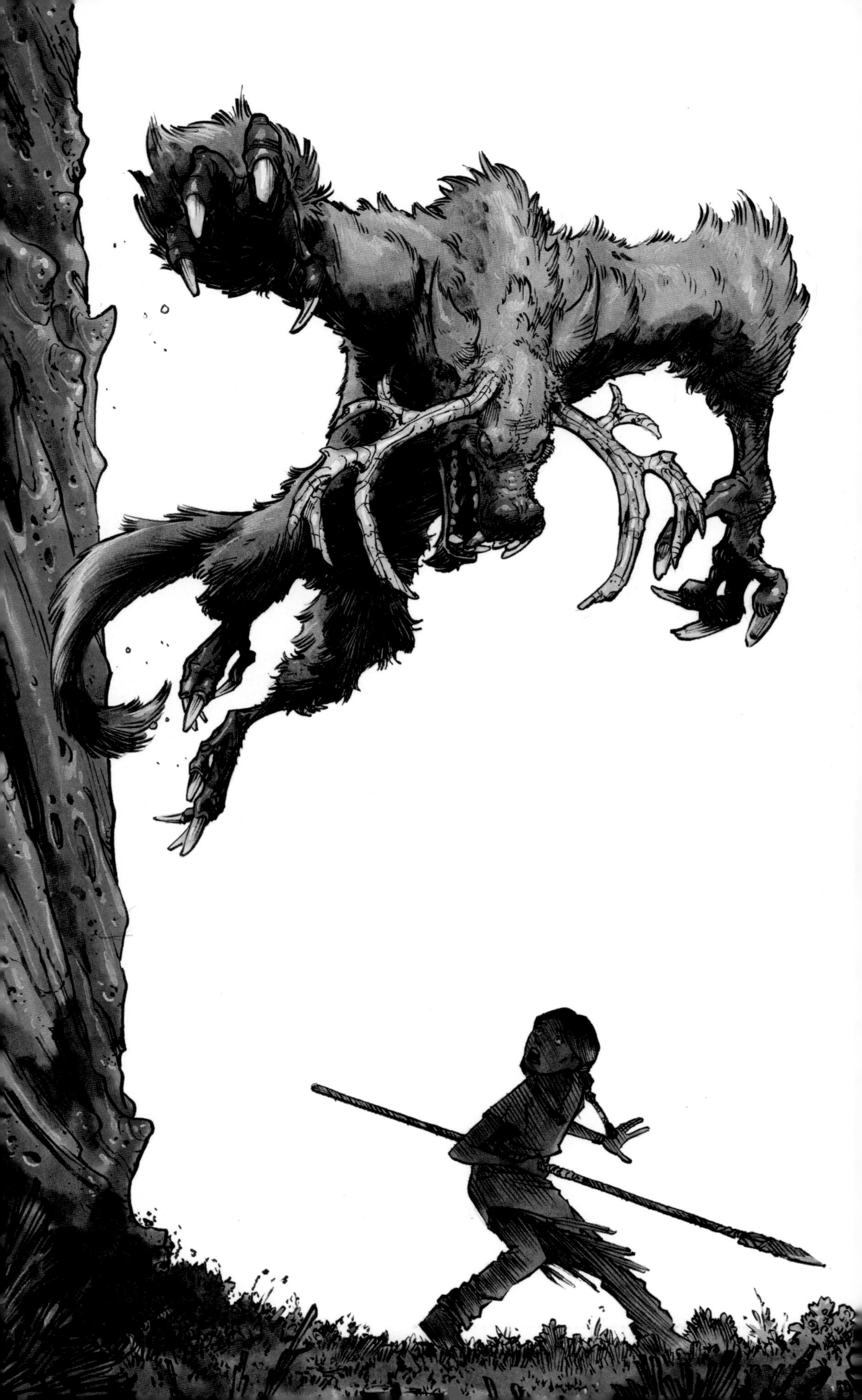

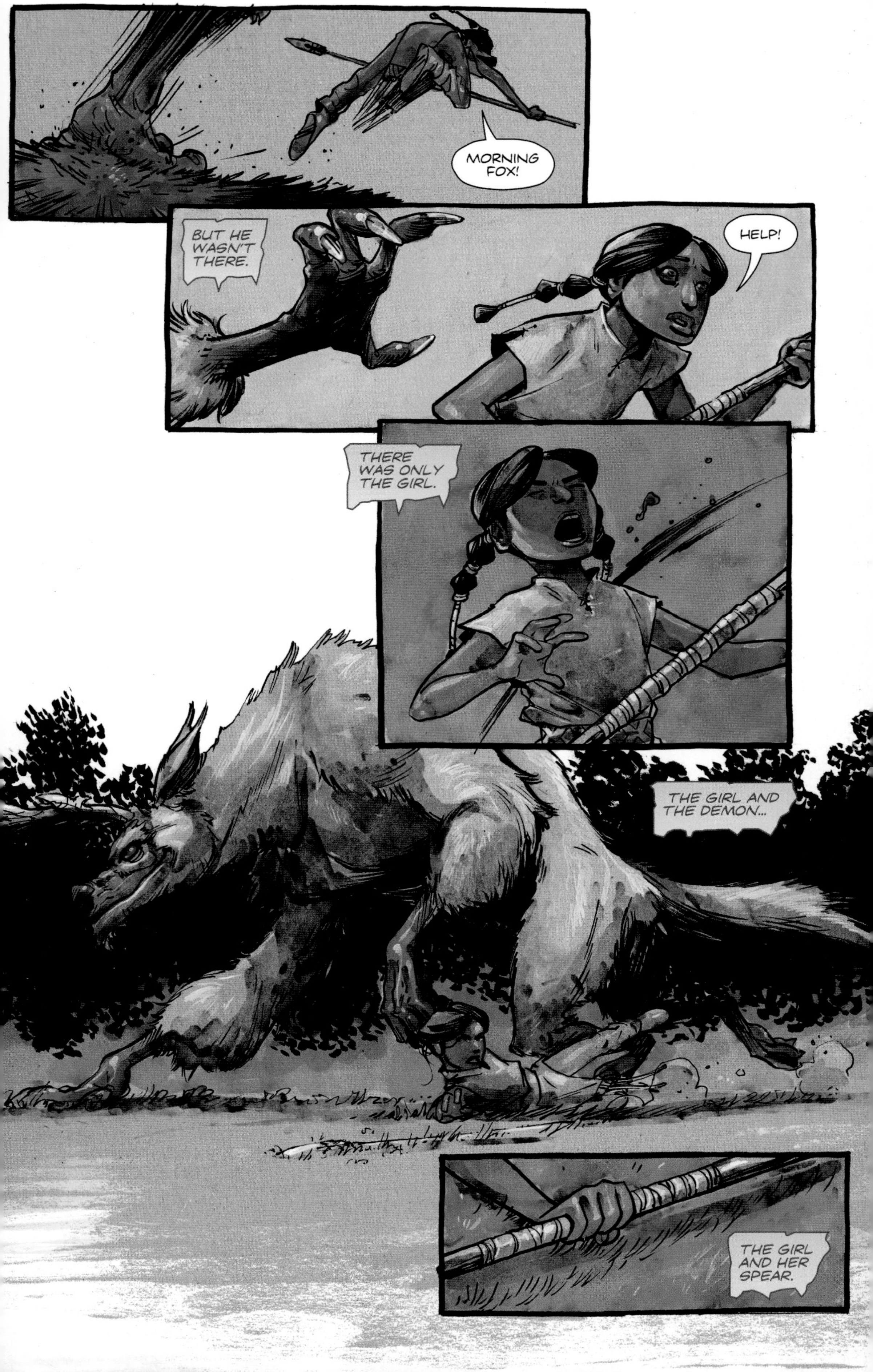
MORNING FOX!
BUT HE WASN'T THERE.
HELP!
THERE WAS ONLY THE GIRL.
THE GIRL AND THE DEMON...
THE GIRL AND HER SPEAR.

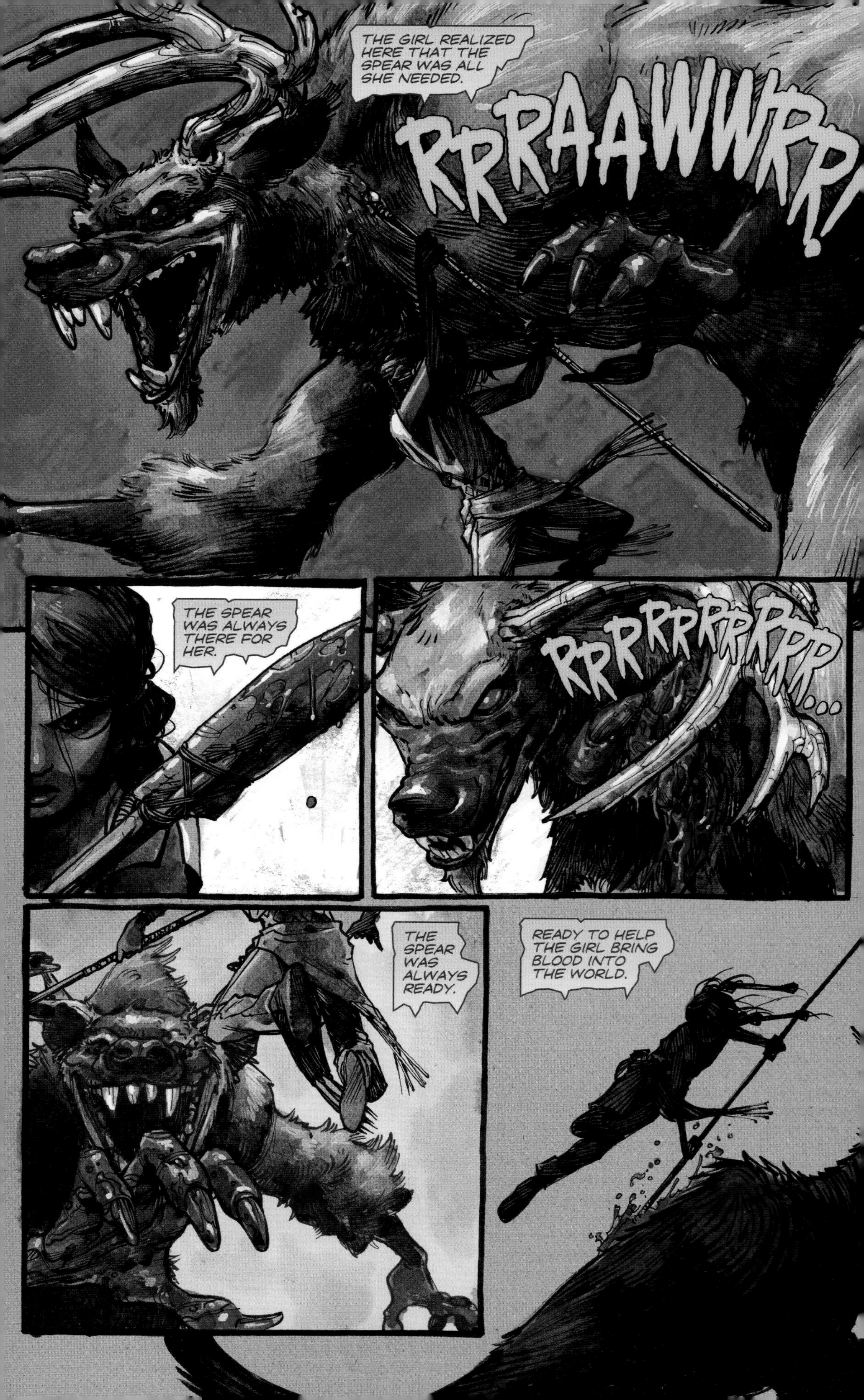
THE GIRL REALIZED HERE THAT THE SPEAR WAS ALL SHE NEEDED.
RRRAAWWRR!
THE SPEAR WAS ALWAYS THERE FOR HER.
RRRRRRRRRR...
THE SPEAR WAS ALWAYS READY.
READY TO HELP THE GIRL BRING BLOOD INTO THE WORLD.

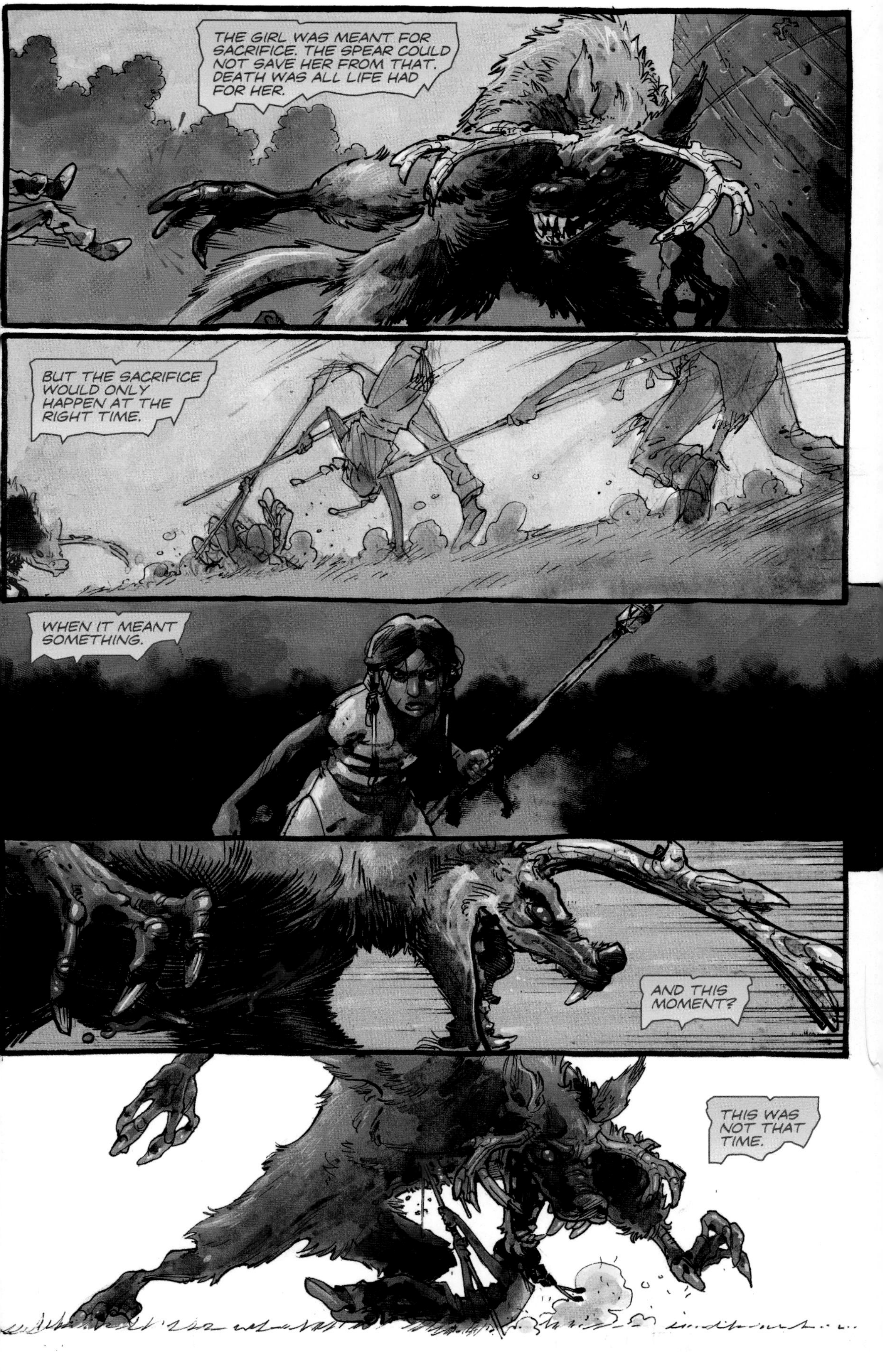
THE GIRL WAS MEANT FOR SACRIFICE. THE SPEAR COULD NOT SAVE HER FROM THAT. DEATH WAS ALL LIFE HAD FOR HER.
BUT THE SACRIFICE WOULD ONLY HAPPEN AT THE RIGHT TIME.
WHEN IT MEANT SOMETHING.
AND THIS MOMENT?
THIS WAS NOT THAT TIME.

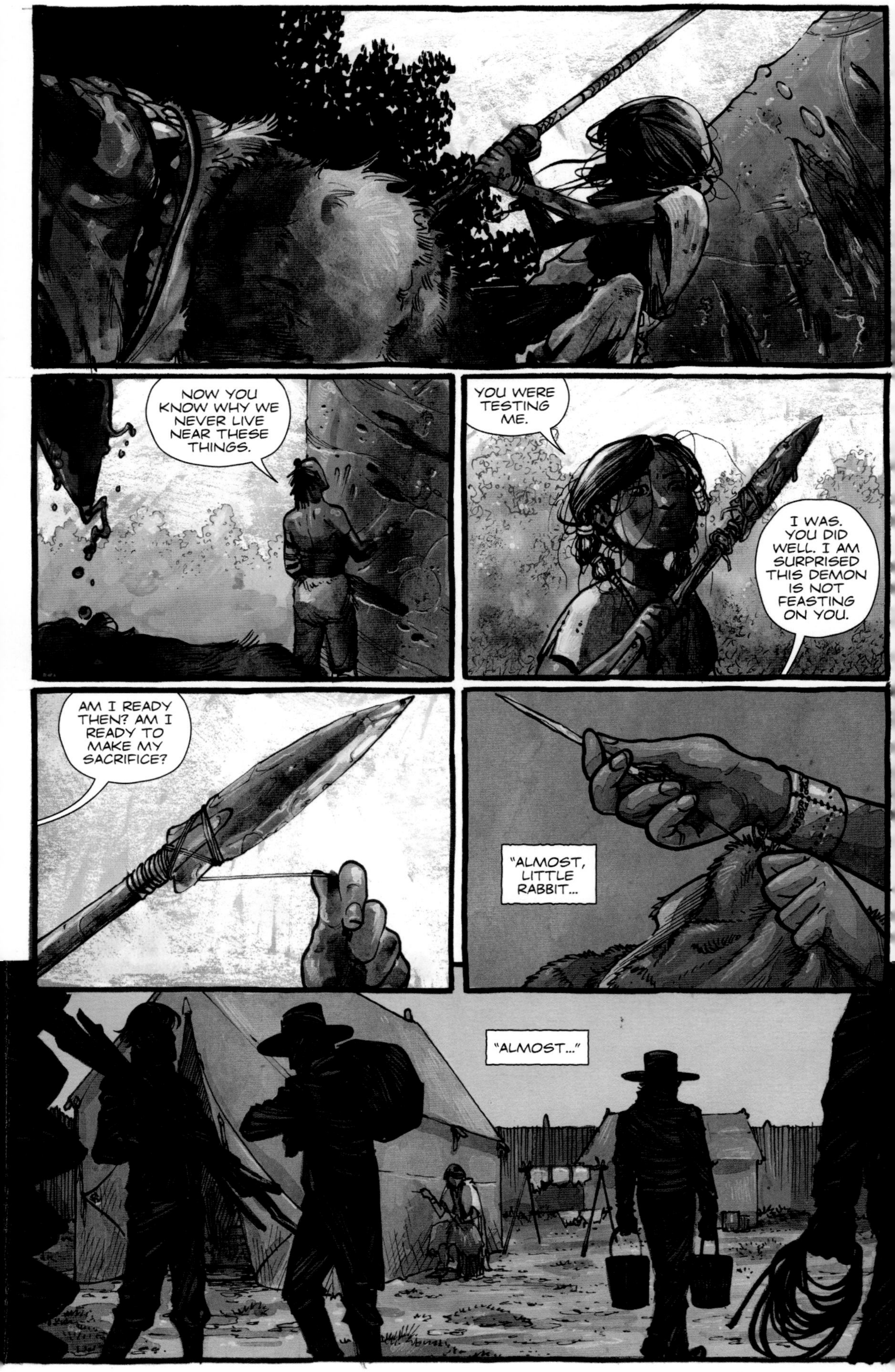
NOW YOU KNOW WHY WE NEVER LIVE NEAR THESE THINGS.
YOU WERE TESTING ME.
I WAS. YOU DID WELL. I AM SURPRISED THIS DEMON IS NOT FEASTING ON YOU.
AM I READY THEN? AM I READY TO MAKE MY SACRIFICE?
"ALMOST, LITTLE RABBIT...
"ALMOST..."

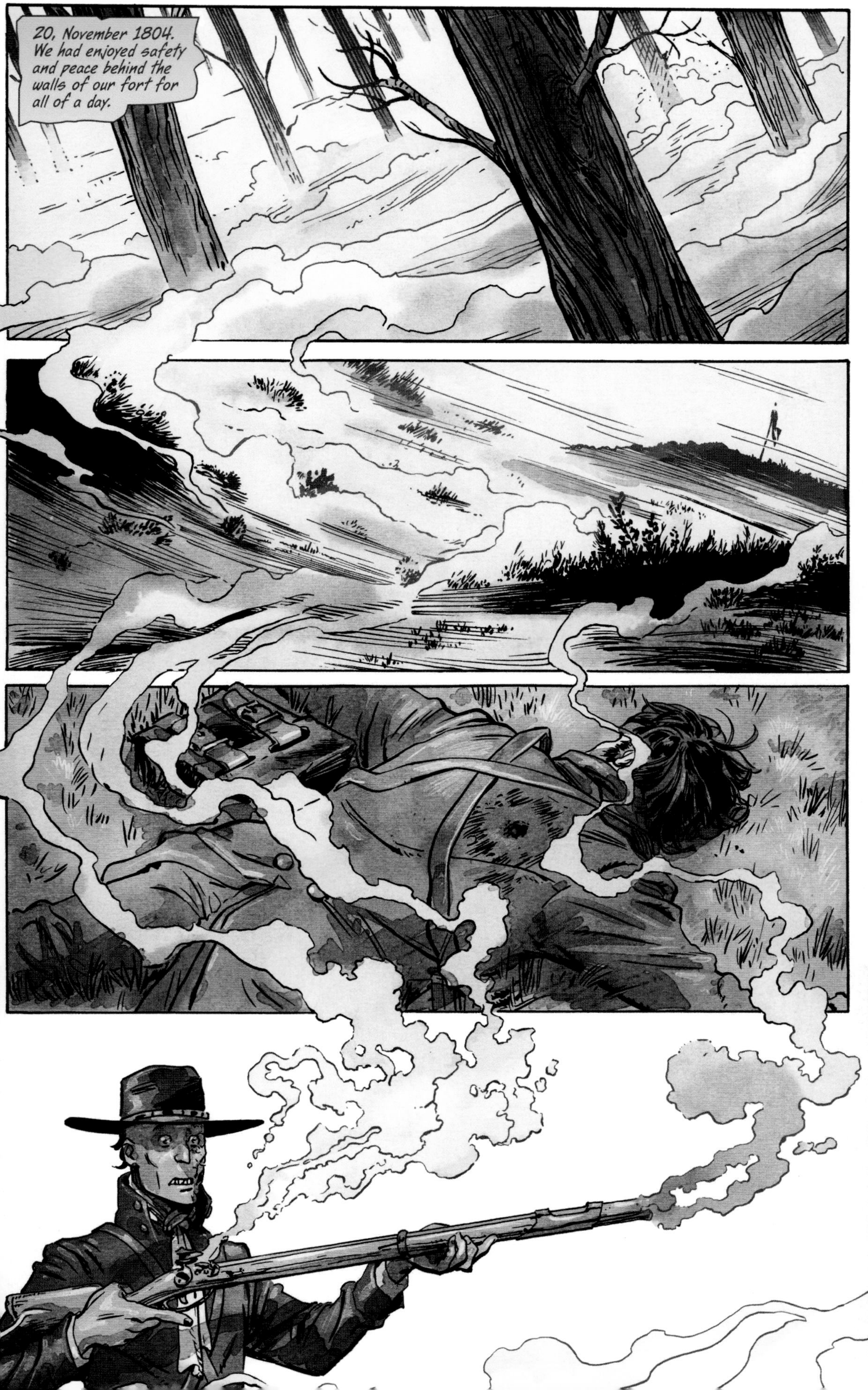
20, November 1804. We had enjoyed safety and peace behind the walls of our fort for all of a day.

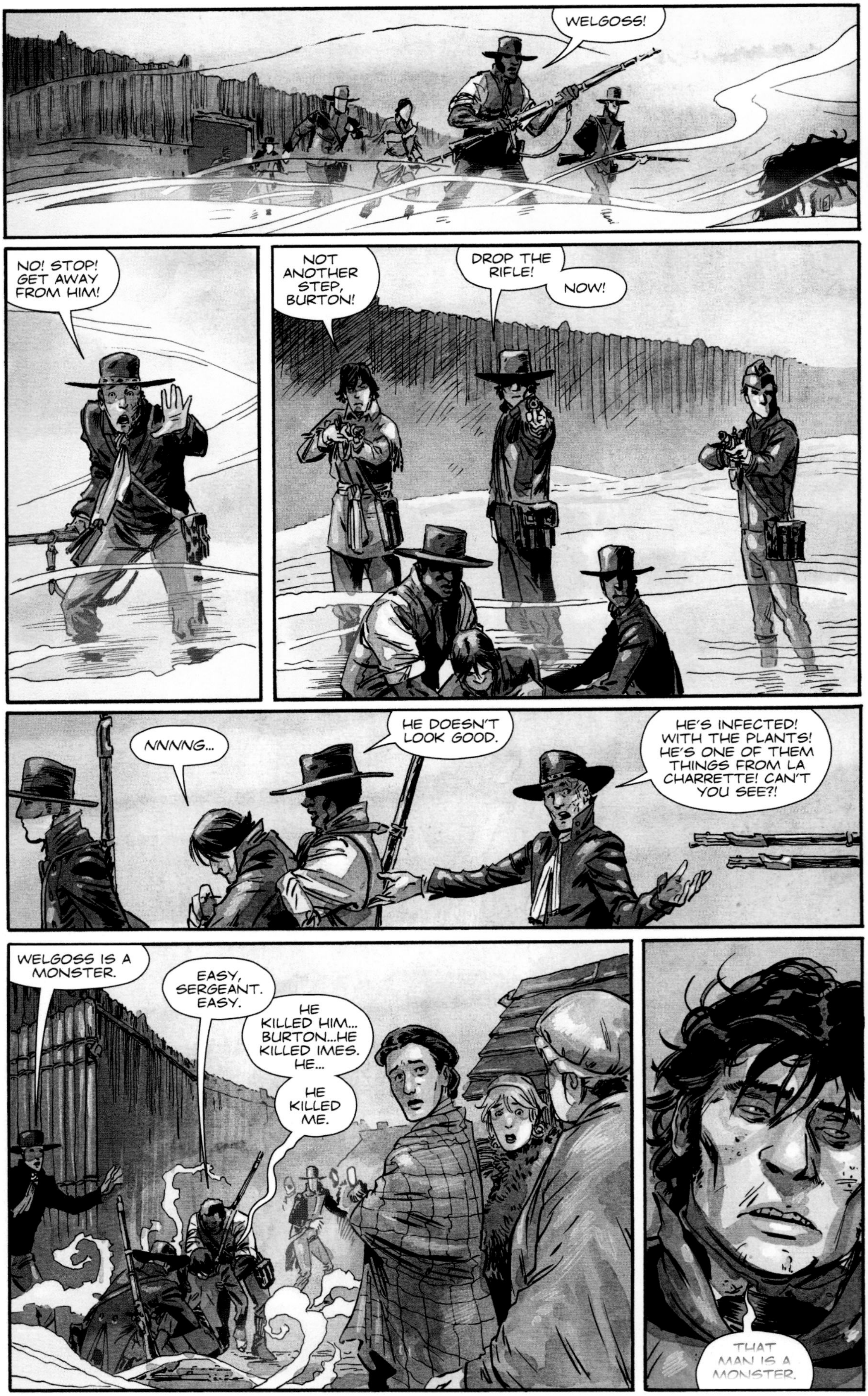
WELGOSS!
NO! STOP! GET AWAY FROM HIM!
NOT ANOTHER STEP, BURTON!
DROP THE RIFLE!
NOW!
NNNNG...
HE DOESN'T LOOK GOOD.
HE'S INFECTED! WITH THE PLANTS! HE'S ONE OF THEM THINGS FROM LA CHARRETTE! CAN'T YOU SEE?!
WELGOSS IS A MONSTER.
EASY, SERGEANT. EASY.
HE KILLED HIM... BURTON...HE KILLED IMES. HE...
HE KILLED ME.
THAT MAN IS A MONSTER.

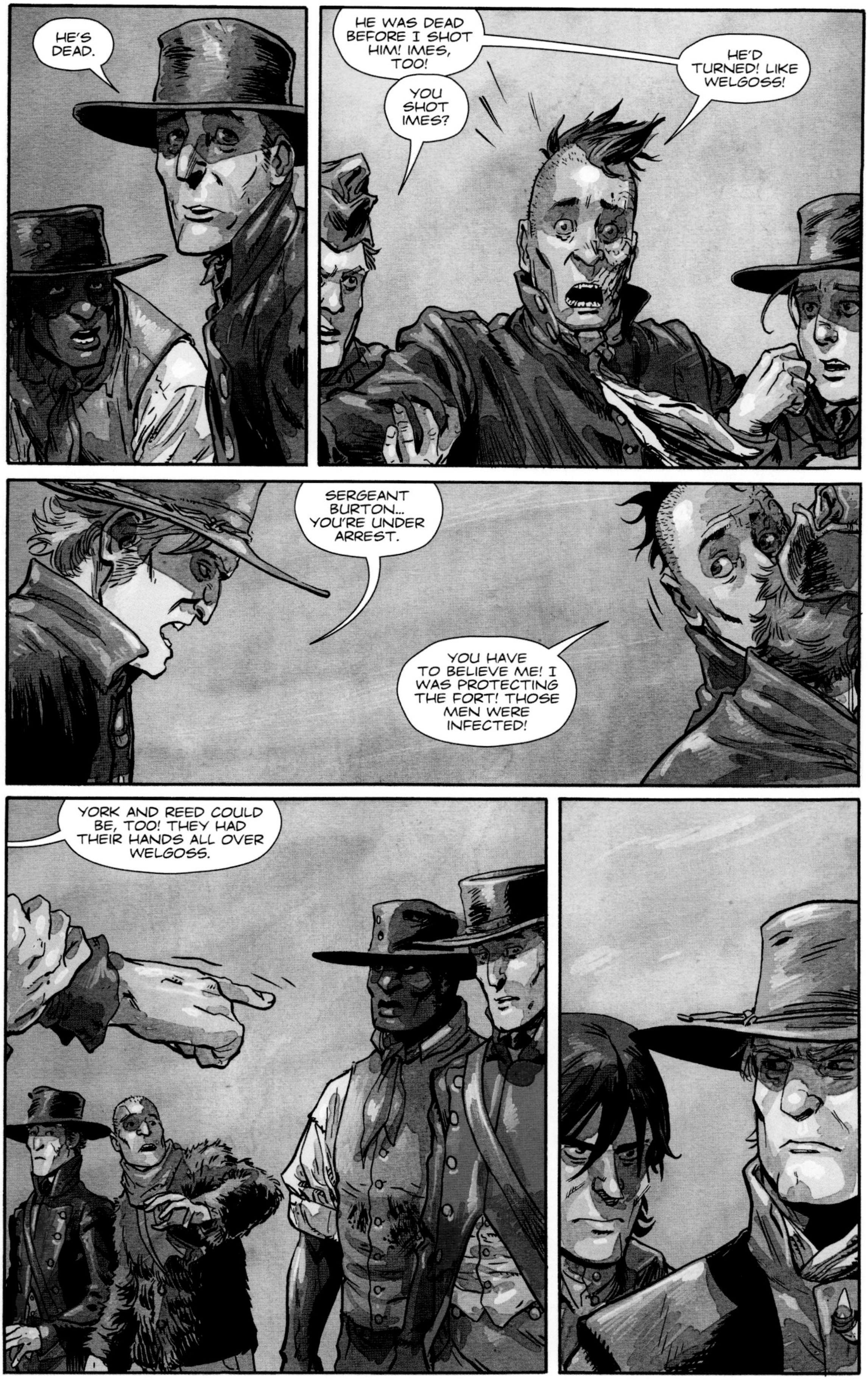
HE'S DEAD.
HE WAS DEAD BEFORE I SHOT HIM! IMES, TOO!
YOU SHOT IMES?
HE'D TURNED! LIKE WELGOSS!
SERGEANT BURTON... YOU'RE UNDER ARREST.
YOU HAVE TO BELIEVE ME! I WAS PROTECTING THE FORT! THOSE MEN WERE INFECTED!
YORK AND REED COULD BE, TOO! THEY HAD THEIR HANDS ALL OVER WELGOSS.

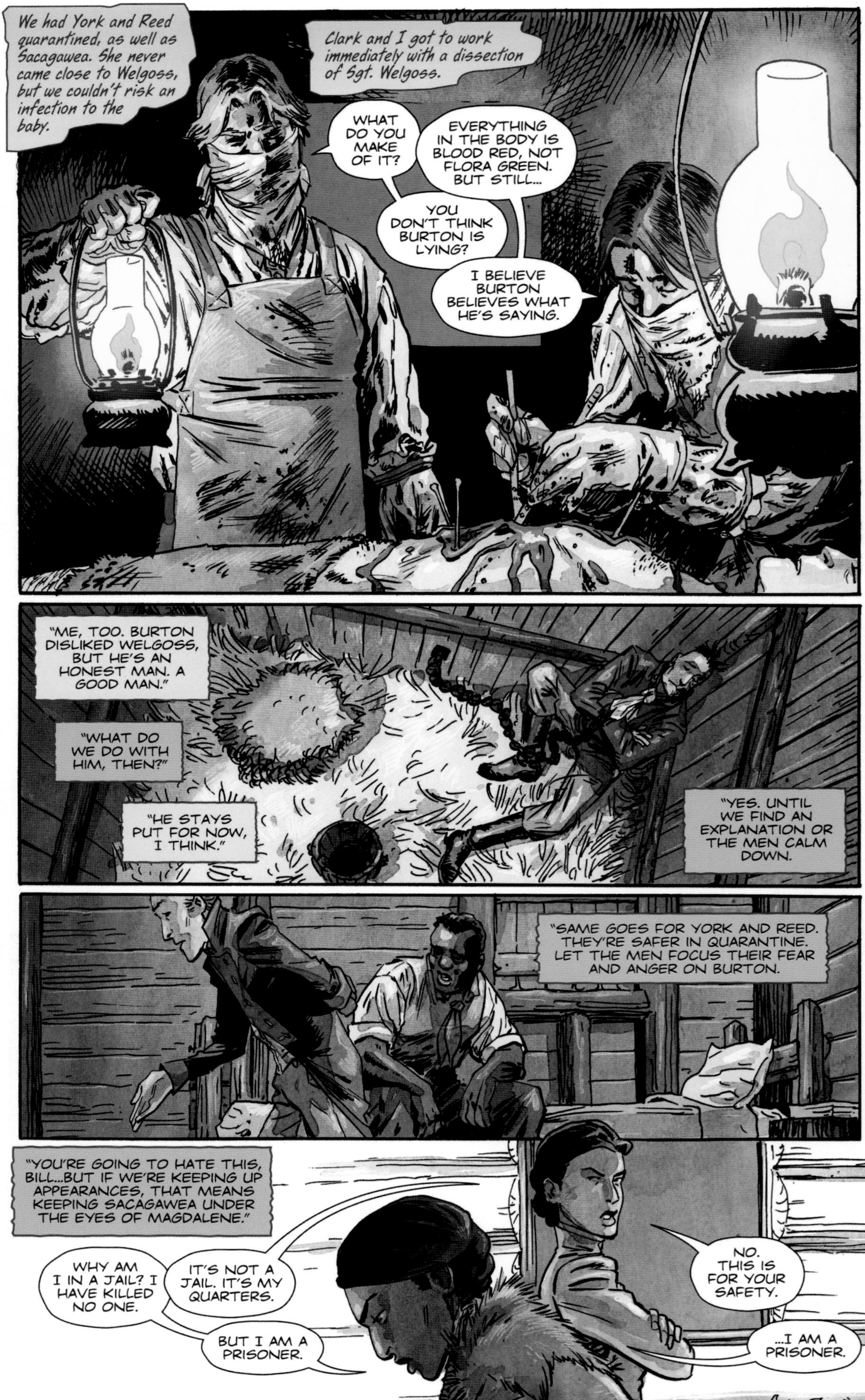
We had York and Reed quarantined, as well as Sacagawea. She never came close to Welgoss, but we couldn't risk an infection to the baby.
Clark and I got to work immediately with a dissection of Sgt. Welgoss.
WHAT DO YOU MAKE OF IT?
EVERYTHING IN THE BODY IS BLOOD RED, NOT FLORA GREEN. BUT STILL...
YOU DON'T THINK BURTON IS LYING?
I BELIEVE BURTON BELIEVES WHAT HE'S SAYING.
"ME, TOO. BURTON DISLIKED WELGOSS, BUT HE'S AN HONEST MAN. A GOOD MAN."
"WHAT DO WE DO WITH HIM, THEN?"
"HE STAYS PUT FOR NOW, I THINK."
"YES. UNTIL WE FIND AN EXPLANATION OR THE MEN CALM DOWN.
"SAME GOES FOR YORK AND REED. THEY'RE SAFER IN QUARANTINE. LET THE MEN FOCUS THEIR FEAR AND ANGER ON BURTON.
"YOU'RE GOING TO HATE THIS, BILL...BUT IF WE'RE KEEPING UP APPEARANCES, THAT MEANS KEEPING SACAGAWEA UNDER THE EYES OF MAGDALENE."
WHY AM I IN A JAIL? I HAVE KILLED NO ONE.
IT'S NOT A JAIL. IT'S MY QUARTERS.
BUT I AM A PRISONER.
NO. THIS IS FOR YOUR SAFETY.
...I AM A PRISONER.

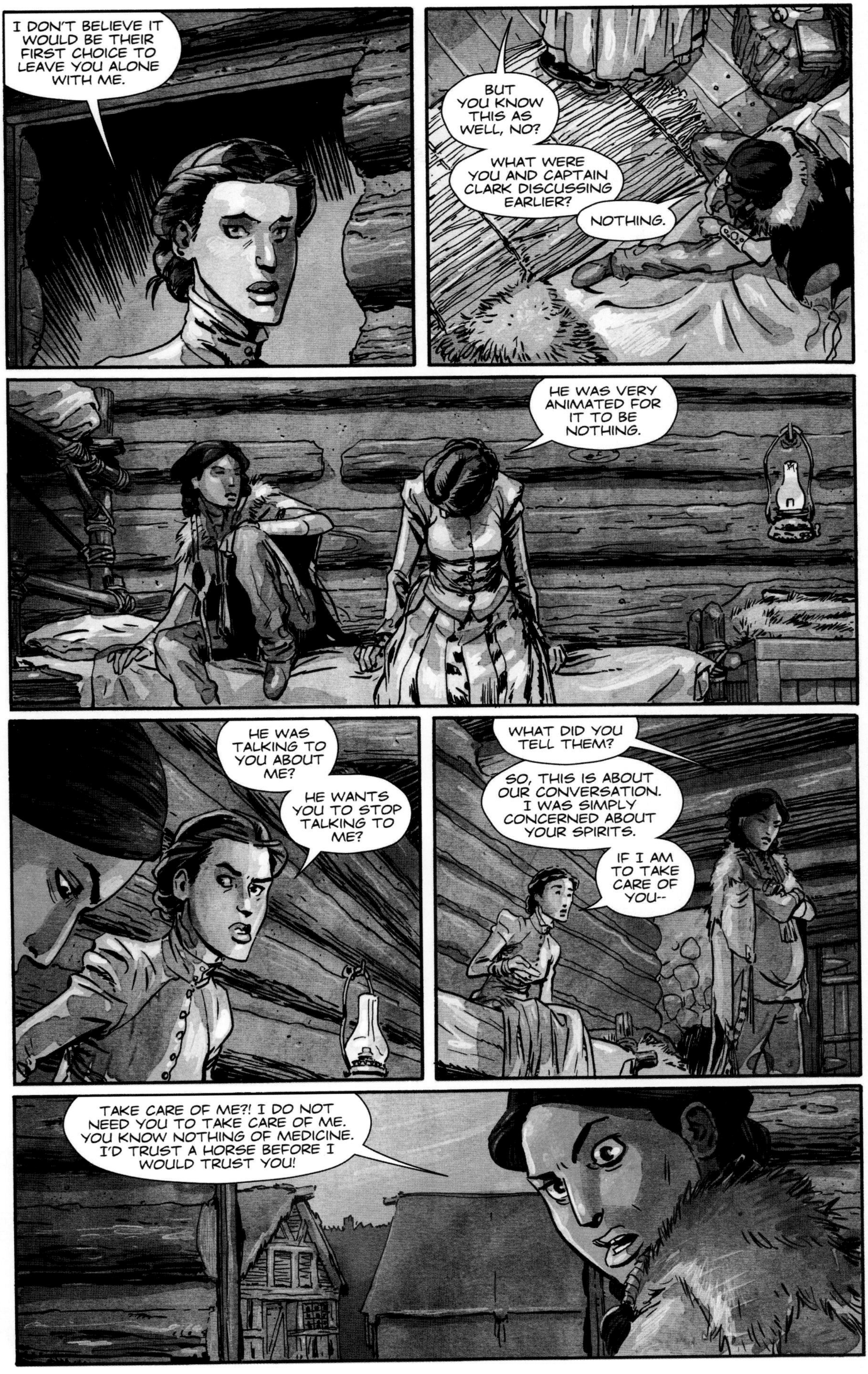
I DON'T BELIEVE IT WOULD BE THEIR FIRST CHOICE TO LEAVE YOU ALONE WITH ME.
BUT YOU KNOW THIS AS WELL, NO?
WHAT WERE YOU AND CAPTAIN CLARK DISCUSSING EARLIER?
NOTHING.
HE WAS VERY ANIMATED FOR IT TO BE NOTHING.
HE WAS TALKING TO YOU ABOUT ME?
HE WANTS YOU TO STOP TALKING TO ME?
WHAT DID YOU TELL THEM?
SO, THIS IS ABOUT OUR CONVERSATION. I WAS SIMPLY CONCERNED ABOUT YOUR SPIRITS.
IF I AM TO TAKE CARE OF YOU--
TAKE CARE OF ME?! I DO NOT NEED YOU TO TAKE CARE OF ME. YOU KNOW NOTHING OF MEDICINE. I'D TRUST A HORSE BEFORE I WOULD TRUST YOU!

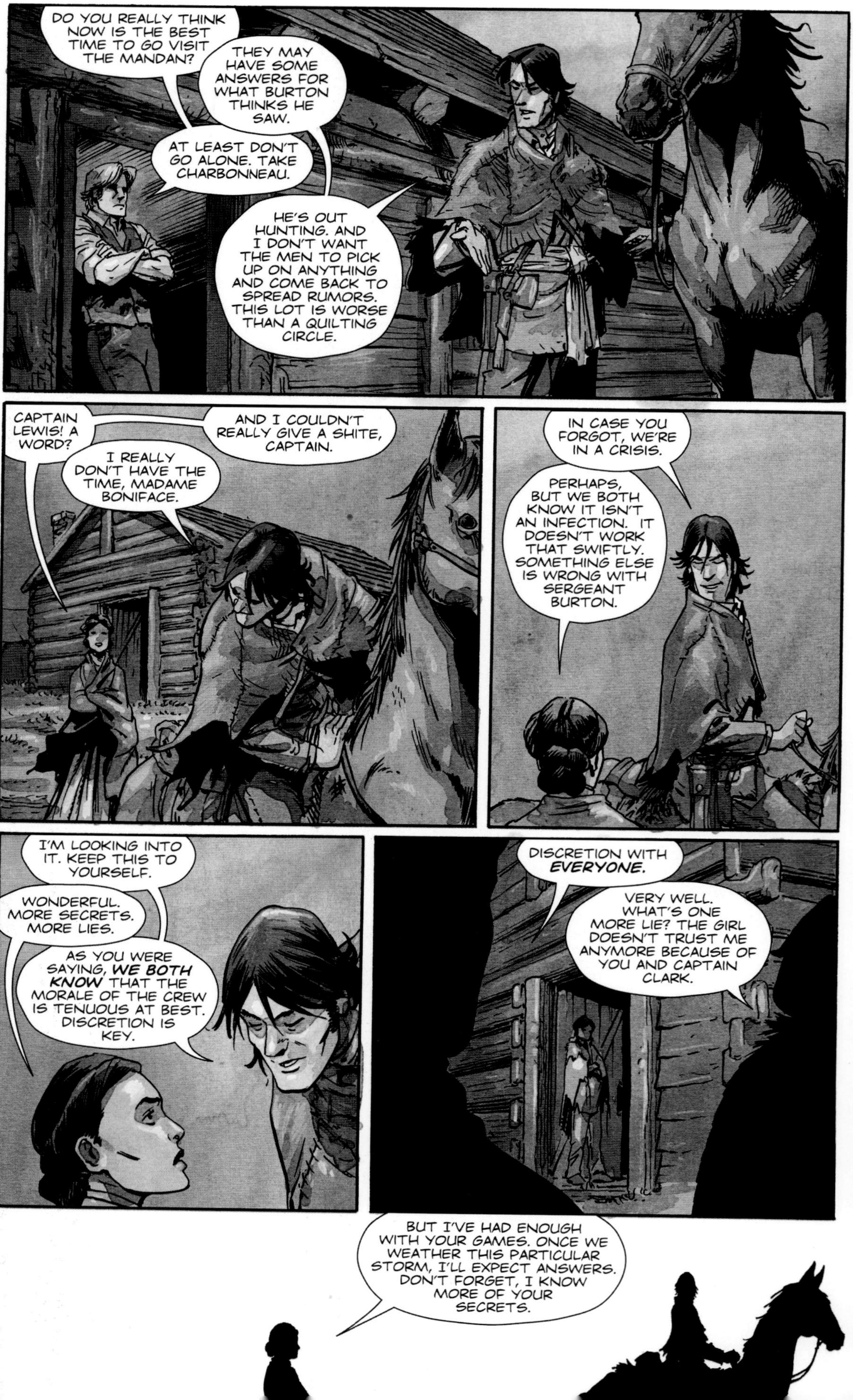
DO YOU REALLY THINK NOW IS THE BEST TIME TO GO VISIT THE MANDAN?
THEY MAY HAVE SOME ANSWERS FOR WHAT BURTON THINKS HE SAW.
AT LEAST DON'T GO ALONE. TAKE CHARBONNEAU.
HE'S OUT HUNTING. AND I DON'T WANT THE MEN TO PICK UP ON ANYTHING AND COME BACK TO SPREAD RUMORS. THIS LOT IS WORSE THAN A QUILTING CIRCLE.
CAPTAIN LEWIS! A WORD?
I REALLY DON'T HAVE THE TIME, MADAME BONIFACE.
AND I COULDN'T REALLY GIVE A SHITE, CAPTAIN.
IN CASE YOU FORGOT, WE'RE IN A CRISIS.
PERHAPS, BUT WE BOTH KNOW IT ISN'T AN INFECTION. IT DOESN'T WORK THAT SWIFTLY. SOMETHING ELSE IS WRONG WITH SERGEANT BURTON.
I'M LOOKING INTO IT. KEEP THIS TO YOURSELF.
WONDERFUL. MORE SECRETS. MORE LIES.
AS YOU WERE SAYING, ***WE BOTH KNOW*** THAT THE MORALE OF THE CREW IS TENUOUS AT BEST. DISCRETION IS KEY.
DISCRETION WITH ***EVERYONE.***
VERY WELL. WHAT'S ONE MORE LIE? THE GIRL DOESN'T TRUST ME ANYMORE BECAUSE OF YOU AND CAPTAIN CLARK.
BUT I'VE HAD ENOUGH WITH YOUR GAMES. ONCE WE WEATHER THIS PARTICULAR STORM, I'LL EXPECT ANSWERS. DON'T FORGET, I KNOW MORE OF YOUR SECRETS.

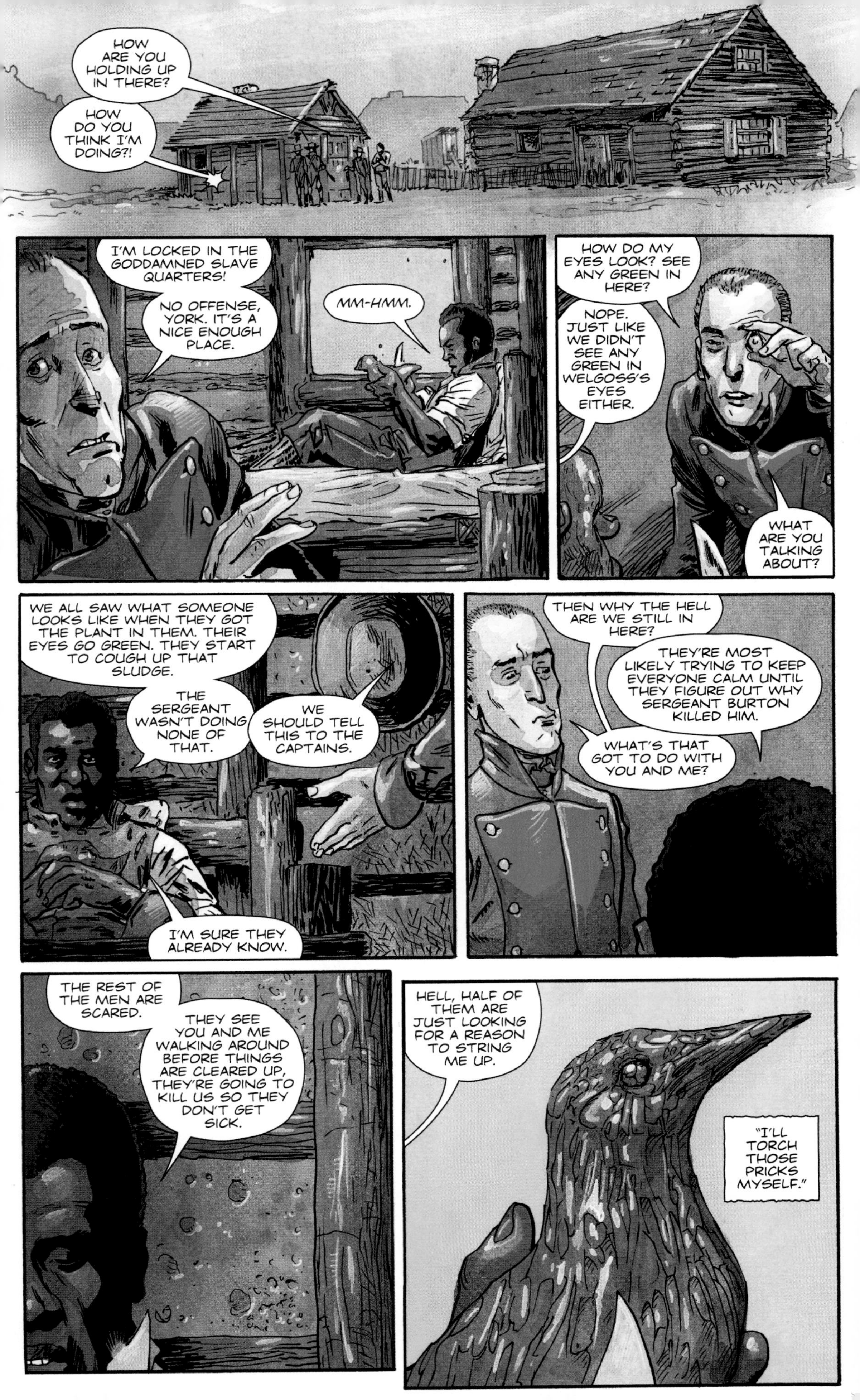
HOW ARE YOU HOLDING UP IN THERE?
HOW DO YOU THINK I'M DOING?!
I'M LOCKED IN THE GODDAMNED SLAVE QUARTERS!
NO OFFENSE, YORK. IT'S A NICE ENOUGH PLACE.
MM-HMM.
HOW DO MY EYES LOOK? SEE ANY GREEN IN HERE?
NOPE. JUST LIKE WE DIDN'T SEE ANY GREEN IN WELGOSS'S EYES EITHER.
WHAT ARE YOU TALKING ABOUT?
WE ALL SAW WHAT SOMEONE LOOKS LIKE WHEN THEY GOT THE PLANT IN THEM. THEIR EYES GO GREEN. THEY START TO COUGH UP THAT SLUDGE.
THE SERGEANT WASN'T DOING NONE OF THAT.
WE SHOULD TELL THIS TO THE CAPTAINS.
I'M SURE THEY ALREADY KNOW.
THEN WHY THE HELL ARE WE STILL IN HERE?
THEY'RE MOST LIKELY TRYING TO KEEP EVERYONE CALM UNTIL THEY FIGURE OUT WHY SERGEANT BURTON KILLED HIM.
WHAT'S THAT GOT TO DO WITH YOU AND ME?
THE REST OF THE MEN ARE SCARED.
THEY SEE YOU AND ME WALKING AROUND BEFORE THINGS ARE CLEARED UP, THEY'RE GOING TO KILL US SO THEY DON'T GET SICK.
HELL, HALF OF THEM ARE JUST LOOKING FOR A REASON TO STRING ME UP.
"I'LL TORCH THOSE PRICKS MYSELF."

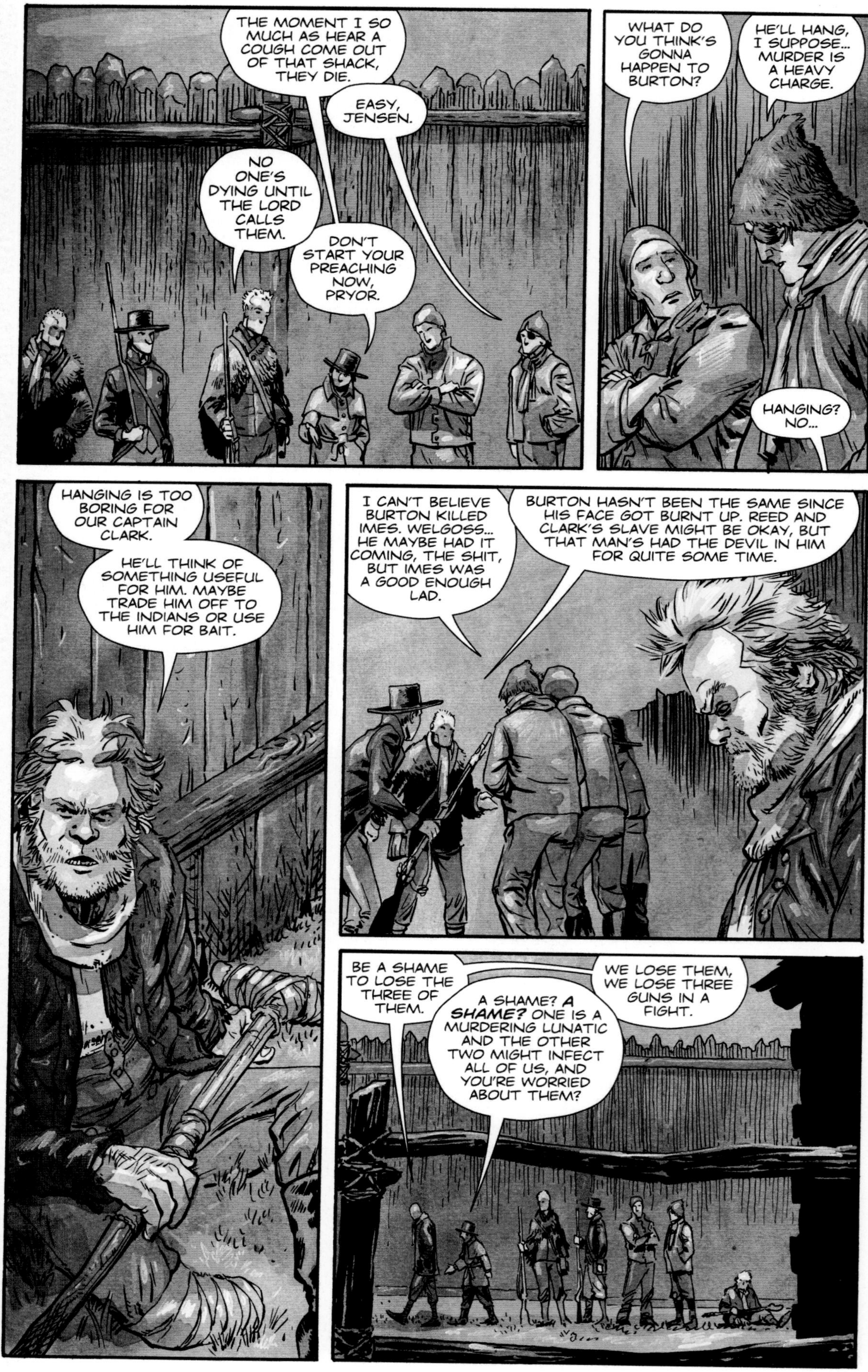
THE MOMENT I SO MUCH AS HEAR A COUGH COME OUT OF THAT SHACK, THEY DIE.
EASY, JENSEN.
NO ONE'S DYING UNTIL THE LORD CALLS THEM.
DON'T START YOUR PREACHING NOW, PRYOR.
WHAT DO YOU THINK'S GONNA HAPPEN TO BURTON?
HE'LL HANG, I SUPPOSE... MURDER IS A HEAVY CHARGE.
HANGING? NO...
HANGING IS TOO BORING FOR OUR CAPTAIN CLARK.
HE'LL THINK OF SOMETHING USEFUL FOR HIM. MAYBE TRADE HIM OFF TO THE INDIANS OR USE HIM FOR BAIT.
I CAN'T BELIEVE BURTON KILLED IMES. WELGOSS... HE MAYBE HAD IT COMING, THE SHIT, BUT IMES WAS A GOOD ENOUGH LAD.
BURTON HASN'T BEEN THE SAME SINCE HIS FACE GOT BURNT UP. REED AND CLARK'S SLAVE MIGHT BE OKAY, BUT THAT MAN'S HAD THE DEVIL IN HIM FOR QUITE SOME TIME.
BE A SHAME TO LOSE THE THREE OF THEM.
WE LOSE THEM, WE LOSE THREE GUNS IN A FIGHT.
A SHAME? A SHAME? ONE IS A MURDERING LUNATIC AND THE OTHER TWO MIGHT INFECT ALL OF US, AND YOU'RE WORRIED ABOUT THEM?

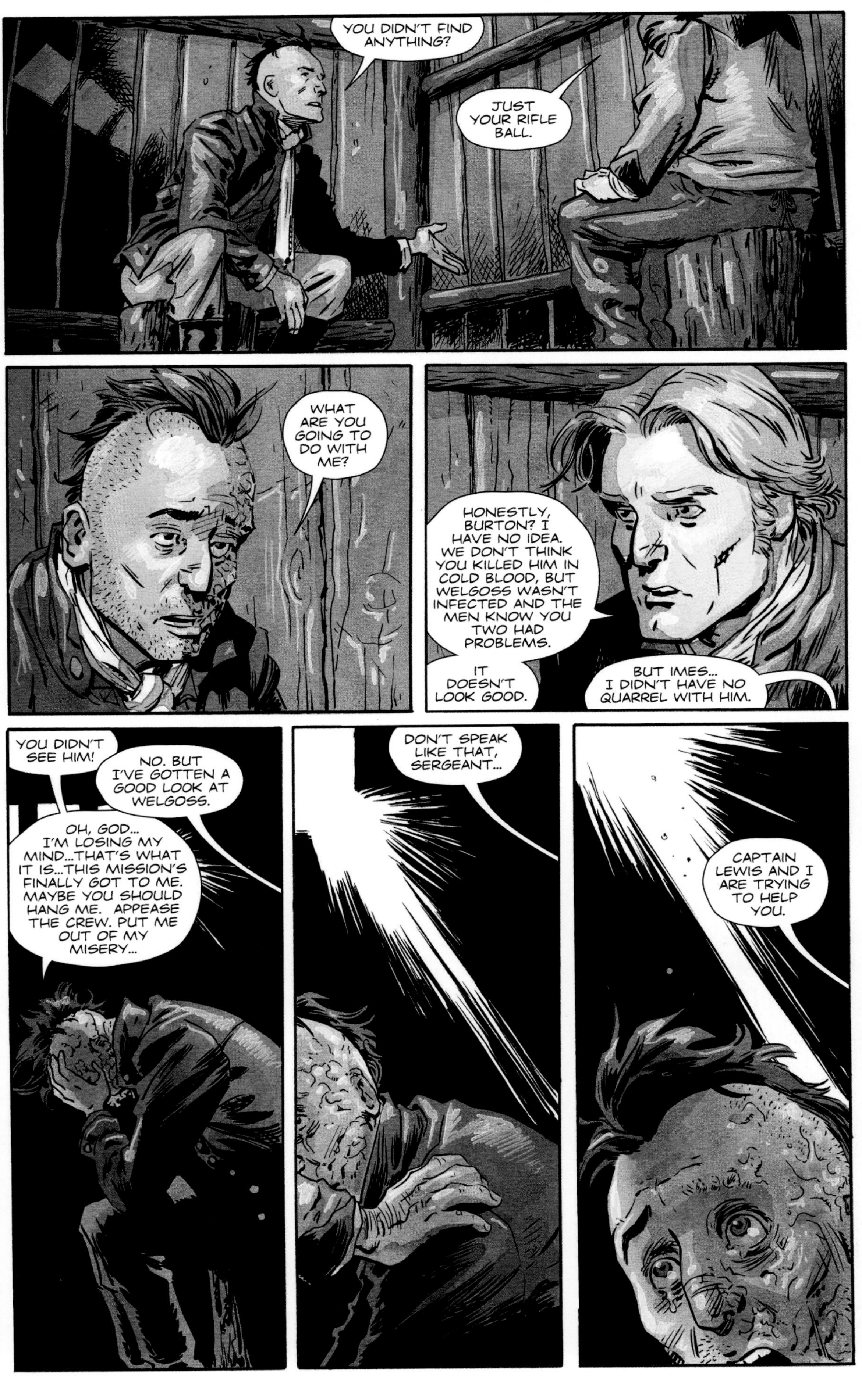
YOU DIDN'T FIND ANYTHING?
JUST YOUR RIFLE BALL.
WHAT ARE YOU GOING TO DO WITH ME?
HONESTLY, BURTON? I HAVE NO IDEA. WE DON'T THINK YOU KILLED HIM IN COLD BLOOD, BUT WELGOSS WASN'T INFECTED AND THE MEN KNOW YOU TWO HAD PROBLEMS.
IT DOESN'T LOOK GOOD.
BUT IMES... I DIDN'T HAVE NO QUARREL WITH HIM.
YOU DIDN'T SEE HIM!
NO. BUT I'VE GOTTEN A GOOD LOOK AT WELGOSS.
OH, GOD... I'M LOSING MY MIND...THAT'S WHAT IT IS...THIS MISSION'S FINALLY GOT TO ME. MAYBE YOU SHOULD HANG ME. APPEASE THE CREW. PUT ME OUT OF MY MISERY...
DON'T SPEAK LIKE THAT, SERGEANT...
CAPTAIN LEWIS AND I ARE TRYING TO HELP YOU.

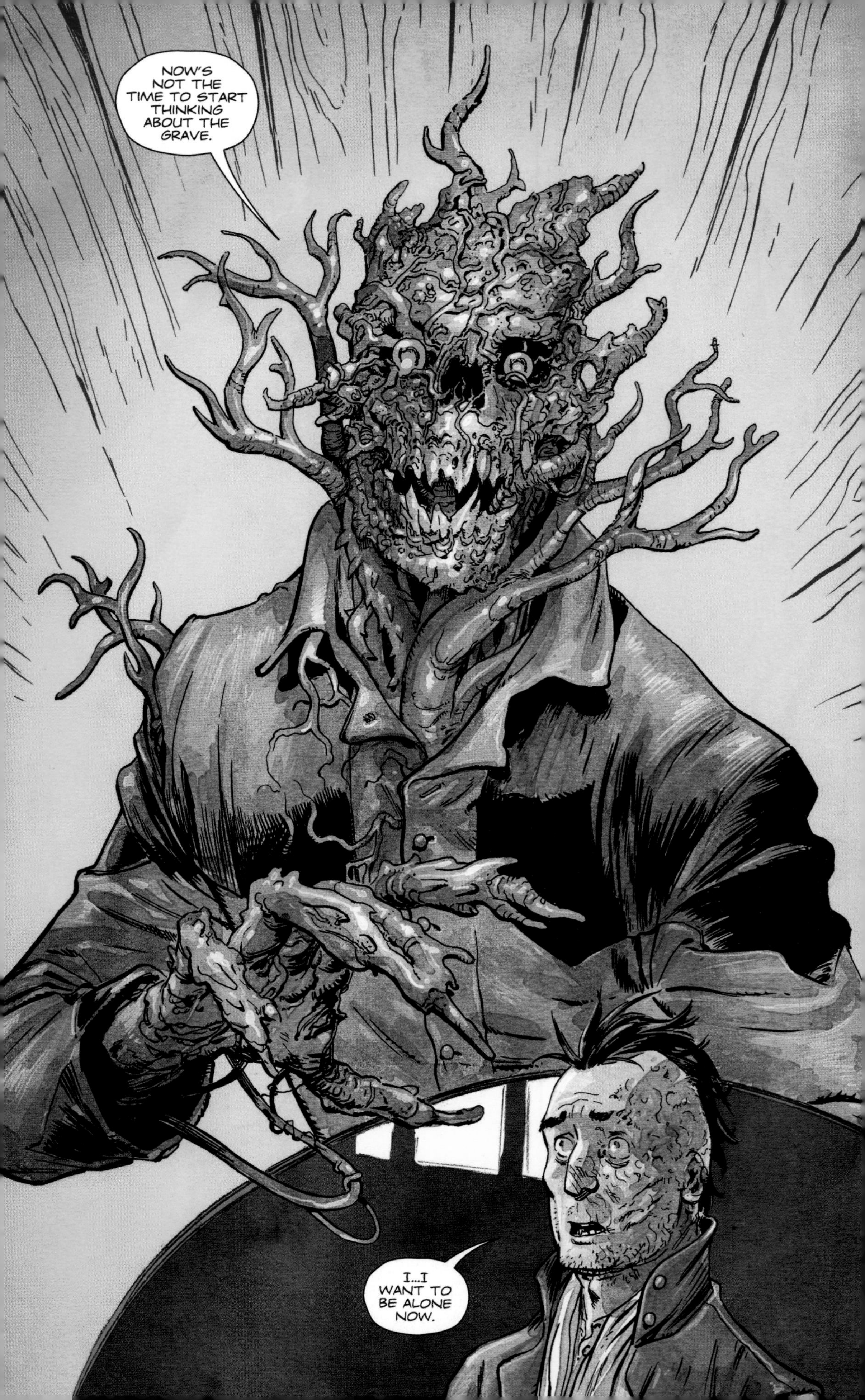
NOW'S NOT THE TIME TO START THINKING ABOUT THE GRAVE.
I...I WANT TO BE ALONE NOW.

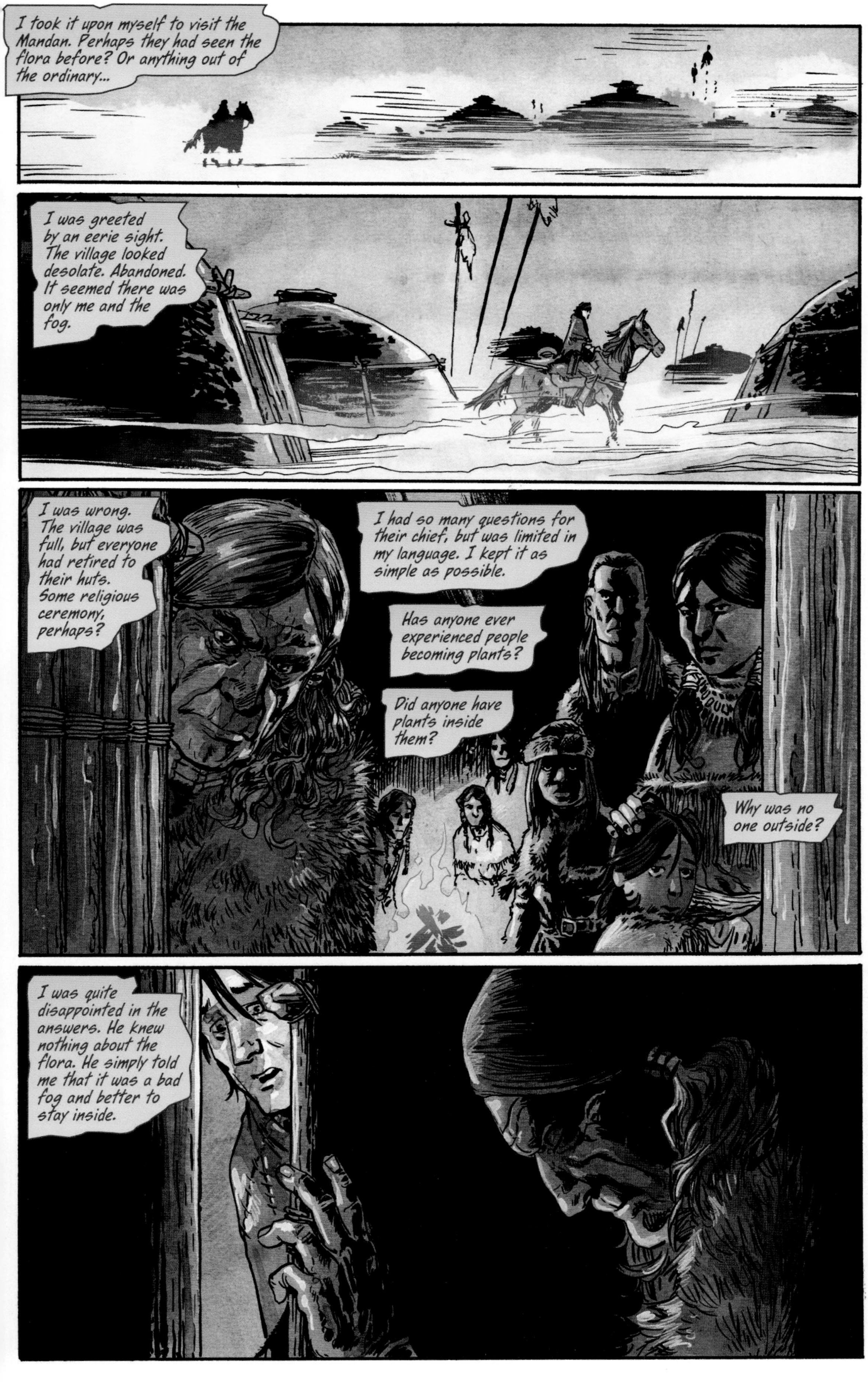
I took it upon myself to visit the Mandan. Perhaps they had seen the flora before? Or anything out of the ordinary...
I was greeted by an eerie sight. The village looked desolate. Abandoned. It seemed there was only me and the fog.
I was wrong. The village was full, but everyone had retired to their huts. Some religious ceremony, perhaps?
I had so many questions for their chief, but was limited in my language. I kept it as simple as possible.
Has anyone ever experienced people becoming plants?
Did anyone have plants inside them?
Why was no one outside?
I was quite disappointed in the answers. He knew nothing about the flora. He simply told me that it was a bad fog and better to stay inside.

He is not wrong about the fog. It hindered my visibility and added an extra hour to my return trip.

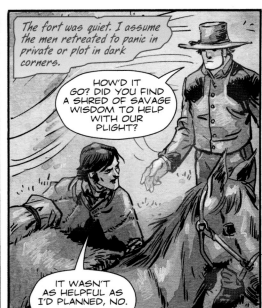

The fort was quiet. I assume the men retreated to panic in private or plot in dark corners.

HOW'D IT GO? DID YOU FIND A SHRED OF SAVAGE WISDOM TO HELP WITH OUR PLIGHT?

IT WASN'T AS HELPFUL AS I'D PLANNED, NO.

HOW ARE THINGS HERE?

TENSE. BUT NO LYNCH MOBS YET. SO IT'S A SMALL VICTORY.

AND BURTON?

BECOMING MORE UNHINGED BY THE MOMENT.

PERHAPS I SHOULD CHECK ON HIM.

I'D HOLD OFF ON THAT. I GOT THE FEELING HE WAS STARTING TO LOOK AT ME AS THOUGH I RESEMBLED WELGOSS.

DIDN'T THINK THIS FOG COULD GET ANY THICKER.

IT'S A SOUP, ALRIGHT. I'M NOT EVEN SURE WHAT THE POINT OF GUARD DUTY IS IN THIS MUCK.

"IF ANYTHING WANTED TO CREEP UP ON US, NOW'S THE TIME."

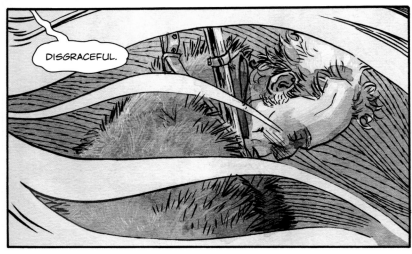

DISGRACEFUL.

STILL PATHETIC, I SEE.

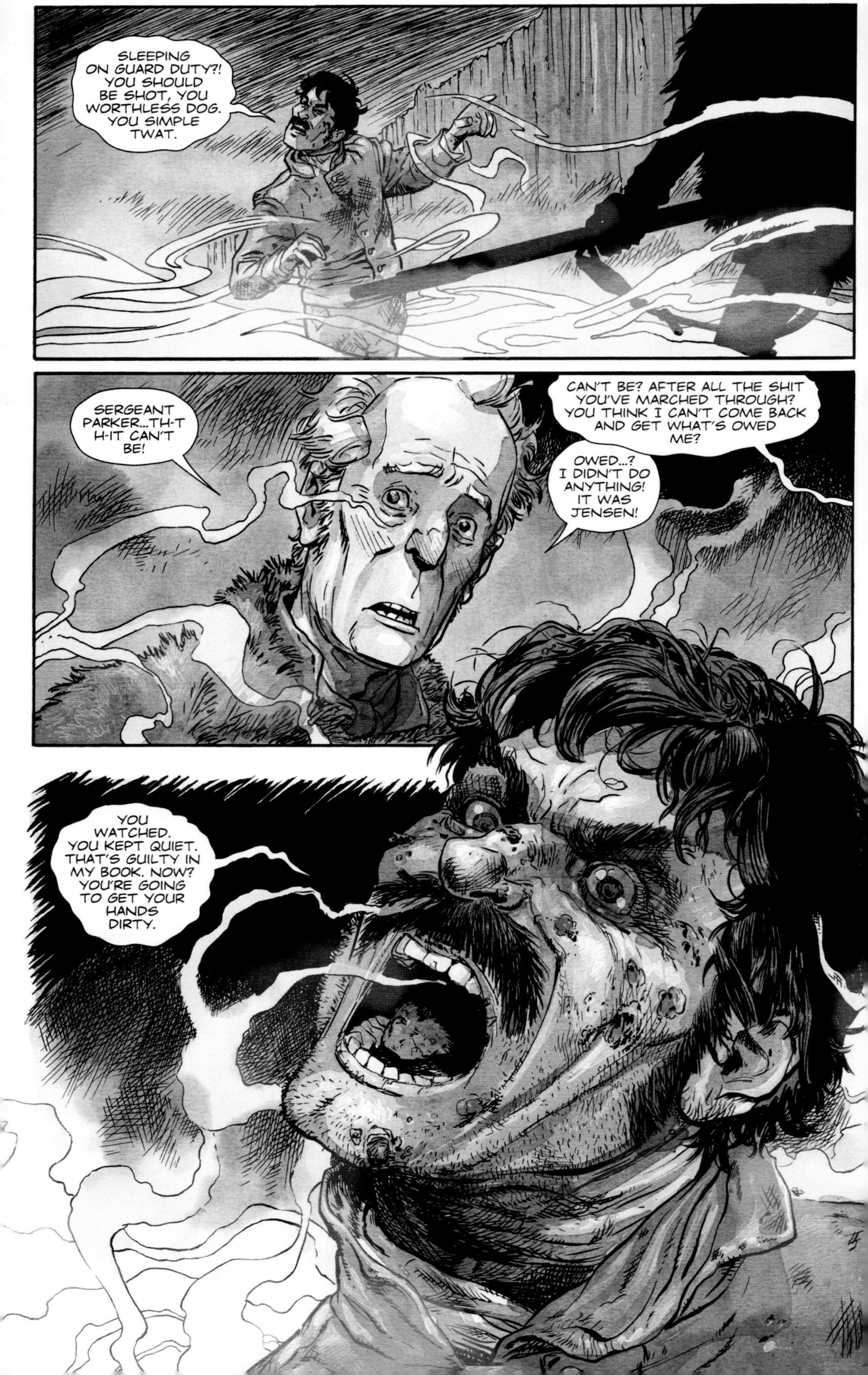
SLEEPING ON GUARD DUTY?! YOU SHOULD BE SHOT, YOU WORTHLESS DOG. YOU SIMPLE TWAT.
SERGEANT PARKER...TH-TH-IT CAN'T BE!
CAN'T BE? AFTER ALL THE SHIT YOU'VE MARCHED THROUGH? YOU THINK I CAN'T COME BACK AND GET WHAT'S OWED ME?
OWED...? I DIDN'T DO ANYTHING! IT WAS JENSEN!
YOU WATCHED. YOU KEPT QUIET. THAT'S GUILTY IN MY BOOK. NOW? YOU'RE GOING TO GET YOUR HANDS DIRTY.

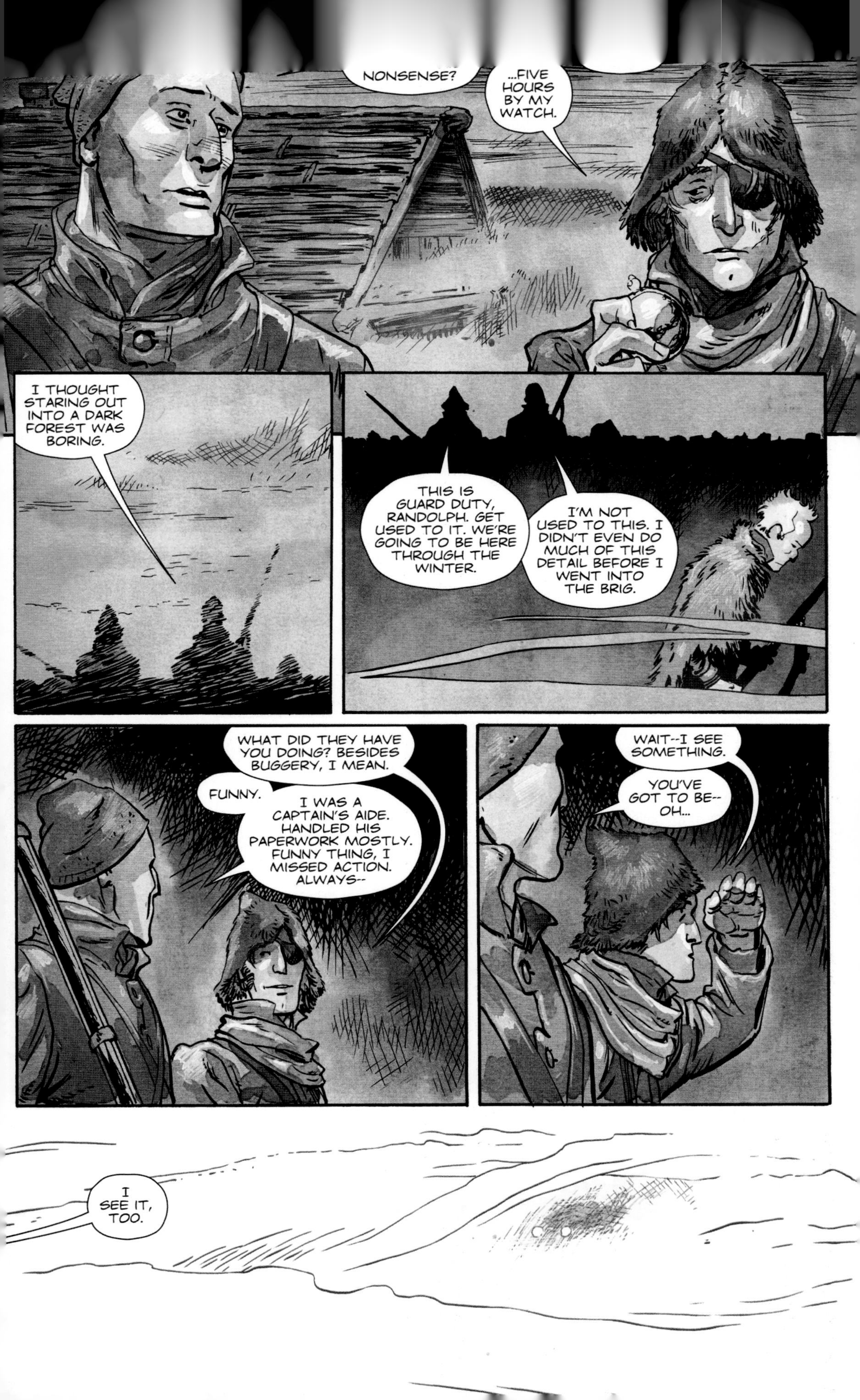
NONSENSE?
...FIVE HOURS BY MY WATCH.
I THOUGHT STARING OUT INTO A DARK FOREST WAS BORING.
THIS IS GUARD DUTY, RANDOLPH. GET USED TO IT. WE'RE GOING TO BE HERE THROUGH THE WINTER.
I'M NOT USED TO THIS. I DIDN'T EVEN DO MUCH OF THIS DETAIL BEFORE I WENT INTO THE BRIG.
WHAT DID THEY HAVE YOU DOING? BESIDES BUGGERY, I MEAN.
FUNNY.
I WAS A CAPTAIN'S AIDE. HANDLED HIS PAPERWORK MOSTLY. FUNNY THING, I MISSED ACTION. ALWAYS--
WAIT--I SEE SOMETHING.
YOU'VE GOT TO BE-- OH...
I SEE IT, TOO.

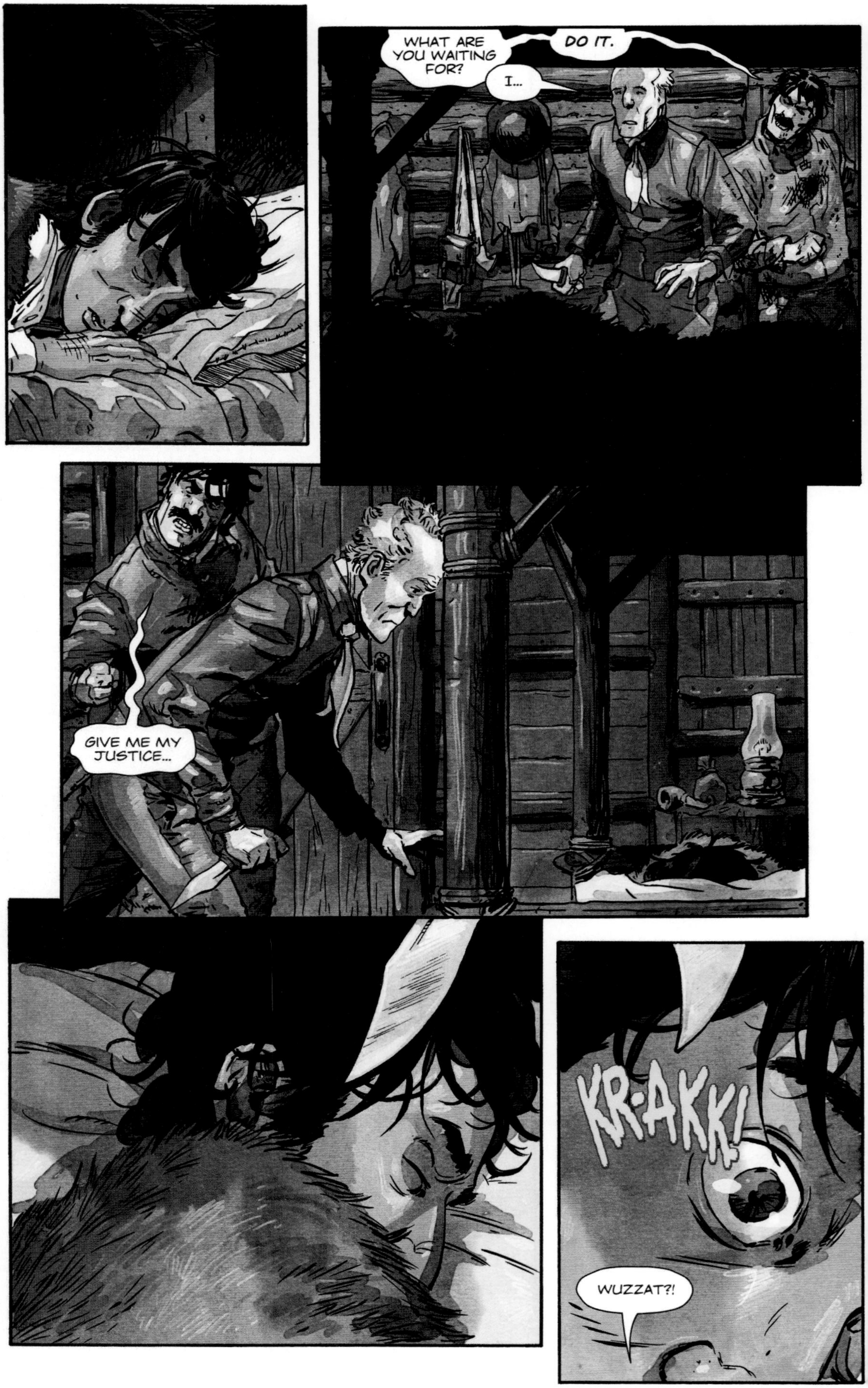
WHAT ARE YOU WAITING FOR?
DO IT.
I...
GIVE ME MY JUSTICE...
KR-AKK!
WUZZAT?!

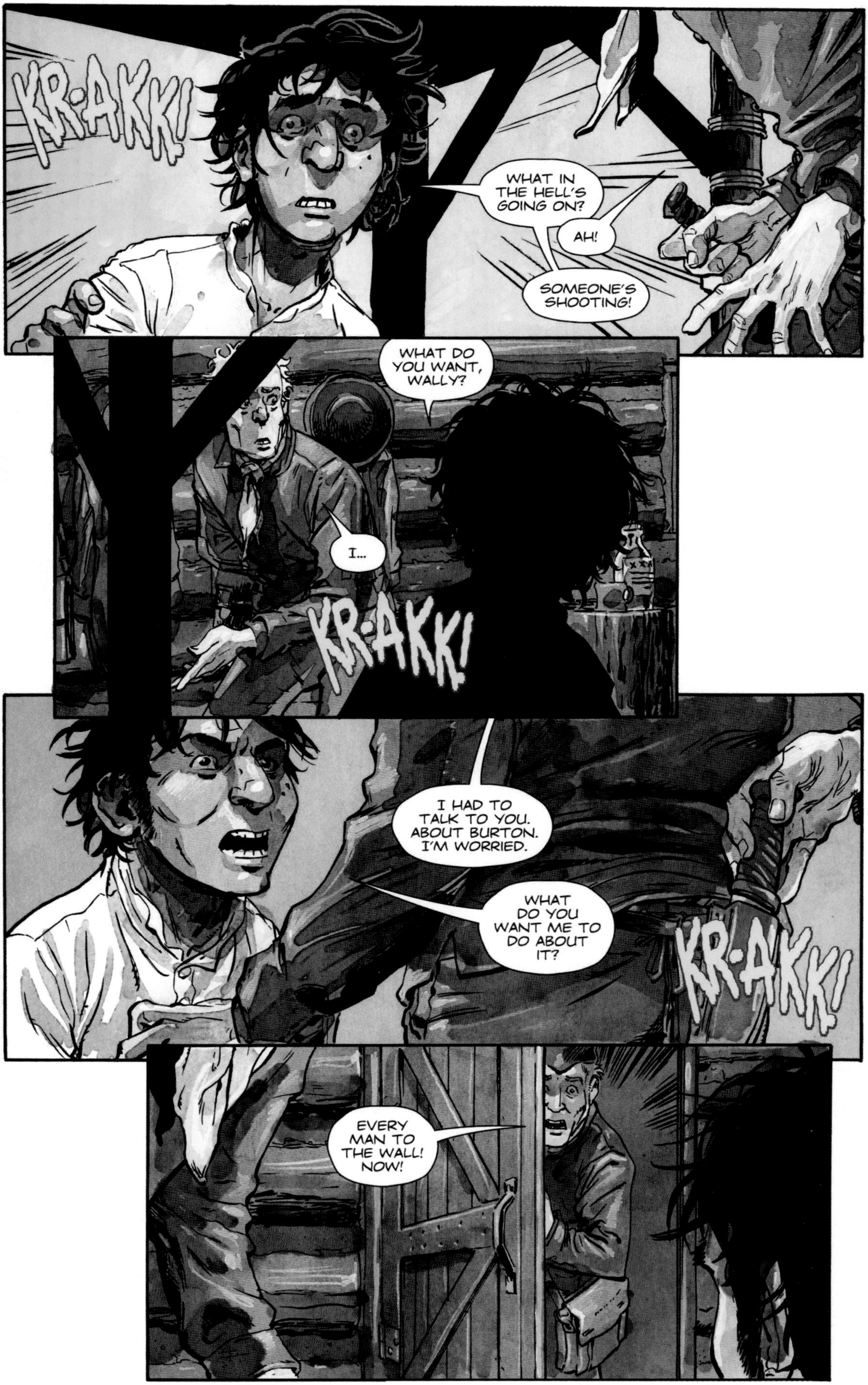
KR-AKK!
WHAT IN THE HELL'S GOING ON?
AH!
SOMEONE'S SHOOTING!
WHAT DO YOU WANT, WALLY?
I...
KR-AKK!
I HAD TO TALK TO YOU. ABOUT BURTON. I'M WORRIED.
WHAT DO YOU WANT ME TO DO ABOUT IT?
KR-AKK!
EVERY MAN TO THE WALL! NOW!

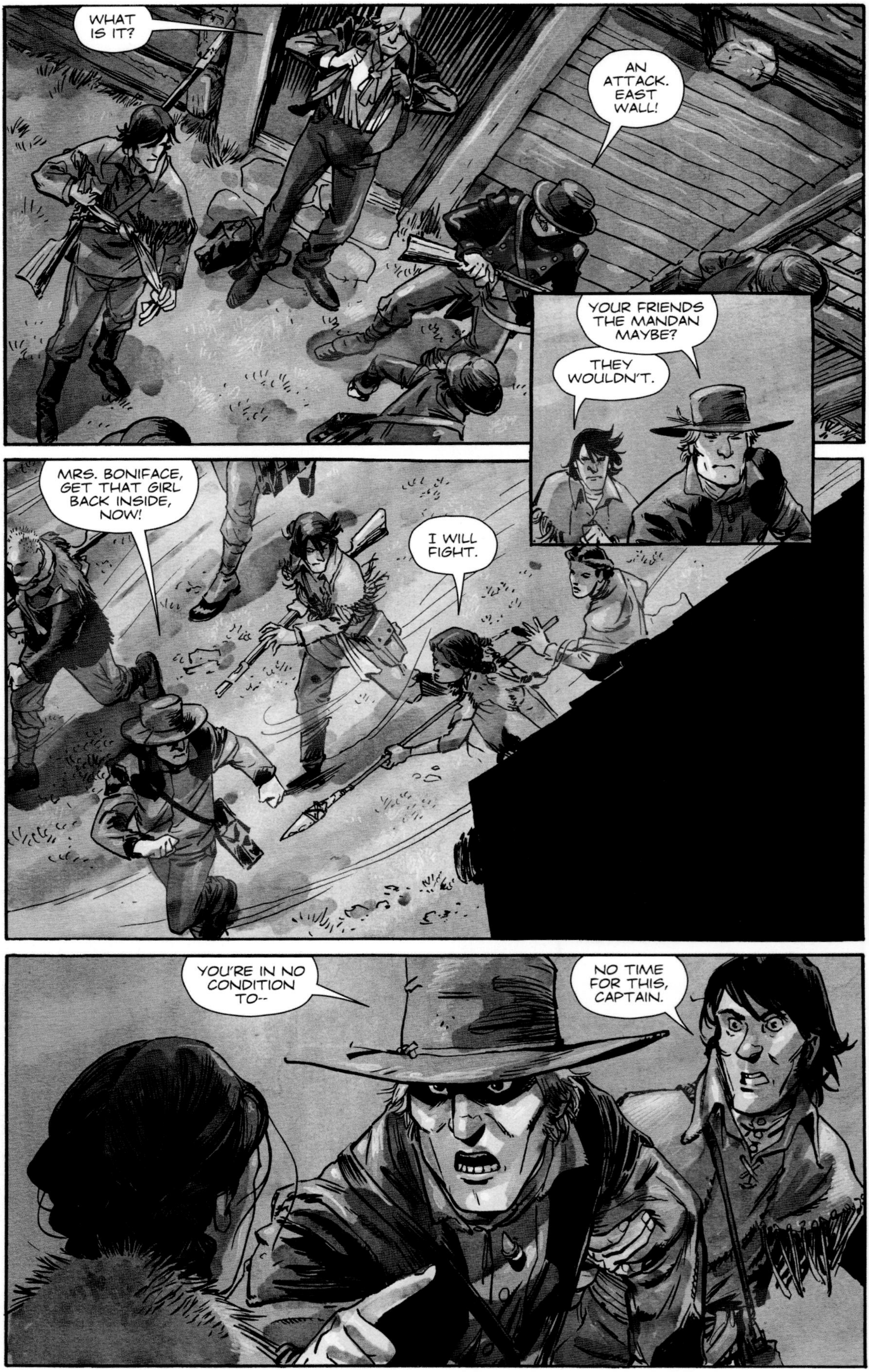
WHAT IS IT?
AN ATTACK. EAST WALL!
YOUR FRIENDS THE MANDAN MAYBE?
THEY WOULDN'T.
MRS. BONIFACE, GET THAT GIRL BACK INSIDE, NOW!
I WILL FIGHT.
YOU'RE IN NO CONDITION TO--
NO TIME FOR THIS, CAPTAIN.

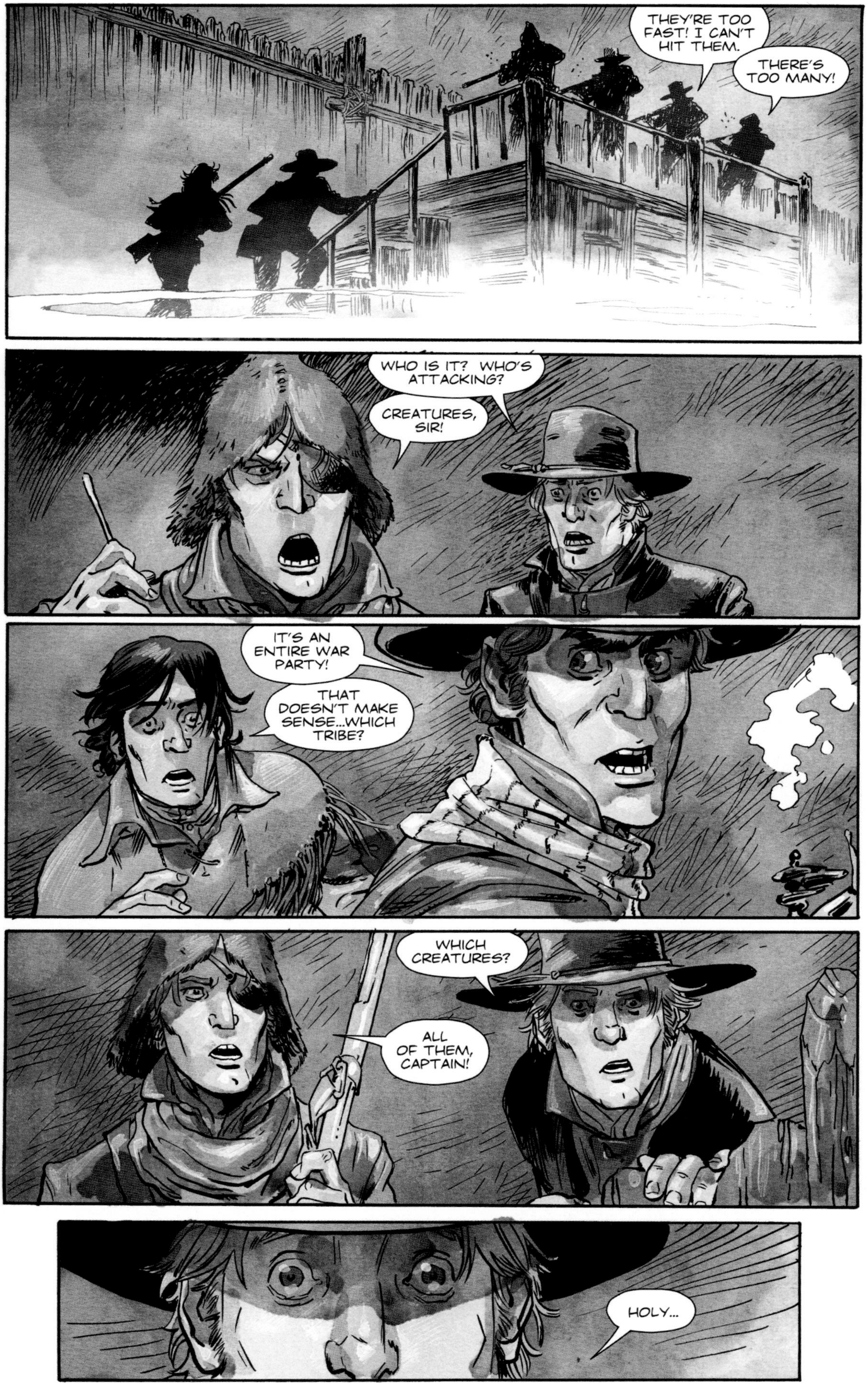
THEY'RE TOO FAST! I CAN'T HIT THEM.
THERE'S TOO MANY!
WHO IS IT? WHO'S ATTACKING?
CREATURES, SIR!
IT'S AN ENTIRE WAR PARTY!
THAT DOESN'T MAKE SENSE...WHICH TRIBE?
WHICH CREATURES?
ALL OF THEM, CAPTAIN!
HOLY...

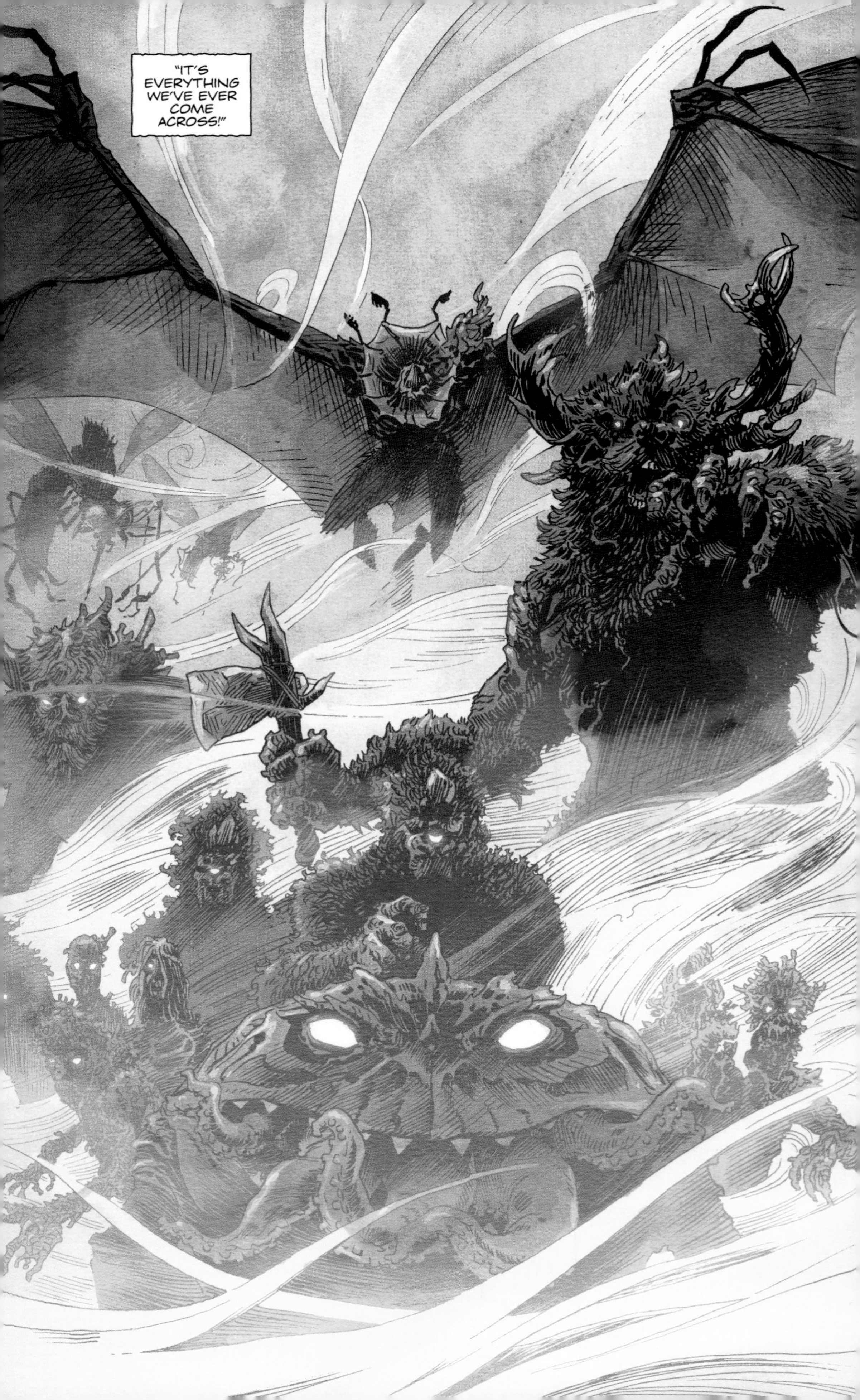
"IT'S EVERYTHING WE'VE EVER COME ACROSS!"

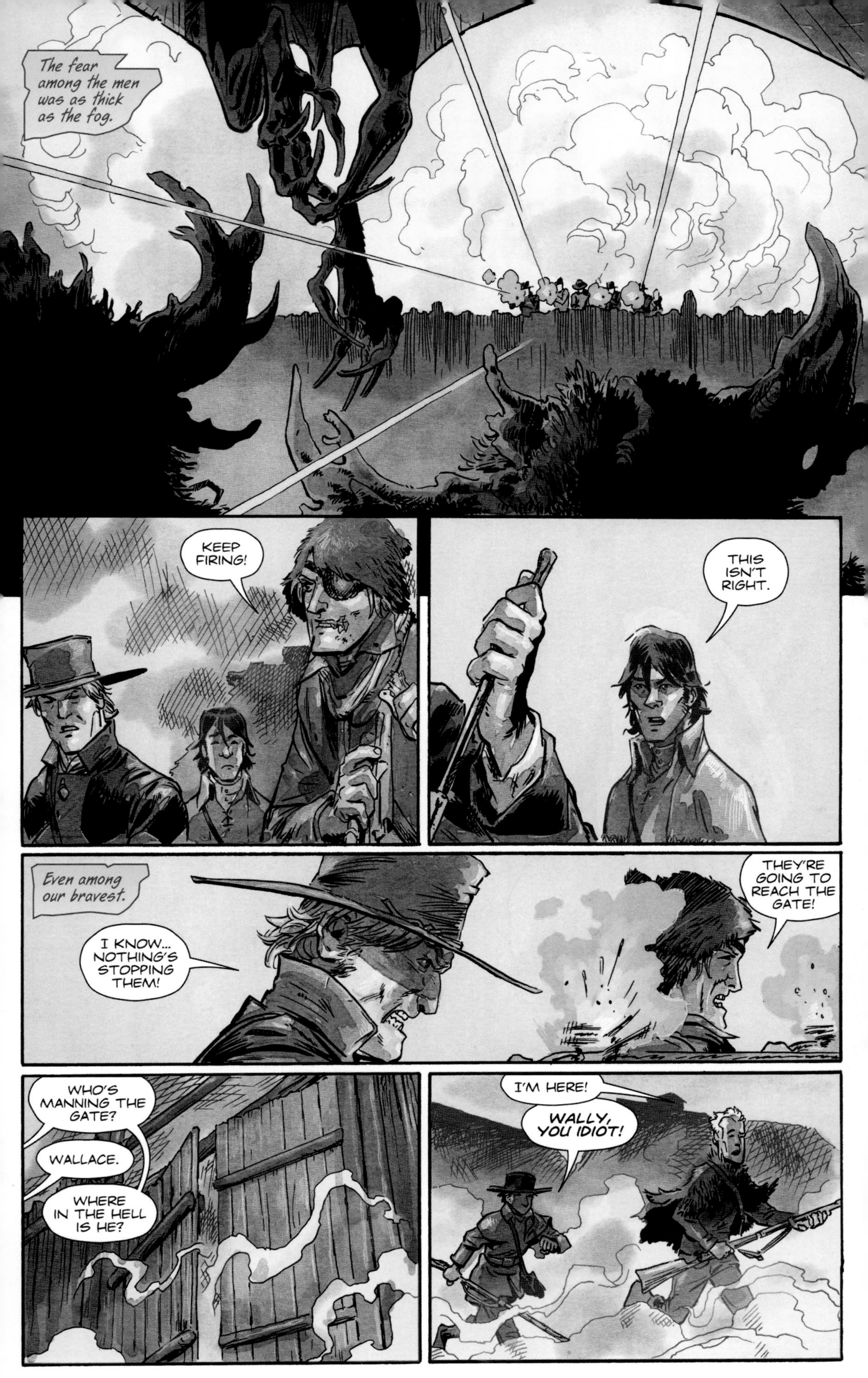
The fear among the men was as thick as the fog.
KEEP FIRING!
THIS ISN'T RIGHT.
Even among our bravest.
I KNOW... NOTHING'S STOPPING THEM!
THEY'RE GOING TO REACH THE GATE!
WHO'S MANNING THE GATE?
WALLACE.
WHERE IN THE HELL IS HE?
I'M HERE!
WALLY, YOU IDIOT!

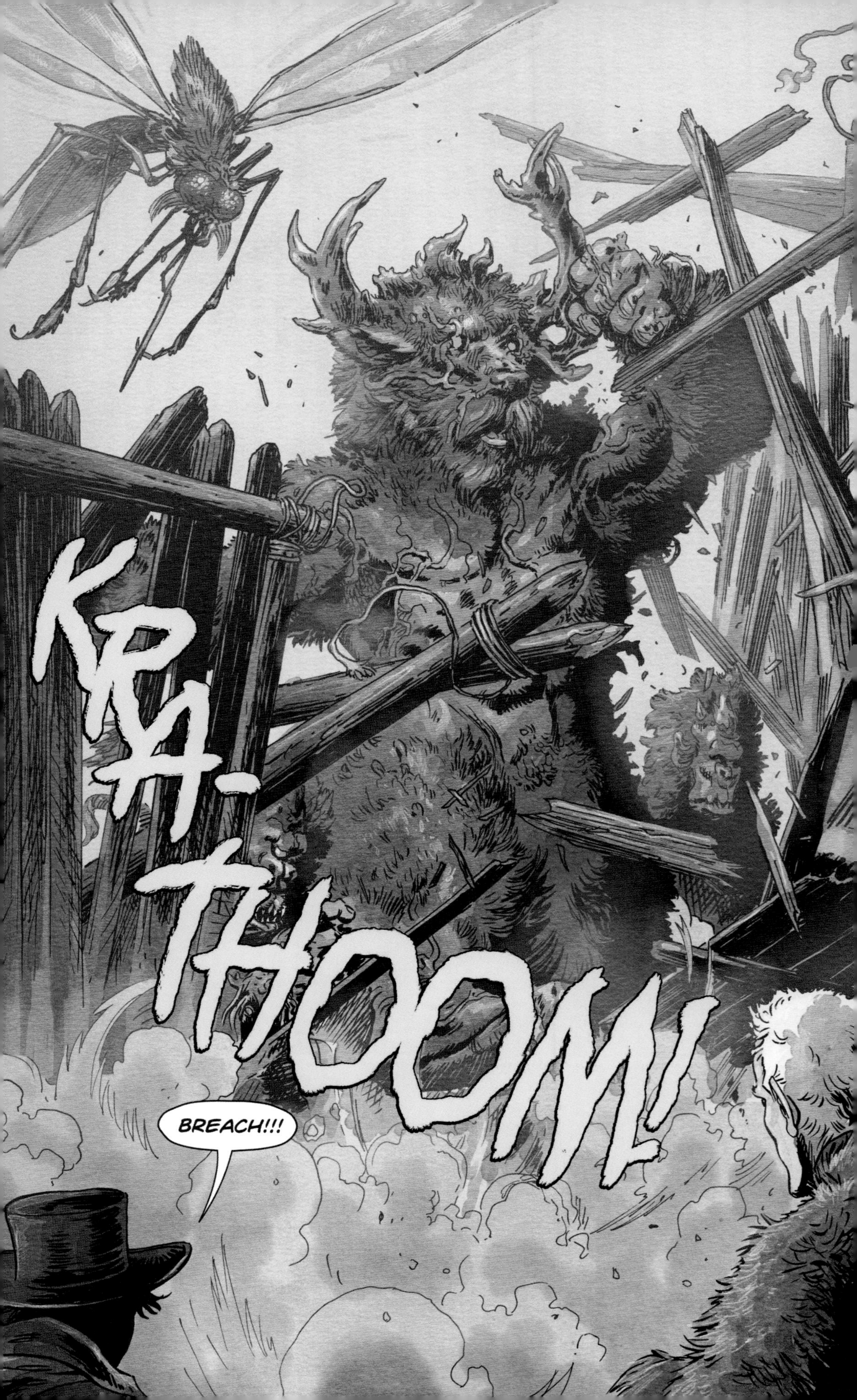
KRA-THOOM!
BREACH!!!

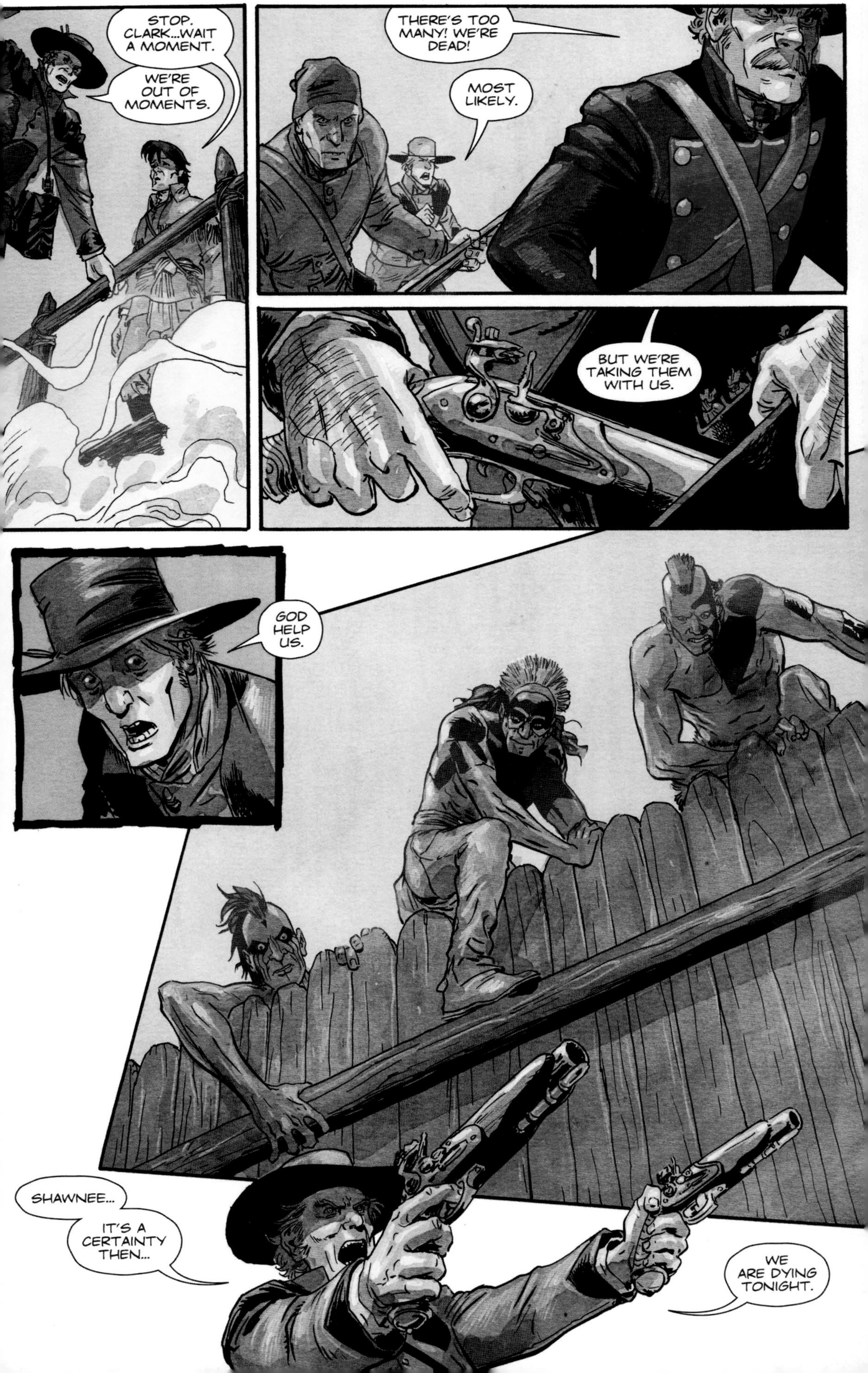
STOP. CLARK...WAIT A MOMENT.
WE'RE OUT OF MOMENTS.
THERE'S TOO MANY! WE'RE DEAD!
MOST LIKELY.
BUT WE'RE TAKING THEM WITH US.
GOD HELP US.
SHAWNEE...
IT'S A CERTAINTY THEN...
WE ARE DYING TONIGHT.

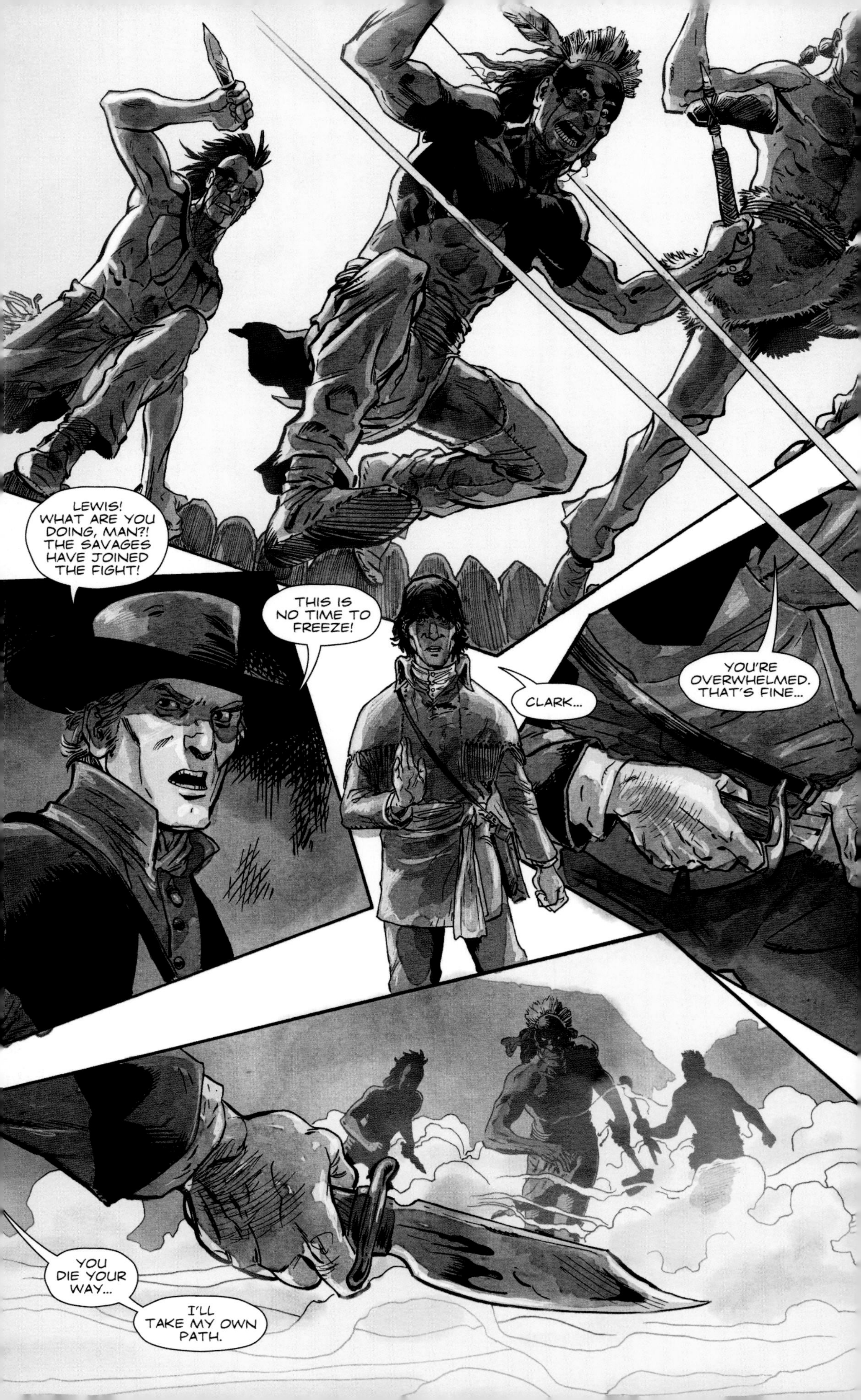
LEWIS! WHAT ARE YOU DOING, MAN?! THE SAVAGES HAVE JOINED THE FIGHT!
THIS IS NO TIME TO FREEZE!
CLARK...
YOU'RE OVERWHELMED. THAT'S FINE...
YOU DIE YOUR WAY...
I'LL TAKE MY OWN PATH.

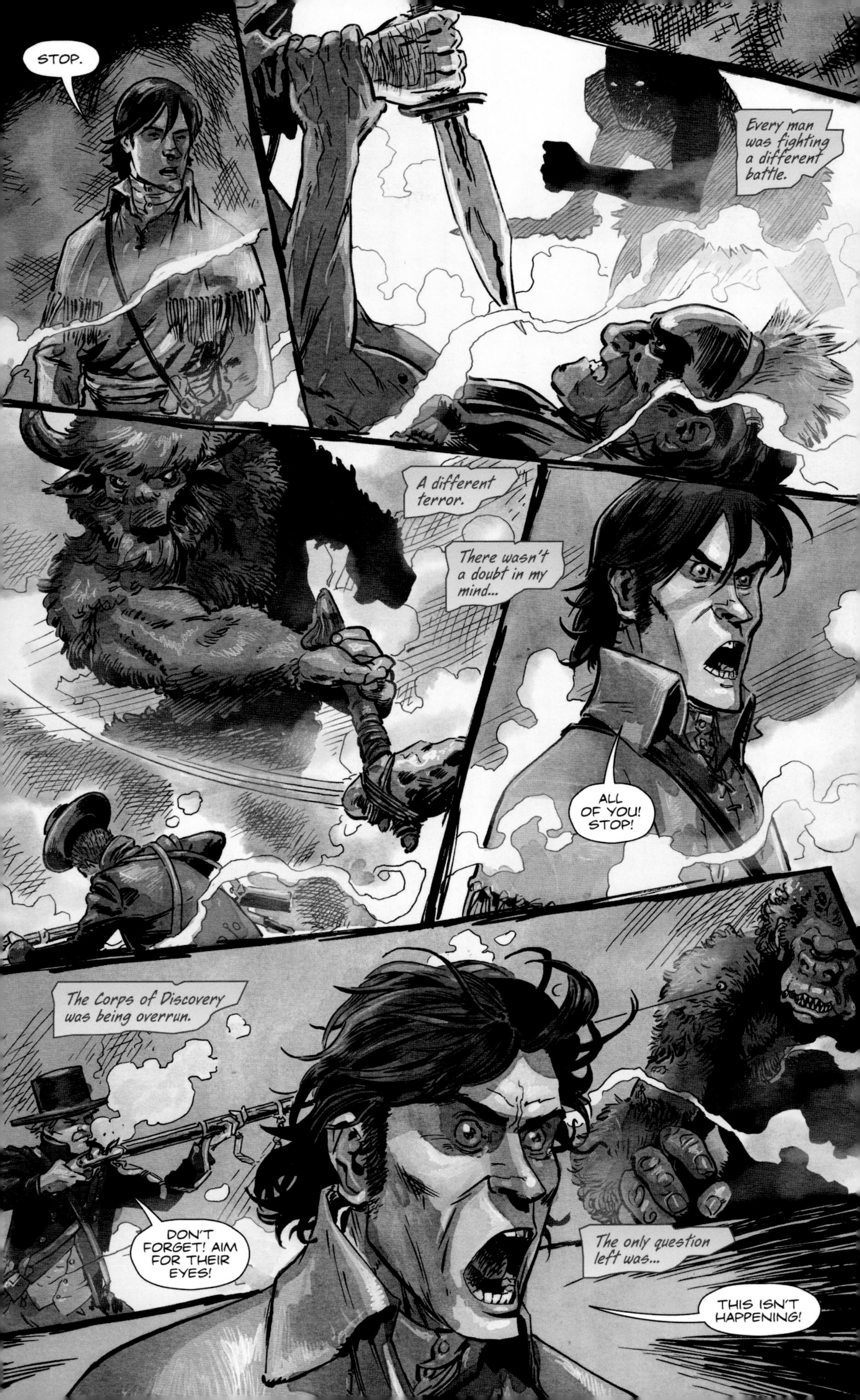
STOP.
Every man was fighting a different battle.
A different terror.
There wasn't a doubt in my mind...
ALL OF YOU! STOP!
The Corps of Discovery was being overrun.
DON'T FORGET! AIM FOR THEIR EYES!
The only question left was...
THIS ISN'T HAPPENING!

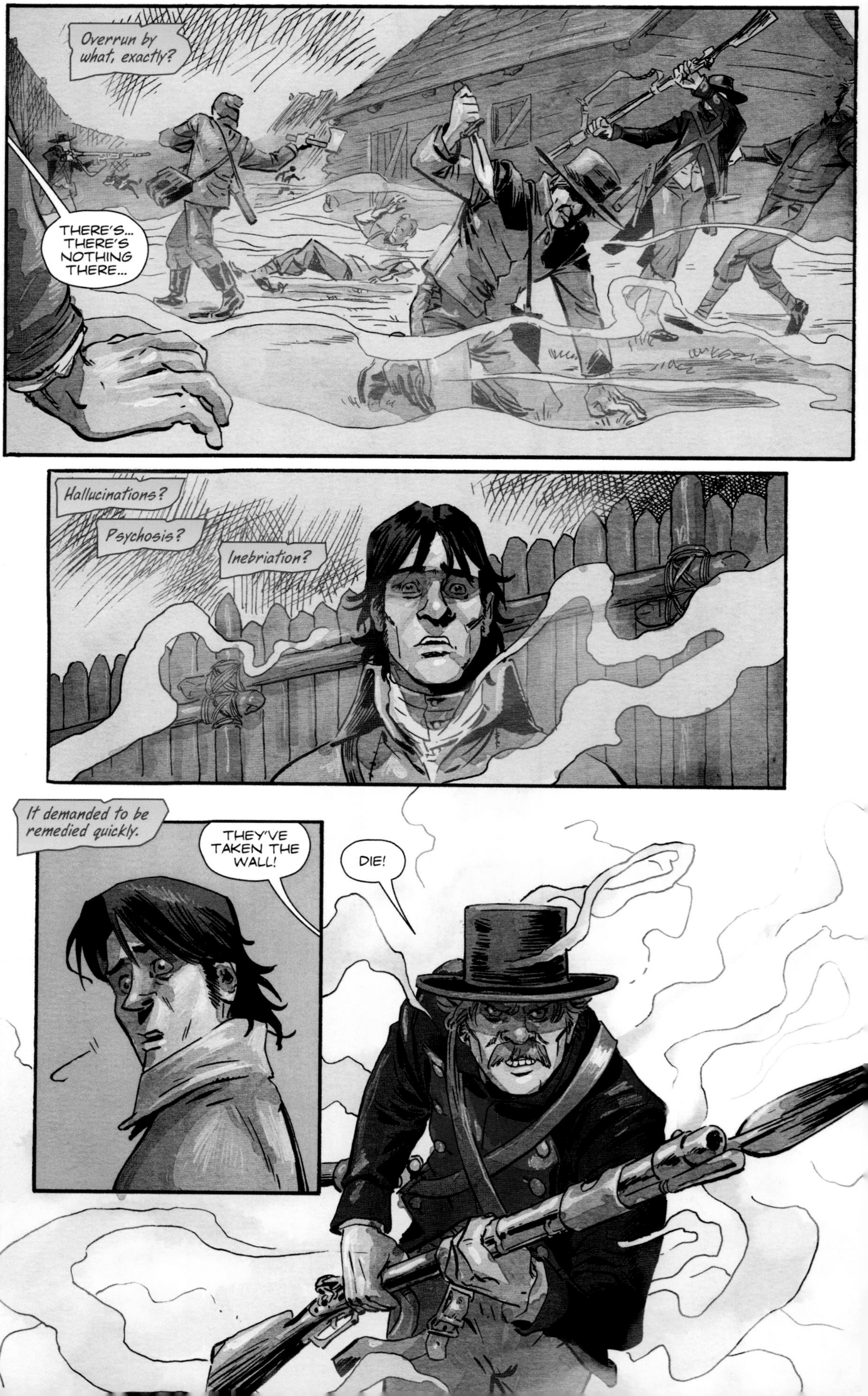
Overrun by what, exactly?
THERE'S... THERE'S NOTHING THERE...
Hallucinations?
Psychosis?
Inebriation?
It demanded to be remedied quickly.
THEY'VE TAKEN THE WALL!
DIE!

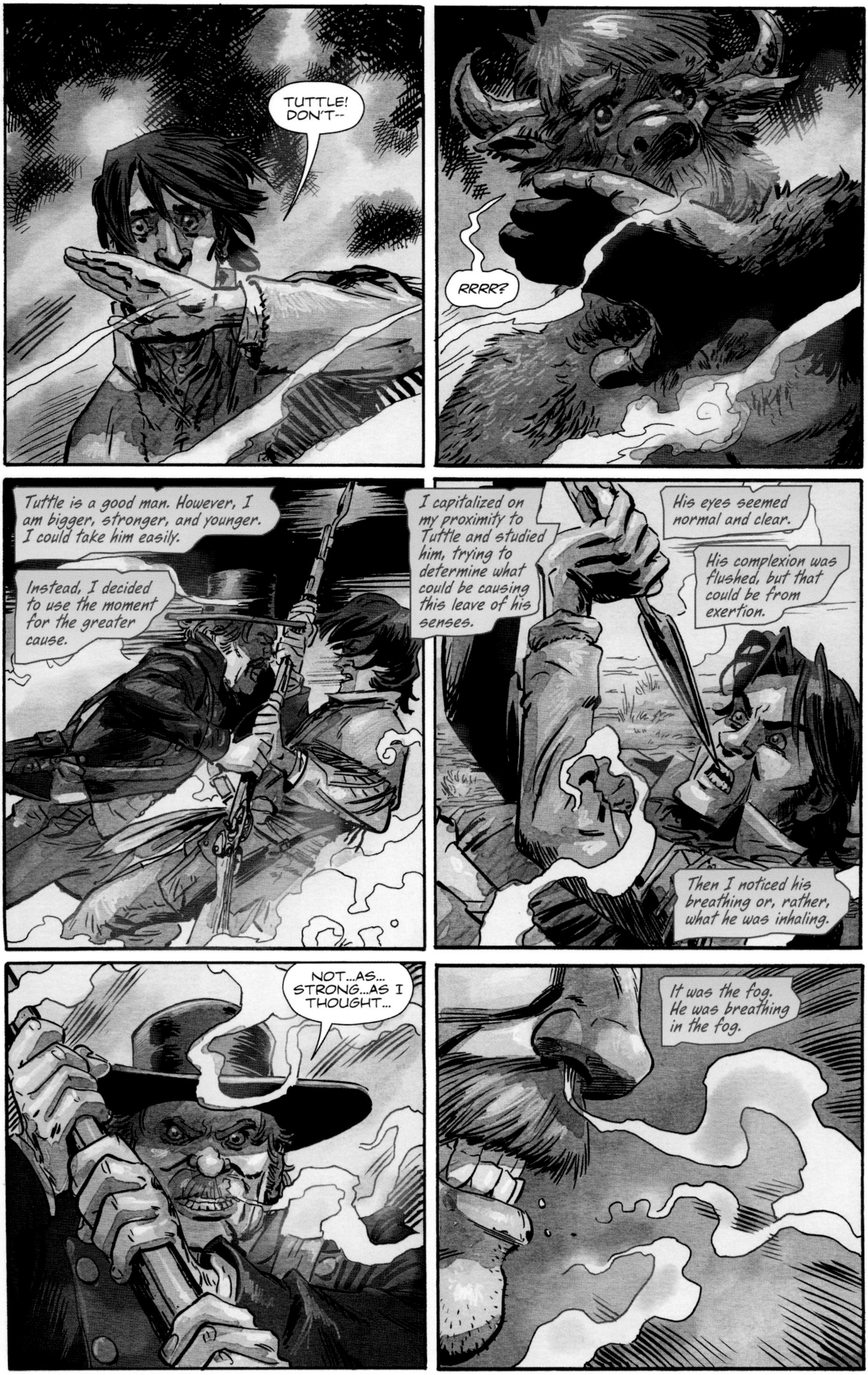
TUTTLE! DON'T--
RRRR?
Tuttle is a good man. However, I am bigger, stronger, and younger. I could take him easily.
Instead, I decided to use the moment for the greater cause.
I capitalized on my proximity to Tuttle and studied him, trying to determine what could be causing this leave of his senses.
His eyes seemed normal and clear.
His complexion was flushed, but that could be from exertion.
Then I noticed his breathing or, rather, what he was inhaling.
NOT...AS... STRONG...AS I THOUGHT...
It was the fog. He was breathing in the fog.

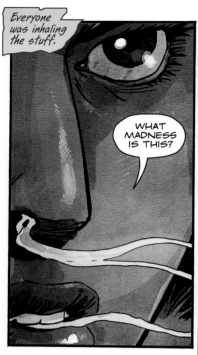

Everyone was inhaling the stuff.

WHAT MADNESS IS THIS?

ARE THEY FIGHTING EACH OTHER?

IT APPEARS. BUT THERE'S MORE. SOME FIGHT NO ONE AND SCREAM INTO THE NIGHT.

WHO CAN TELL A THING WITH ALL OF THIS FOG?

I AM GOING OUT THERE.

YOU'LL DO NO SUCH THING. IT'S TOO DANGEROUS FOR YOU.

PLEASE, GIRL...THINK OF YOUR BABY.

IT'S DANGEROUS IN HERE. IF I DIE, IT WILL BE FIGHTING. NOT WAITING IN A BOX AS CAGED MEAT FOR WHATEVER IS OUTSIDE.

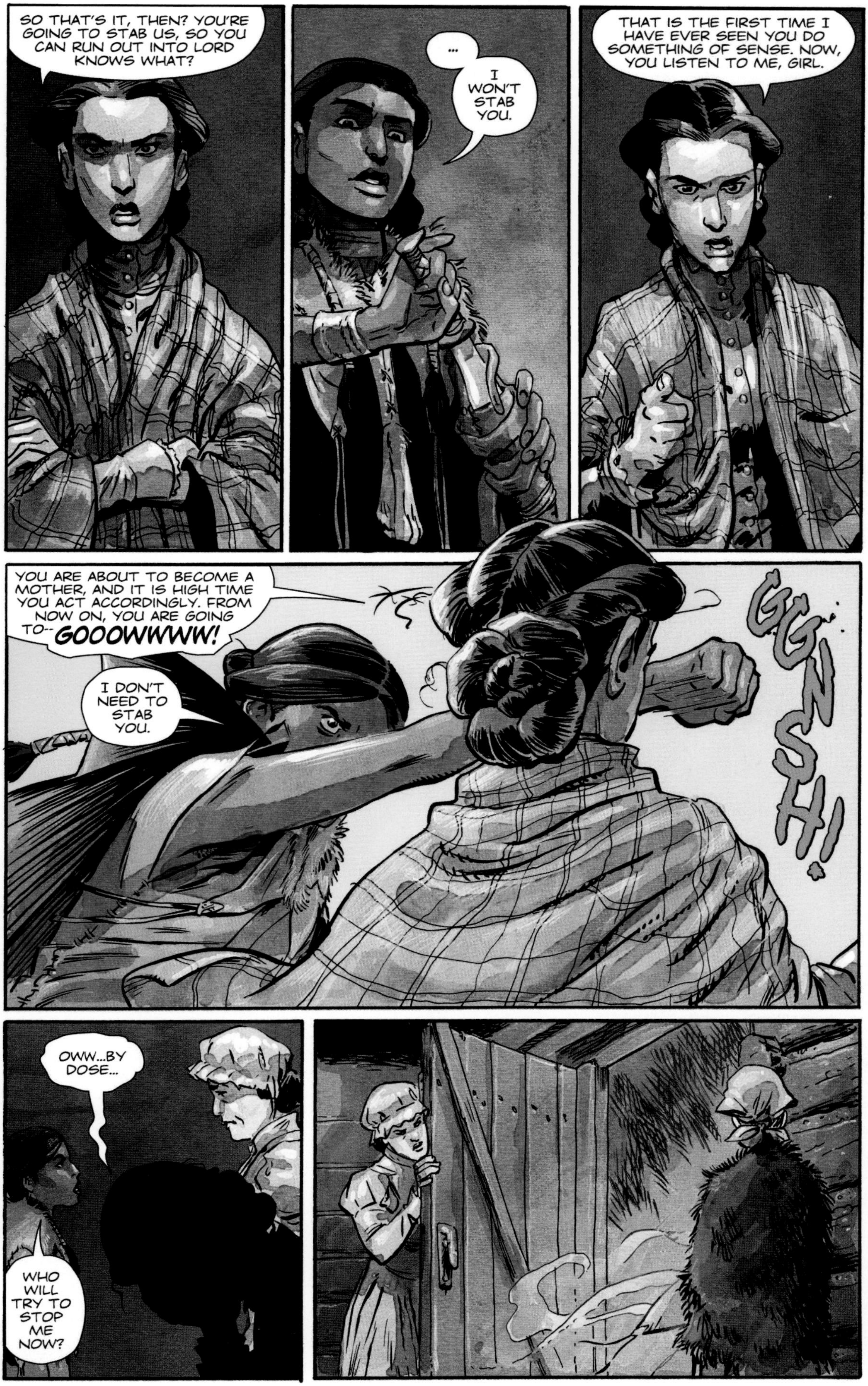
SO THAT'S IT, THEN? YOU'RE GOING TO STAB US, SO YOU CAN RUN OUT INTO LORD KNOWS WHAT?
...
I WON'T STAB YOU.
THAT IS THE FIRST TIME I HAVE EVER SEEN YOU DO SOMETHING OF SENSE. NOW, YOU LISTEN TO ME, GIRL.
YOU ARE ABOUT TO BECOME A MOTHER, AND IT IS HIGH TIME YOU ACT ACCORDINGLY. FROM NOW ON, YOU ARE GOING TO-- GOOOWWWW!
I DON'T NEED TO STAB YOU.
GGNSH!
OWW...BY DOSE...
WHO WILL TRY TO STOP ME NOW?

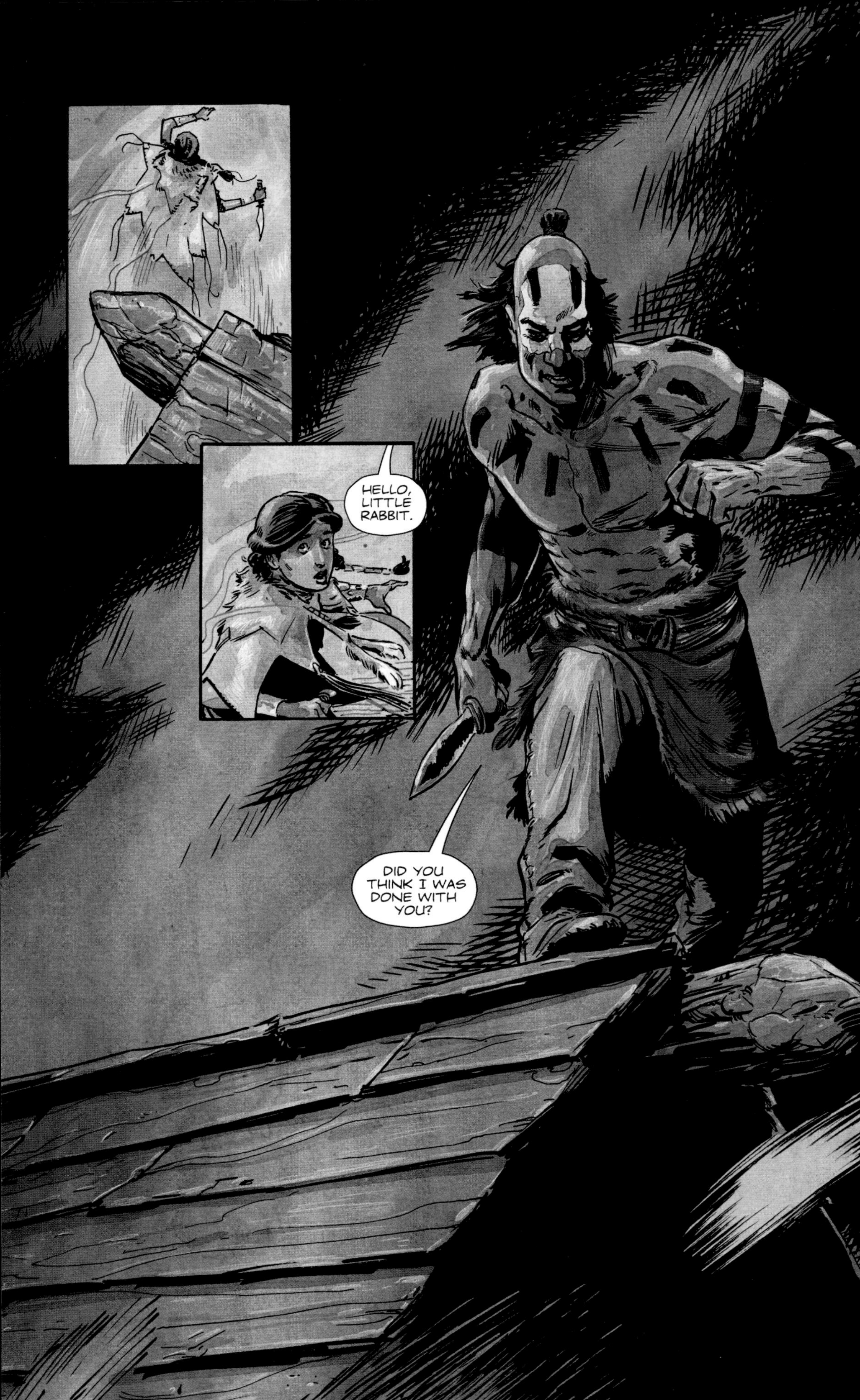
HELLO, LITTLE RABBIT.
DID YOU THINK I WAS DONE WITH YOU?

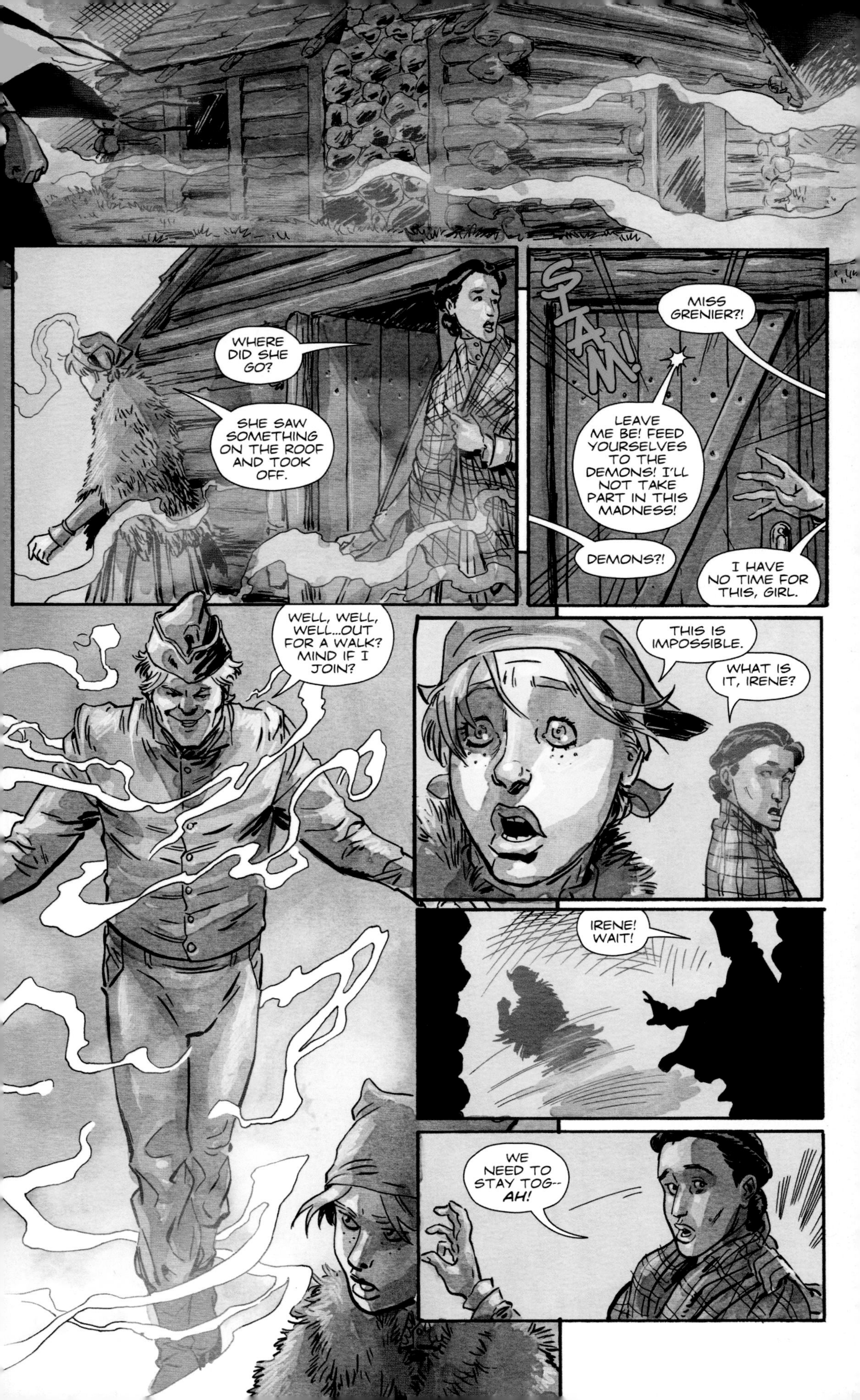
WHERE DID SHE GO?
SHE SAW SOMETHING ON THE ROOF AND TOOK OFF.
SLAM!
MISS GRENIER?!
LEAVE ME BE! FEED YOURSELVES TO THE DEMONS! I'LL NOT TAKE PART IN THIS MADNESS!
DEMONS?!
I HAVE NO TIME FOR THIS, GIRL.
WELL, WELL, WELL...OUT FOR A WALK? MIND IF I JOIN?
THIS IS IMPOSSIBLE.
WHAT IS IT, IRENE?
IRENE! WAIT!
WE NEED TO STAY TOG-- AH!

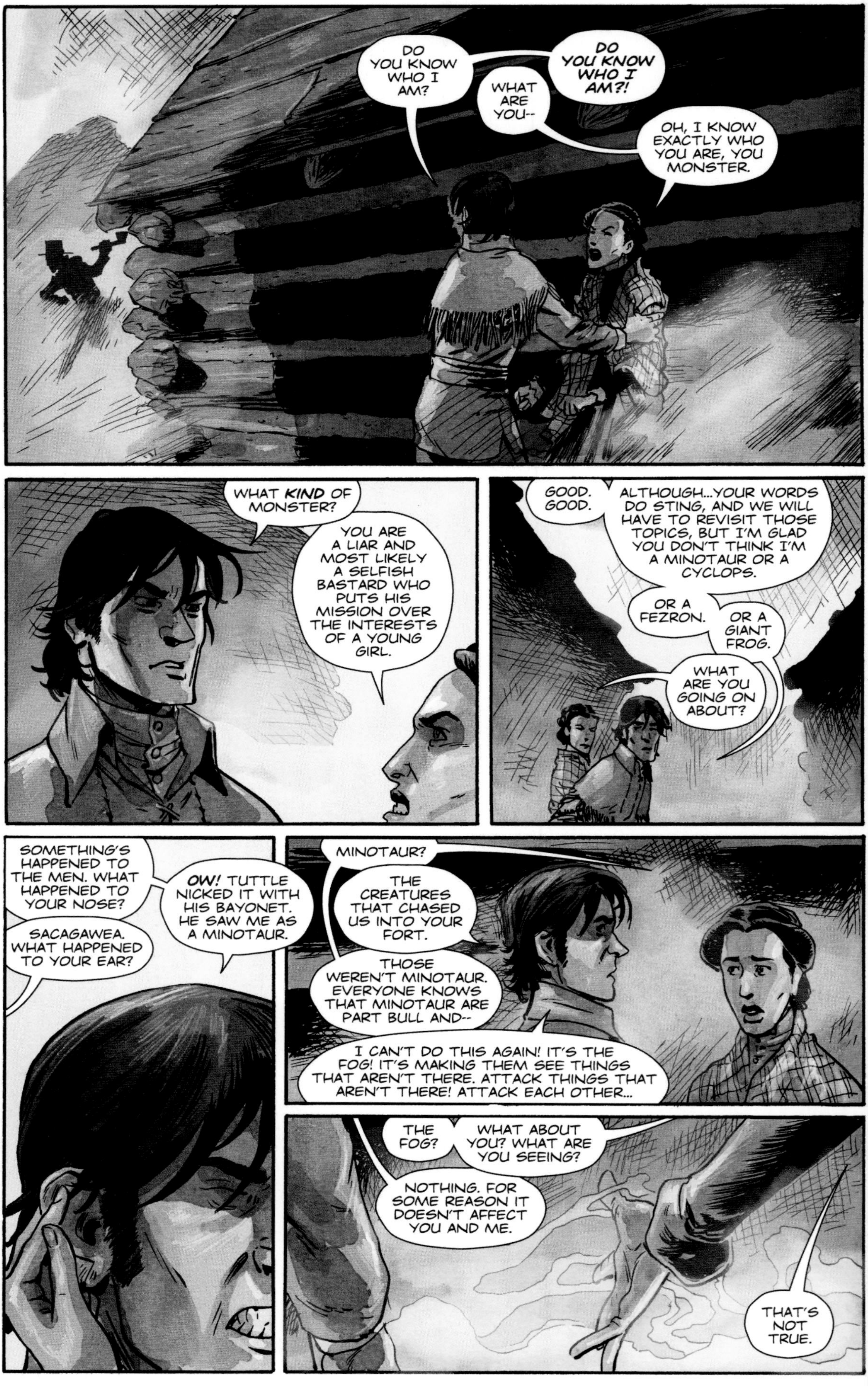
DO YOU KNOW WHO I AM?
WHAT ARE YOU--
DO YOU KNOW WHO I AM?!
OH, I KNOW EXACTLY WHO YOU ARE, YOU MONSTER.
WHAT KIND OF MONSTER?
YOU ARE A LIAR AND MOST LIKELY A SELFISH BASTARD WHO PUTS HIS MISSION OVER THE INTERESTS OF A YOUNG GIRL.
GOOD. GOOD.
ALTHOUGH...YOUR WORDS DO STING, AND WE WILL HAVE TO REVISIT THOSE TOPICS, BUT I'M GLAD YOU DON'T THINK I'M A MINOTAUR OR A CYCLOPS.
OR A FEZRON.
OR A GIANT FROG.
WHAT ARE YOU GOING ON ABOUT?
SOMETHING'S HAPPENED TO THE MEN. WHAT HAPPENED TO YOUR NOSE?
OW! TUTTLE NICKED IT WITH HIS BAYONET. HE SAW ME AS A MINOTAUR.
SACAGAWEA. WHAT HAPPENED TO YOUR EAR?
MINOTAUR?
THE CREATURES THAT CHASED US INTO YOUR FORT.
THOSE WEREN'T MINOTAUR. EVERYONE KNOWS THAT MINOTAUR ARE PART BULL AND--
I CAN'T DO THIS AGAIN! IT'S THE FOG! IT'S MAKING THEM SEE THINGS THAT AREN'T THERE. ATTACK THINGS THAT AREN'T THERE! ATTACK EACH OTHER...
THE FOG?
WHAT ABOUT YOU? WHAT ARE YOU SEEING?
NOTHING. FOR SOME REASON IT DOESN'T AFFECT YOU AND ME.
THAT'S NOT TRUE.

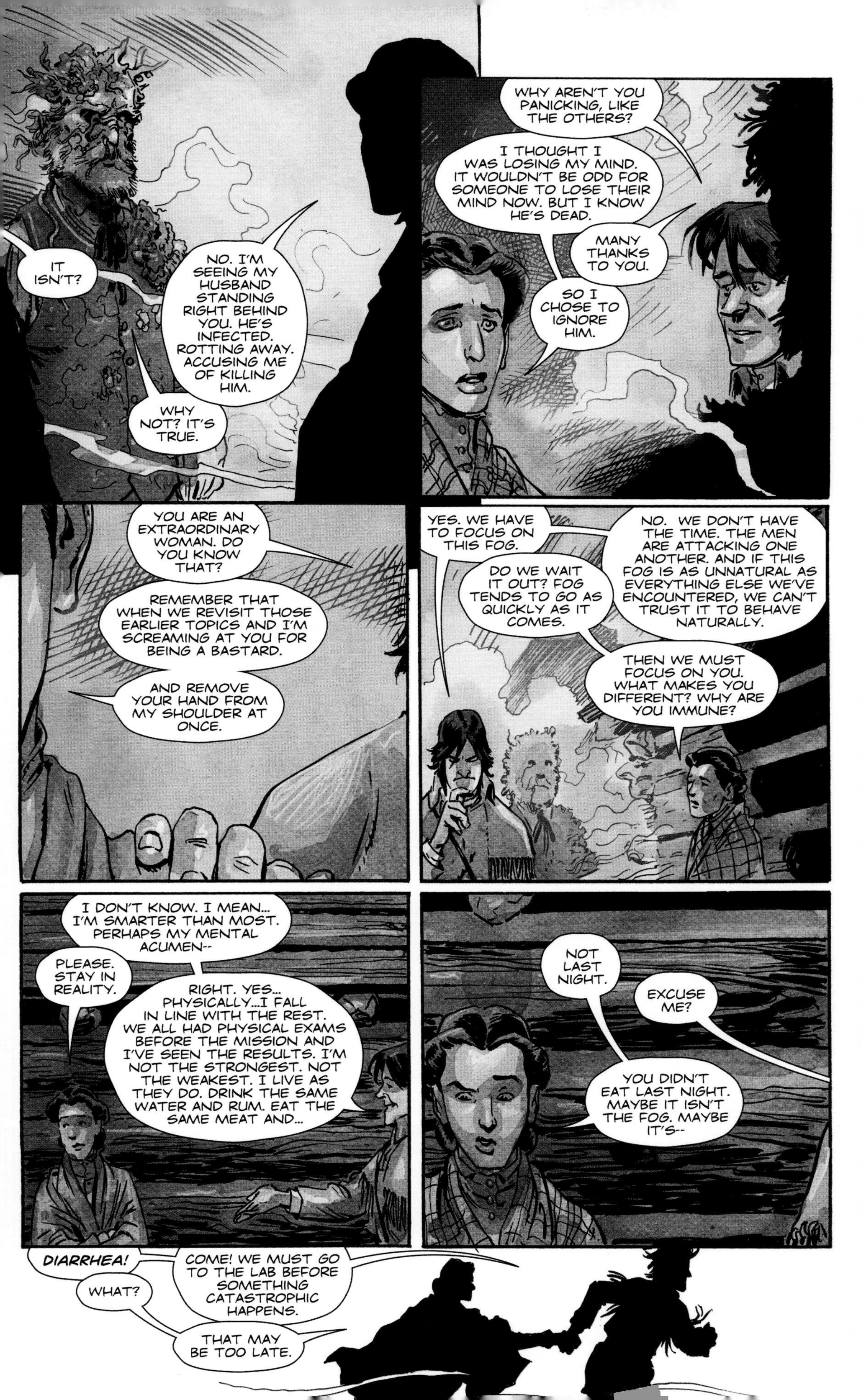
IT ISN'T?
NO. I'M SEEING MY HUSBAND STANDING RIGHT BEHIND YOU. HE'S INFECTED. ROTTING AWAY. ACCUSING ME OF KILLING HIM.
WHY NOT? IT'S TRUE.
WHY AREN'T YOU PANICKING, LIKE THE OTHERS?
I THOUGHT I WAS LOSING MY MIND. IT WOULDN'T BE ODD FOR SOMEONE TO LOSE THEIR MIND NOW. BUT I KNOW HE'S DEAD.
MANY THANKS TO YOU.
SO I CHOSE TO IGNORE HIM.
YOU ARE AN EXTRAORDINARY WOMAN. DO YOU KNOW THAT?
REMEMBER THAT WHEN WE REVISIT THOSE EARLIER TOPICS AND I'M SCREAMING AT YOU FOR BEING A BASTARD.
AND REMOVE YOUR HAND FROM MY SHOULDER AT ONCE.
YES. WE HAVE TO FOCUS ON THIS FOG.
DO WE WAIT IT OUT? FOG TENDS TO GO AS QUICKLY AS IT COMES.
NO. WE DON'T HAVE THE TIME. THE MEN ARE ATTACKING ONE ANOTHER. AND IF THIS FOG IS AS UNNATURAL AS EVERYTHING ELSE WE'VE ENCOUNTERED, WE CAN'T TRUST IT TO BEHAVE NATURALLY.
THEN WE MUST FOCUS ON YOU. WHAT MAKES YOU DIFFERENT? WHY ARE YOU IMMUNE?
I DON'T KNOW. I MEAN... I'M SMARTER THAN MOST. PERHAPS MY MENTAL ACUMEN--
PLEASE. STAY IN REALITY.
RIGHT. YES... PHYSICALLY...I FALL IN LINE WITH THE REST. WE ALL HAD PHYSICAL EXAMS BEFORE THE MISSION AND I'VE SEEN THE RESULTS. I'M NOT THE STRONGEST. NOT THE WEAKEST. I LIVE AS THEY DO. DRINK THE SAME WATER AND RUM. EAT THE SAME MEAT AND...
NOT LAST NIGHT.
EXCUSE ME?
YOU DIDN'T EAT LAST NIGHT. MAYBE IT ISN'T THE FOG. MAYBE IT'S--
DIARRHEA!
WHAT?
COME! WE MUST GO TO THE LAB BEFORE SOMETHING CATASTROPHIC HAPPENS.
THAT MAY BE TOO LATE.

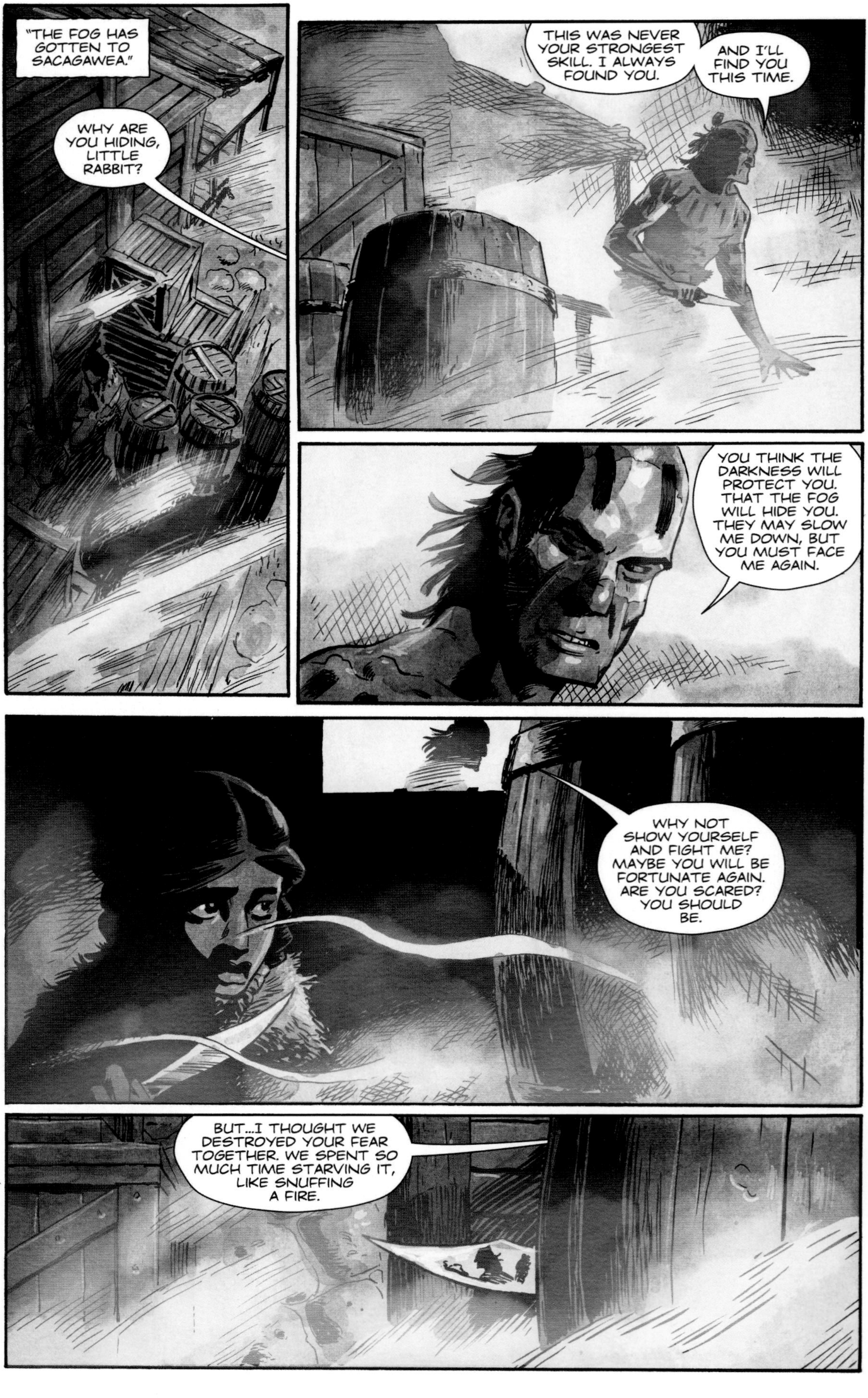
"THE FOG HAS GOTTEN TO SACAGAWEA."
WHY ARE YOU HIDING, LITTLE RABBIT?
THIS WAS NEVER YOUR STRONGEST SKILL. I ALWAYS FOUND YOU.
AND I'LL FIND YOU THIS TIME.
YOU THINK THE DARKNESS WILL PROTECT YOU. THAT THE FOG WILL HIDE YOU. THEY MAY SLOW ME DOWN, BUT YOU MUST FACE ME AGAIN.
WHY NOT SHOW YOURSELF AND FIGHT ME? MAYBE YOU WILL BE FORTUNATE AGAIN. ARE YOU SCARED? YOU SHOULD BE.
BUT...I THOUGHT WE DESTROYED YOUR FEAR TOGETHER. WE SPENT SO MUCH TIME STARVING IT, LIKE SNUFFING A FIRE.

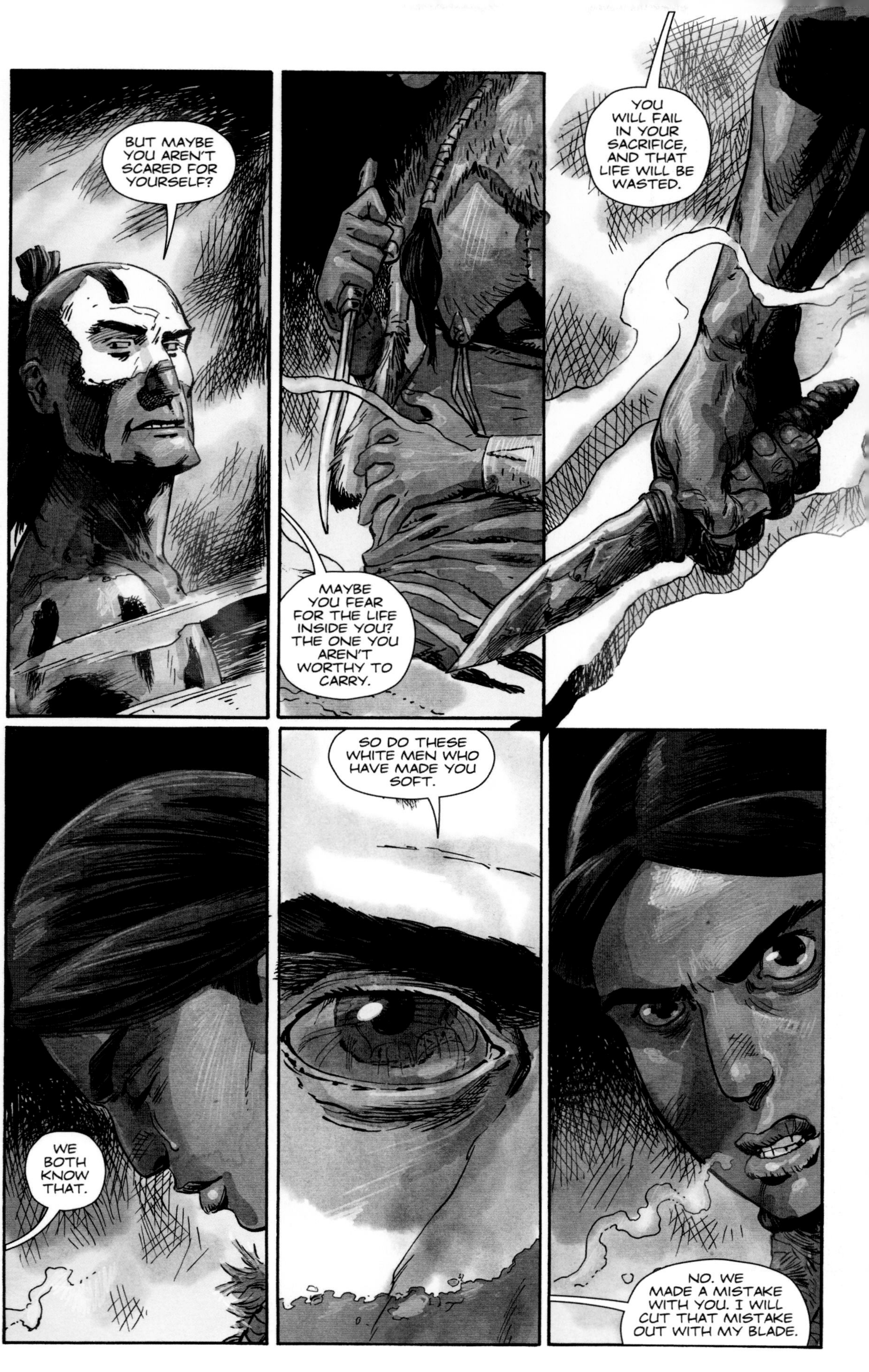
BUT MAYBE YOU AREN'T SCARED FOR YOURSELF?
MAYBE YOU FEAR FOR THE LIFE INSIDE YOU? THE ONE YOU AREN'T WORTHY TO CARRY.
YOU WILL FAIL IN YOUR SACRIFICE, AND THAT LIFE WILL BE WASTED.
WE BOTH KNOW THAT.
SO DO THESE WHITE MEN WHO HAVE MADE YOU SOFT.
NO. WE MADE A MISTAKE WITH YOU. I WILL CUT THAT MISTAKE OUT WITH MY BLADE.

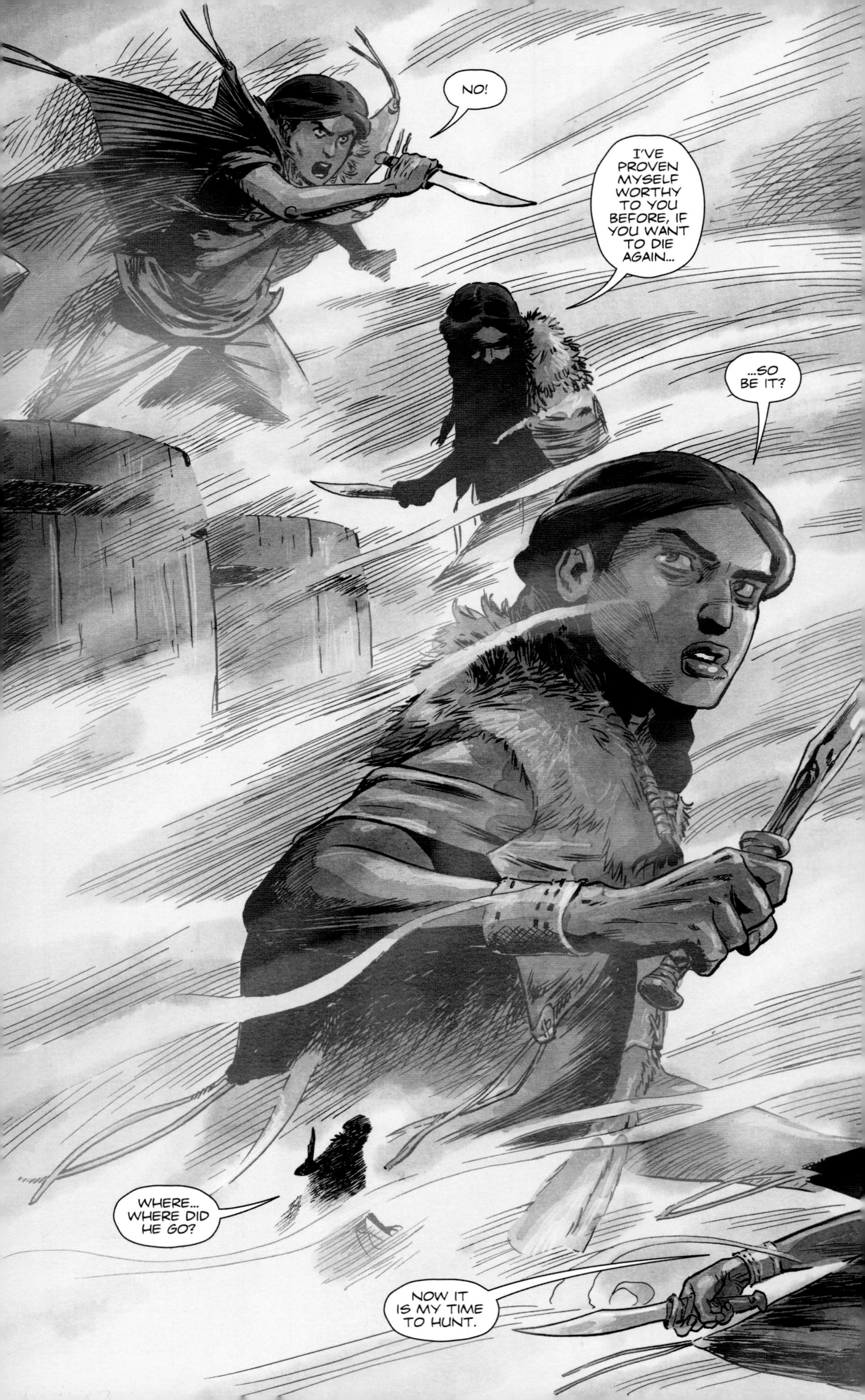
NO!
I'VE PROVEN MYSELF WORTHY TO YOU BEFORE, IF YOU WANT TO DIE AGAIN...
...SO BE IT?
WHERE... WHERE DID HE GO?
NOW IT IS MY TIME TO HUNT.

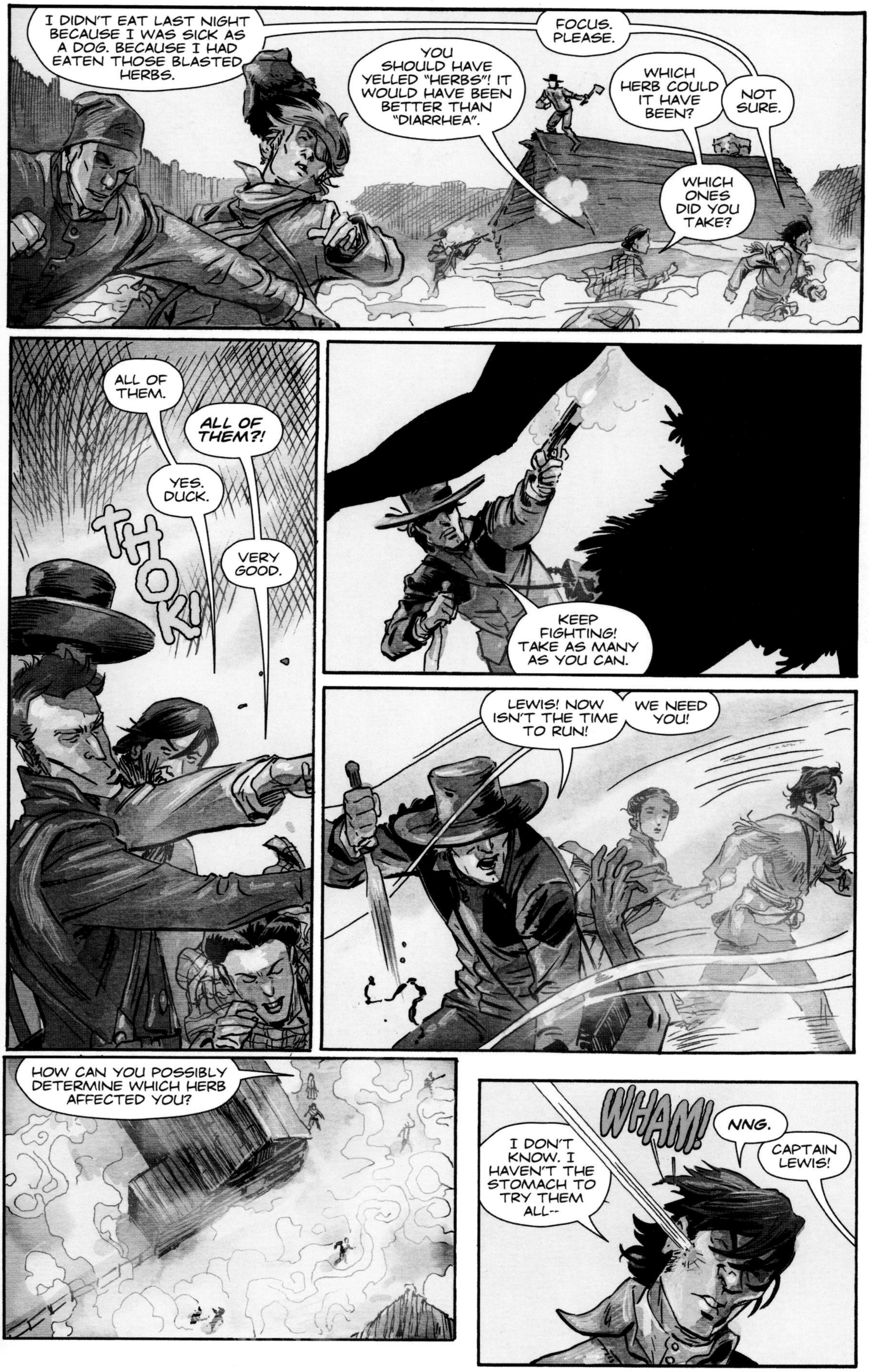
I DIDN'T EAT LAST NIGHT BECAUSE I WAS SICK AS A DOG. BECAUSE I HAD EATEN THOSE BLASTED HERBS.
FOCUS. PLEASE.
YOU SHOULD HAVE YELLED "HERBS"! IT WOULD HAVE BEEN BETTER THAN "DIARRHEA".
WHICH HERB COULD IT HAVE BEEN?
NOT SURE.
WHICH ONES DID YOU TAKE?
ALL OF THEM.
ALL OF THEM?!
YES. DUCK.
THOK!
VERY GOOD.
KEEP FIGHTING! TAKE AS MANY AS YOU CAN.
LEWIS! NOW ISN'T THE TIME TO RUN!
WE NEED YOU!
HOW CAN YOU POSSIBLY DETERMINE WHICH HERB AFFECTED YOU?
I DON'T KNOW. I HAVEN'T THE STOMACH TO TRY THEM ALL--
WHAM!
NNG.
CAPTAIN LEWIS!

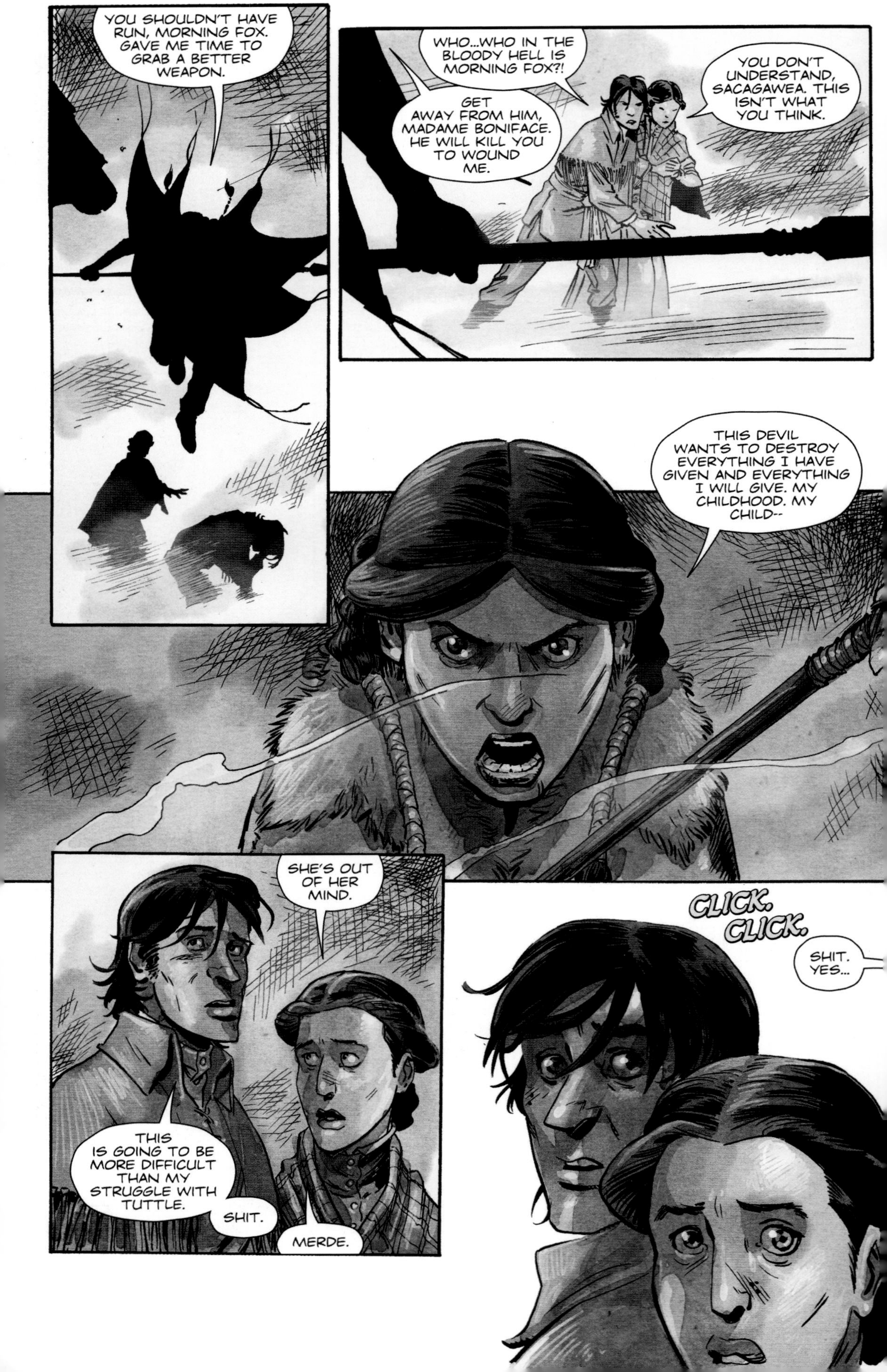
YOU SHOULDN'T HAVE RUN, MORNING FOX. GAVE ME TIME TO GRAB A BETTER WEAPON.
WHO...WHO IN THE BLOODY HELL IS MORNING FOX?!
GET AWAY FROM HIM, MADAME BONIFACE. HE WILL KILL YOU TO WOUND ME.
YOU DON'T UNDERSTAND, SACAGAWEA. THIS ISN'T WHAT YOU THINK.
THIS DEVIL WANTS TO DESTROY EVERYTHING I HAVE GIVEN AND EVERYTHING I WILL GIVE. MY CHILDHOOD. MY CHILD--
SHE'S OUT OF HER MIND.
THIS IS GOING TO BE MORE DIFFICULT THAN MY STRUGGLE WITH TUTTLE.
SHIT.
MERDE.
CLICK. CLICK.
SHIT. YES...

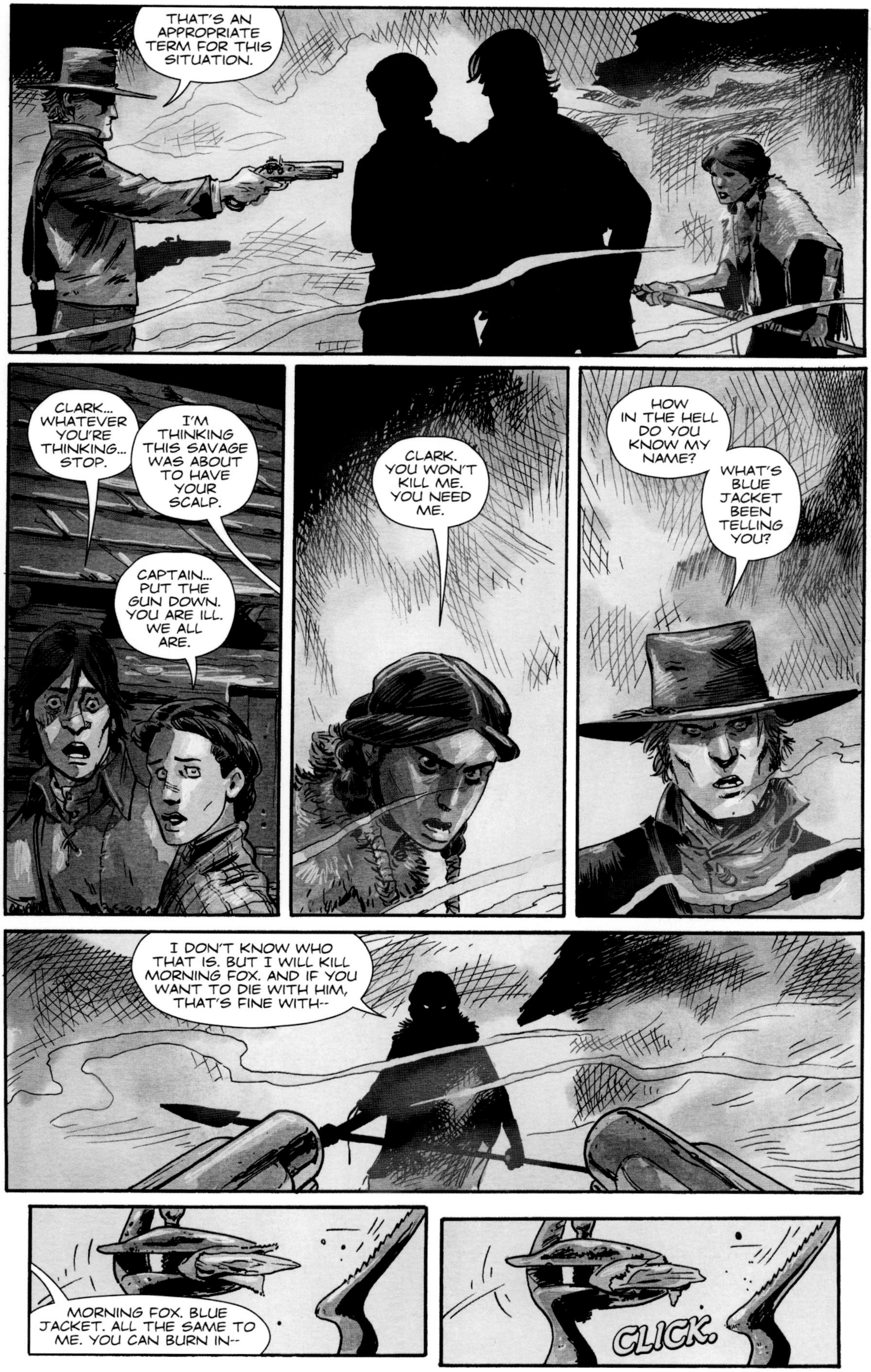
THAT'S AN APPROPRIATE TERM FOR THIS SITUATION.
CLARK... WHATEVER YOU'RE THINKING... STOP.
I'M THINKING THIS SAVAGE WAS ABOUT TO HAVE YOUR SCALP.
CAPTAIN... PUT THE GUN DOWN. YOU ARE ILL. WE ALL ARE.
CLARK. YOU WON'T KILL ME. YOU NEED ME.
HOW IN THE HELL DO YOU KNOW MY NAME?
WHAT'S BLUE JACKET BEEN TELLING YOU?
I DON'T KNOW WHO THAT IS. BUT I WILL KILL MORNING FOX. AND IF YOU WANT TO DIE WITH HIM, THAT'S FINE WITH--
MORNING FOX. BLUE JACKET. ALL THE SAME TO ME. YOU CAN BURN IN--
CLICK.

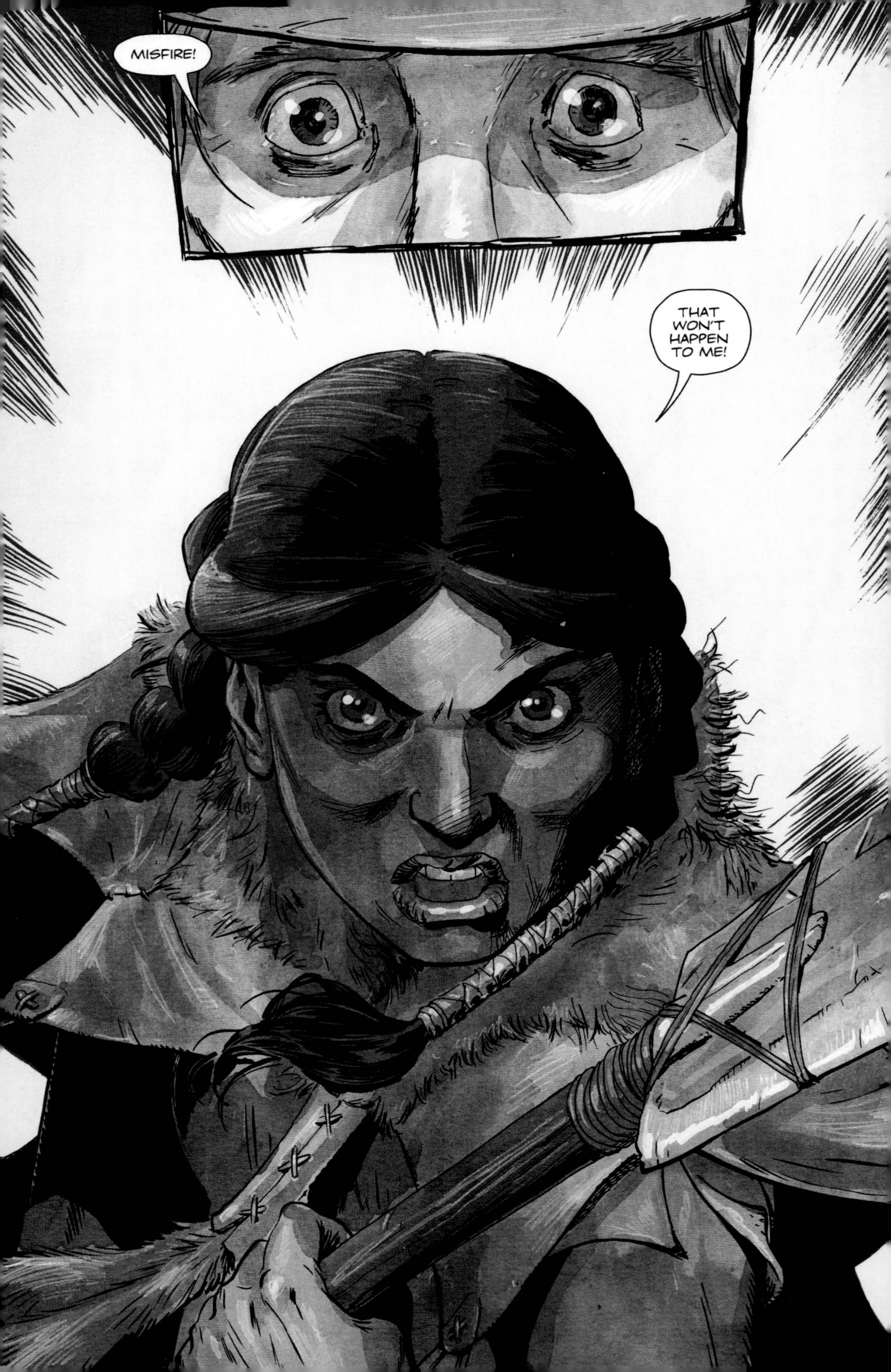
MISFIRE!
THAT WON'T HAPPEN TO ME!

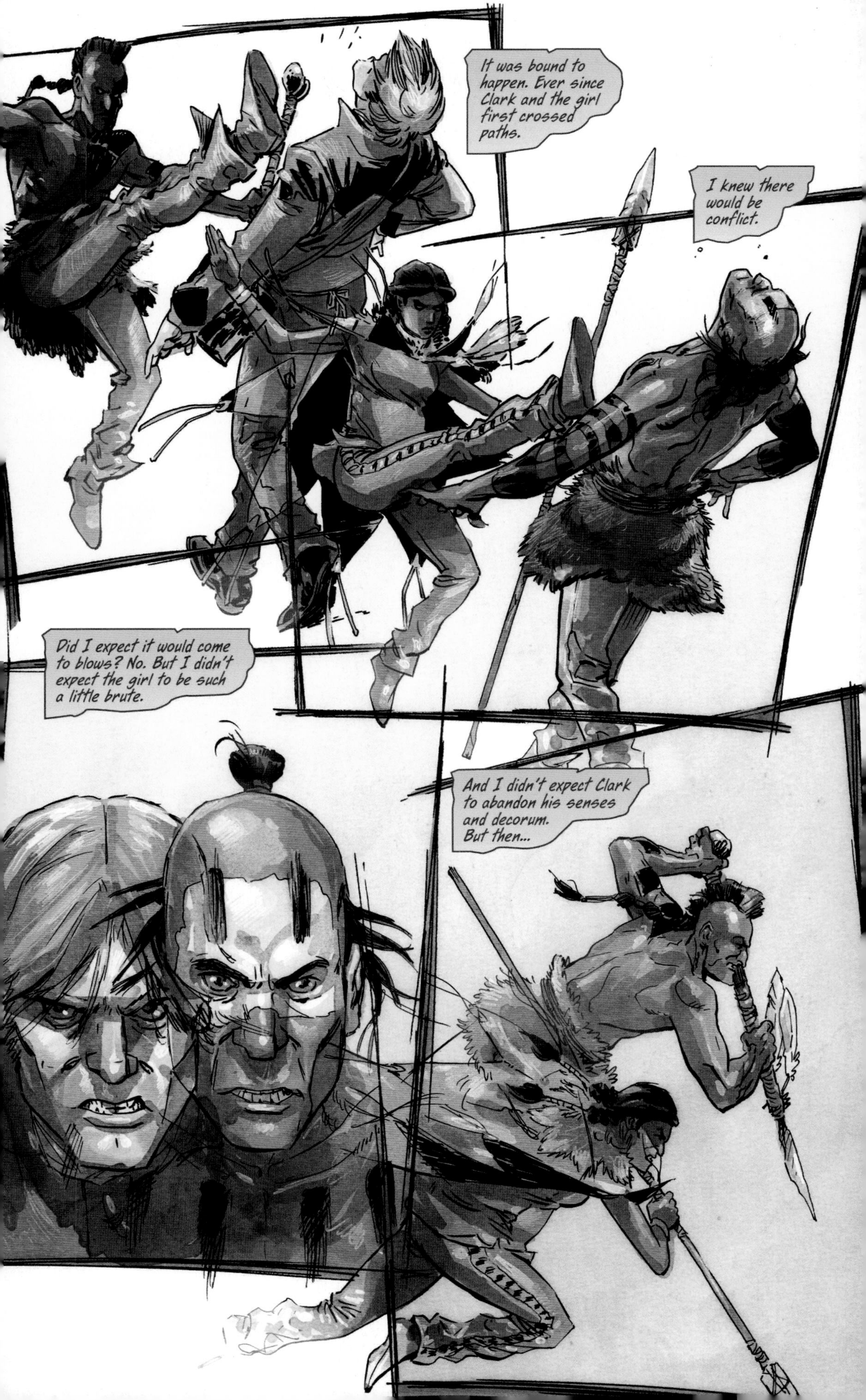
It was bound to happen. Ever since Clark and the girl first crossed paths.
I knew there would be conflict.
Did I expect it would come to blows? No. But I didn't expect the girl to be such a little brute.
And I didn't expect Clark to abandon his senses and decorum. But then...

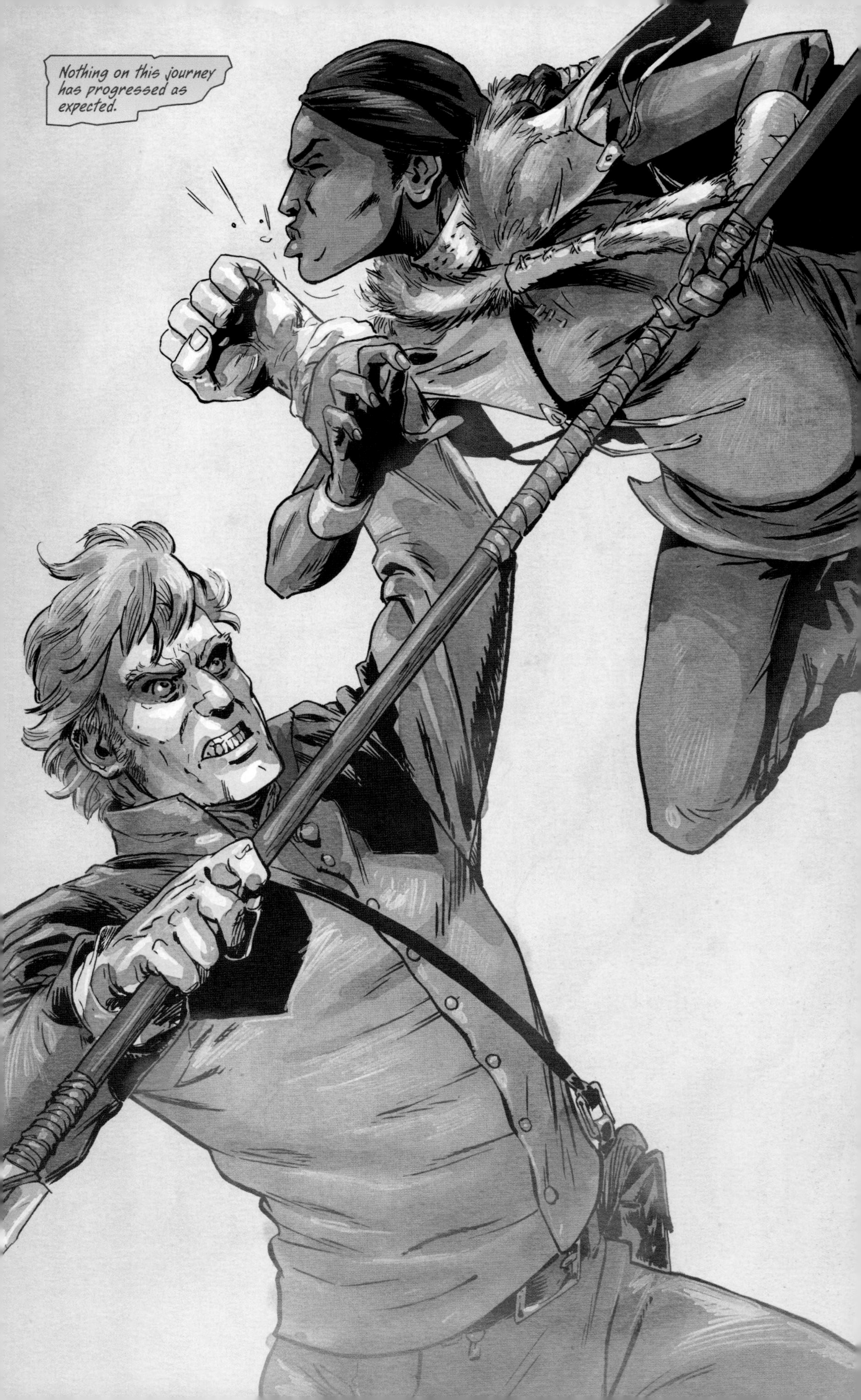
Nothing on this journey has progressed as expected.

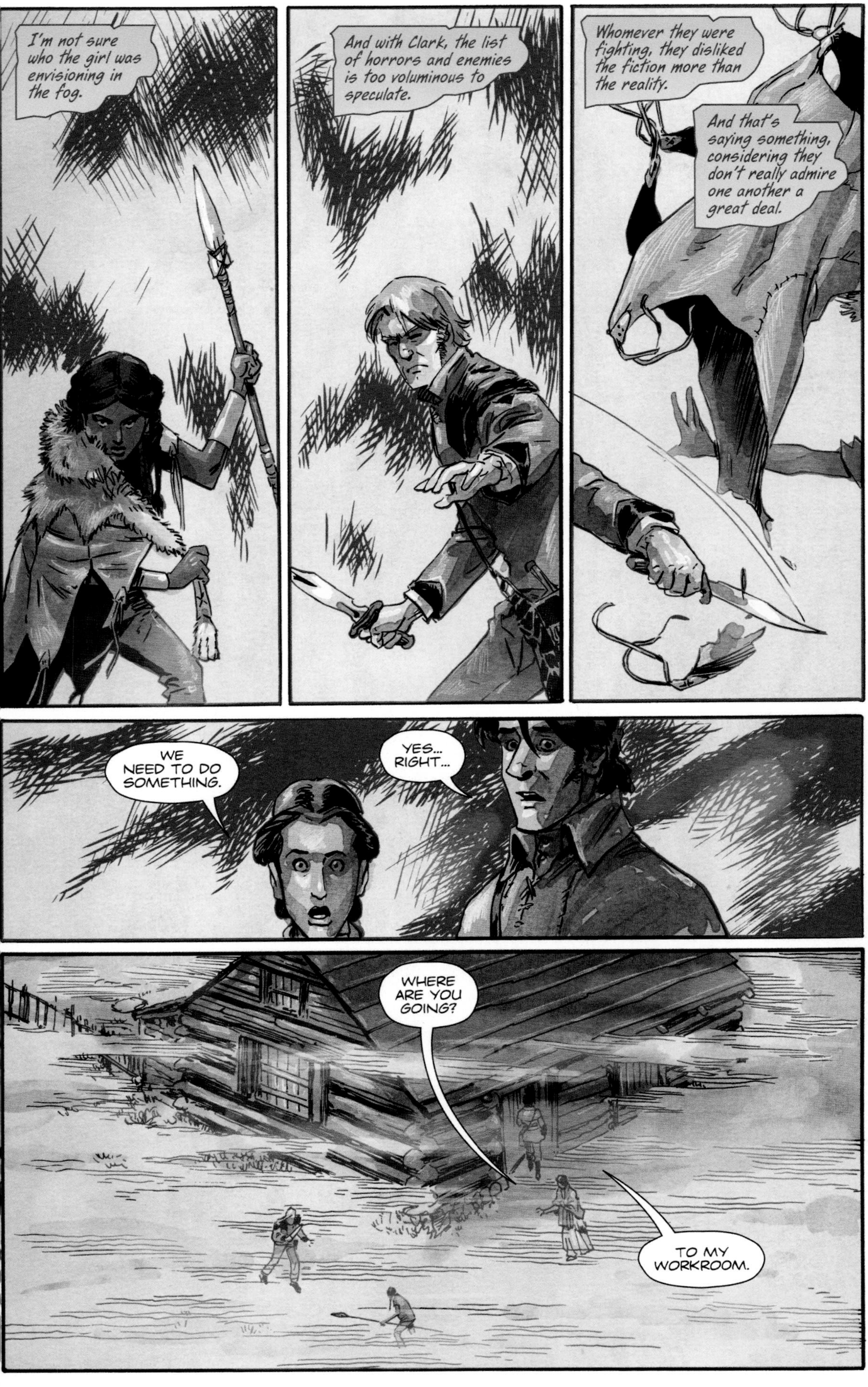

I'm not sure who the girl was envisioning in the fog.
And with Clark, the list of horrors and enemies is too voluminous to speculate.
Whomever they were fighting, they disliked the fiction more than the reality.
And that's saying something, considering they don't really admire one another a great deal.
WE NEED TO DO SOMETHING.
YES... RIGHT...
WHERE ARE YOU GOING?
TO MY WORKROOM.

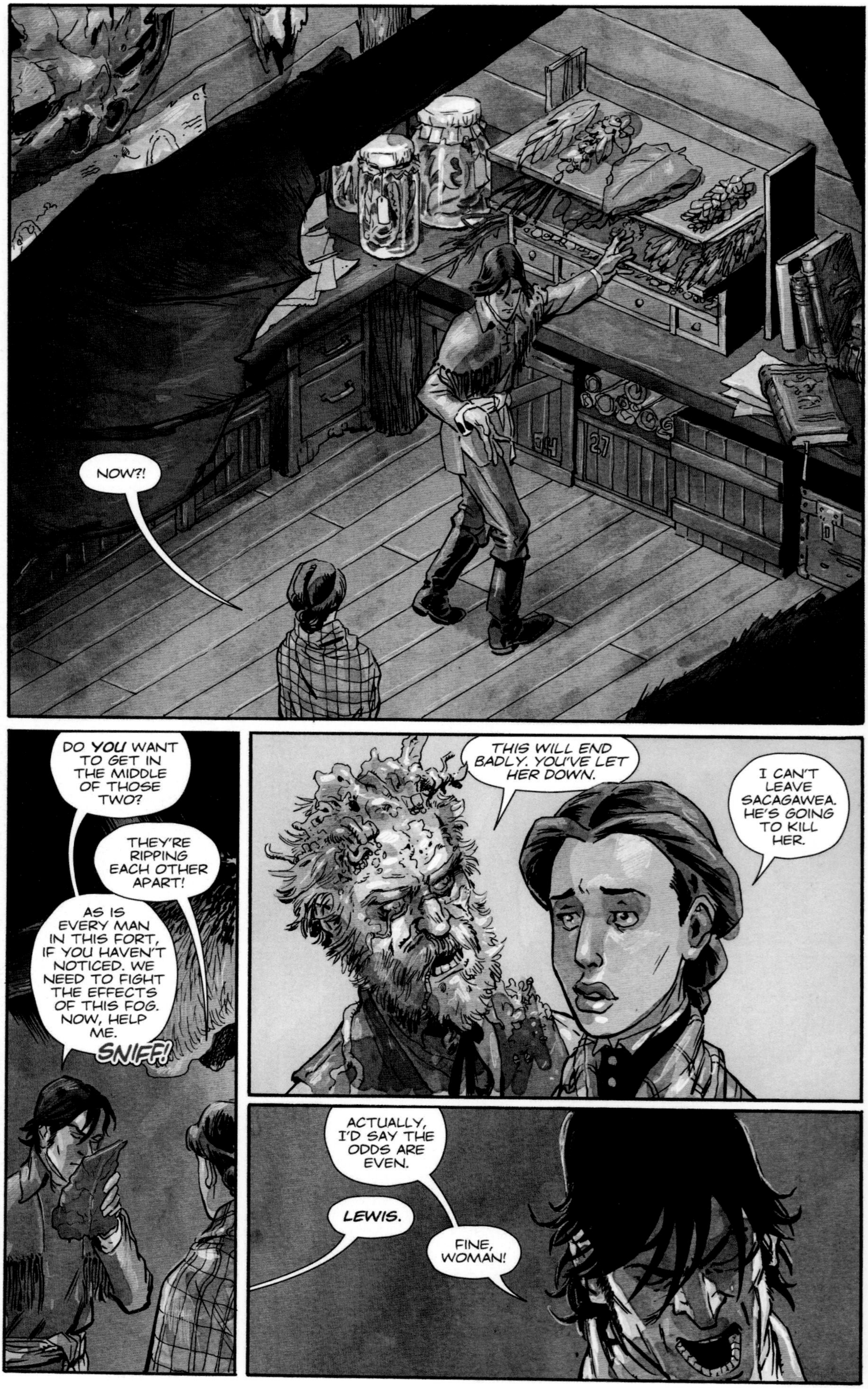
NOW?!
DO YOU WANT TO GET IN THE MIDDLE OF THOSE TWO?
THEY'RE RIPPING EACH OTHER APART!
AS IS EVERY MAN IN THIS FORT, IF YOU HAVEN'T NOTICED. WE NEED TO FIGHT THE EFFECTS OF THIS FOG. NOW, HELP ME.
SNIFF!
THIS WILL END BADLY. YOU'VE LET HER DOWN.
I CAN'T LEAVE SACAGAWEA. HE'S GOING TO KILL HER.
ACTUALLY, I'D SAY THE ODDS ARE EVEN.
LEWIS.
FINE, WOMAN!

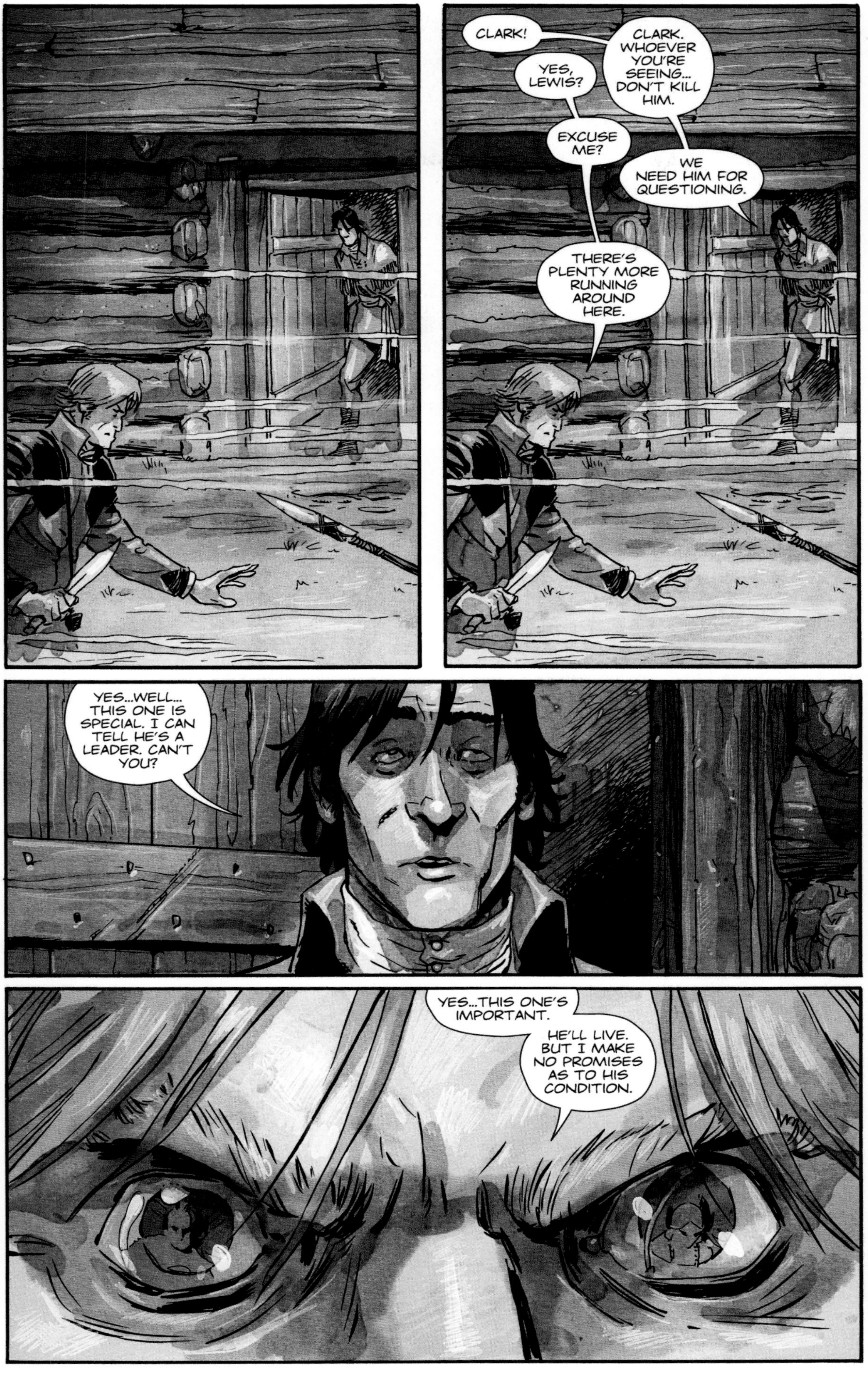
CLARK!
YES, LEWIS?
CLARK. WHOEVER YOU'RE SEEING... DON'T KILL HIM.
EXCUSE ME?
WE NEED HIM FOR QUESTIONING.
THERE'S PLENTY MORE RUNNING AROUND HERE.
YES...WELL... THIS ONE IS SPECIAL. I CAN TELL HE'S A LEADER. CAN'T YOU?
YES...THIS ONE'S IMPORTANT.
HE'LL LIVE. BUT I MAKE NO PROMISES AS TO HIS CONDITION.

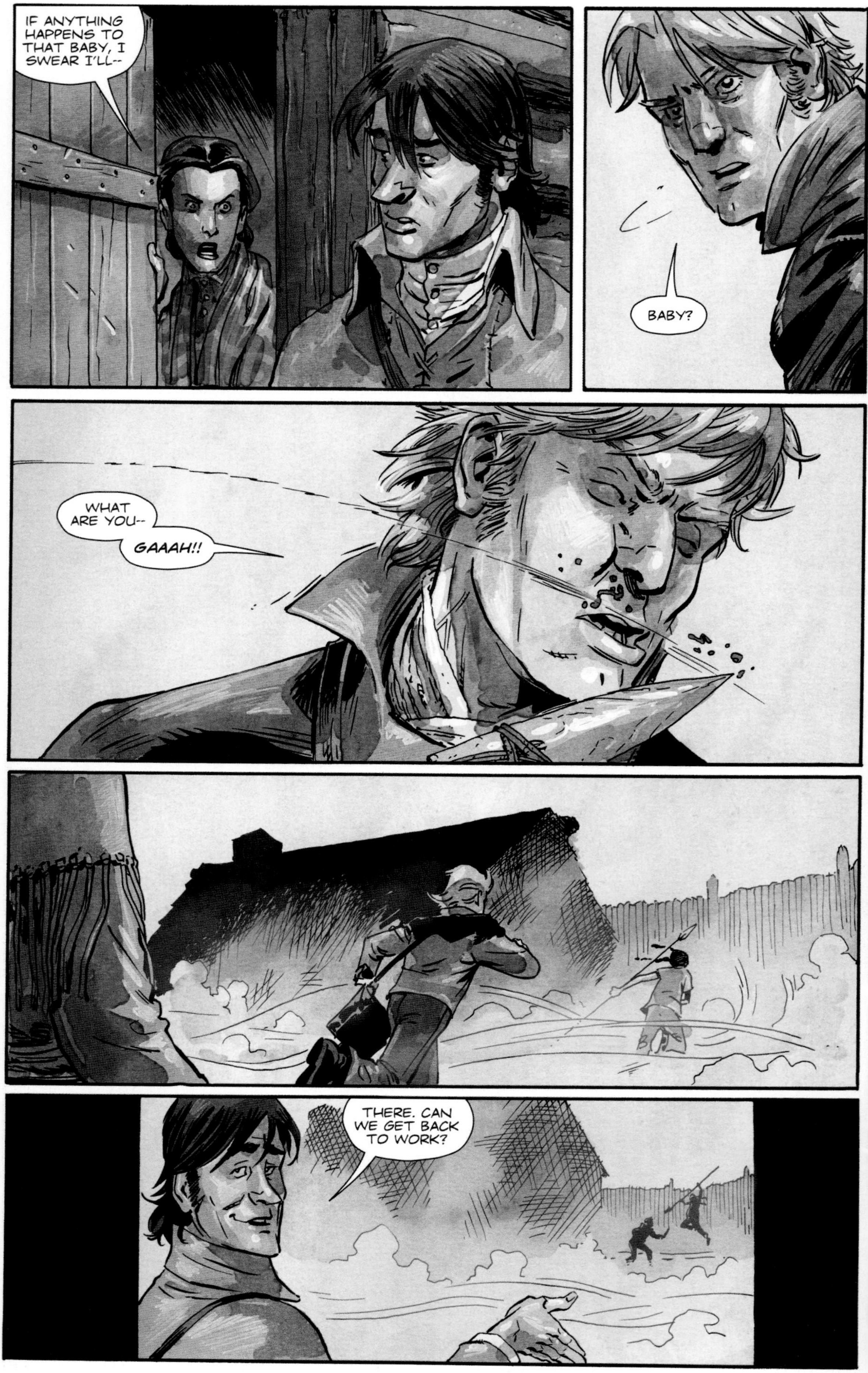
IF ANYTHING HAPPENS TO THAT BABY, I SWEAR I'LL--
BABY?
WHAT ARE YOU--
GAAAH!!
THERE. CAN WE GET BACK TO WORK?

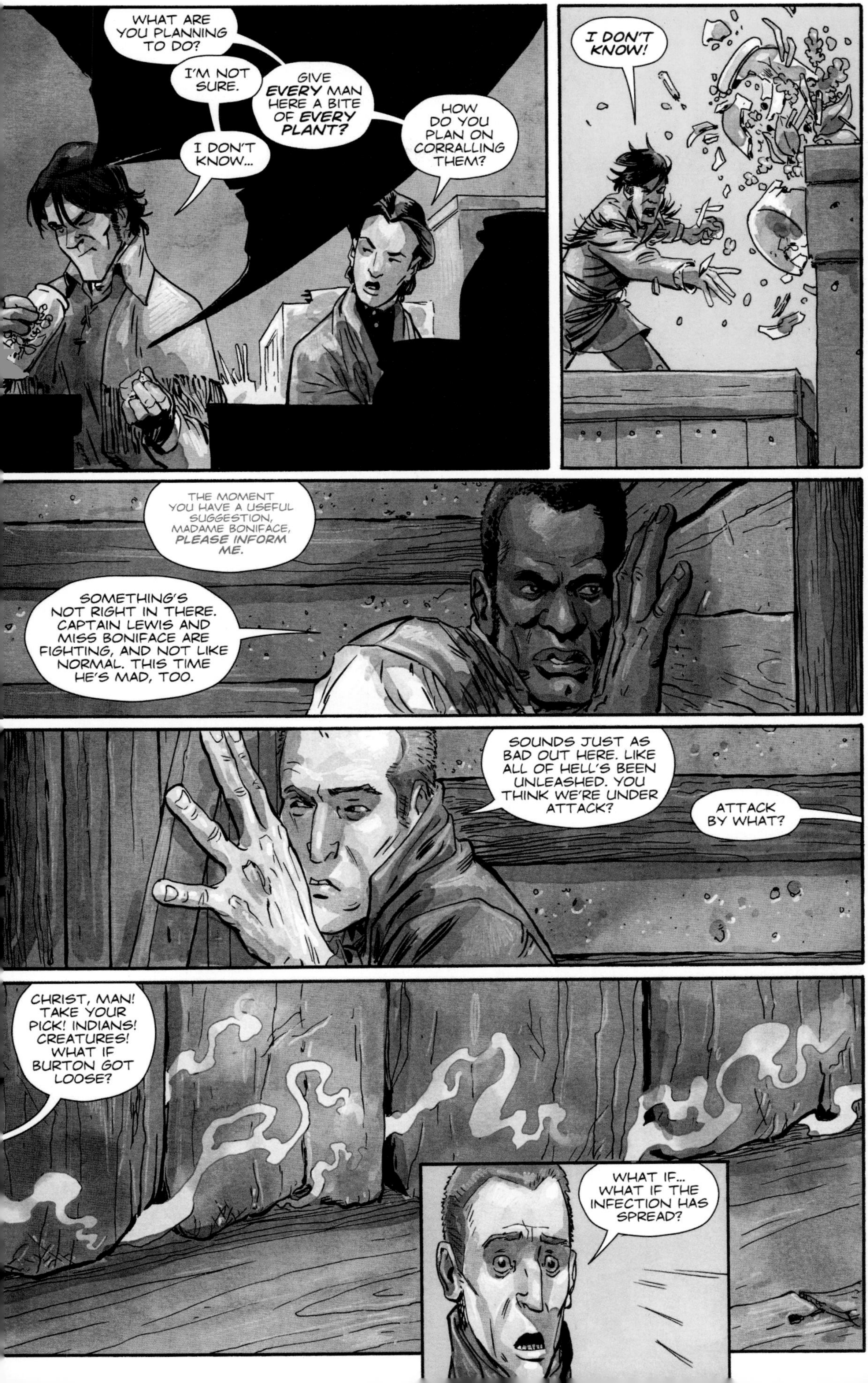
WHAT ARE YOU PLANNING TO DO?
I'M NOT SURE.
I DON'T KNOW...
GIVE EVERY MAN HERE A BITE OF EVERY PLANT?
HOW DO YOU PLAN ON CORRALLING THEM?
I DON'T KNOW!
THE MOMENT YOU HAVE A USEFUL SUGGESTION, MADAME BONIFACE, PLEASE INFORM ME.
SOMETHING'S NOT RIGHT IN THERE. CAPTAIN LEWIS AND MISS BONIFACE ARE FIGHTING, AND NOT LIKE NORMAL. THIS TIME HE'S MAD, TOO.
SOUNDS JUST AS BAD OUT HERE. LIKE ALL OF HELL'S BEEN UNLEASHED. YOU THINK WE'RE UNDER ATTACK?
ATTACK BY WHAT?
CHRIST, MAN! TAKE YOUR PICK! INDIANS! CREATURES! WHAT IF BURTON GOT LOOSE?
WHAT IF... WHAT IF THE INFECTION HAS SPREAD?

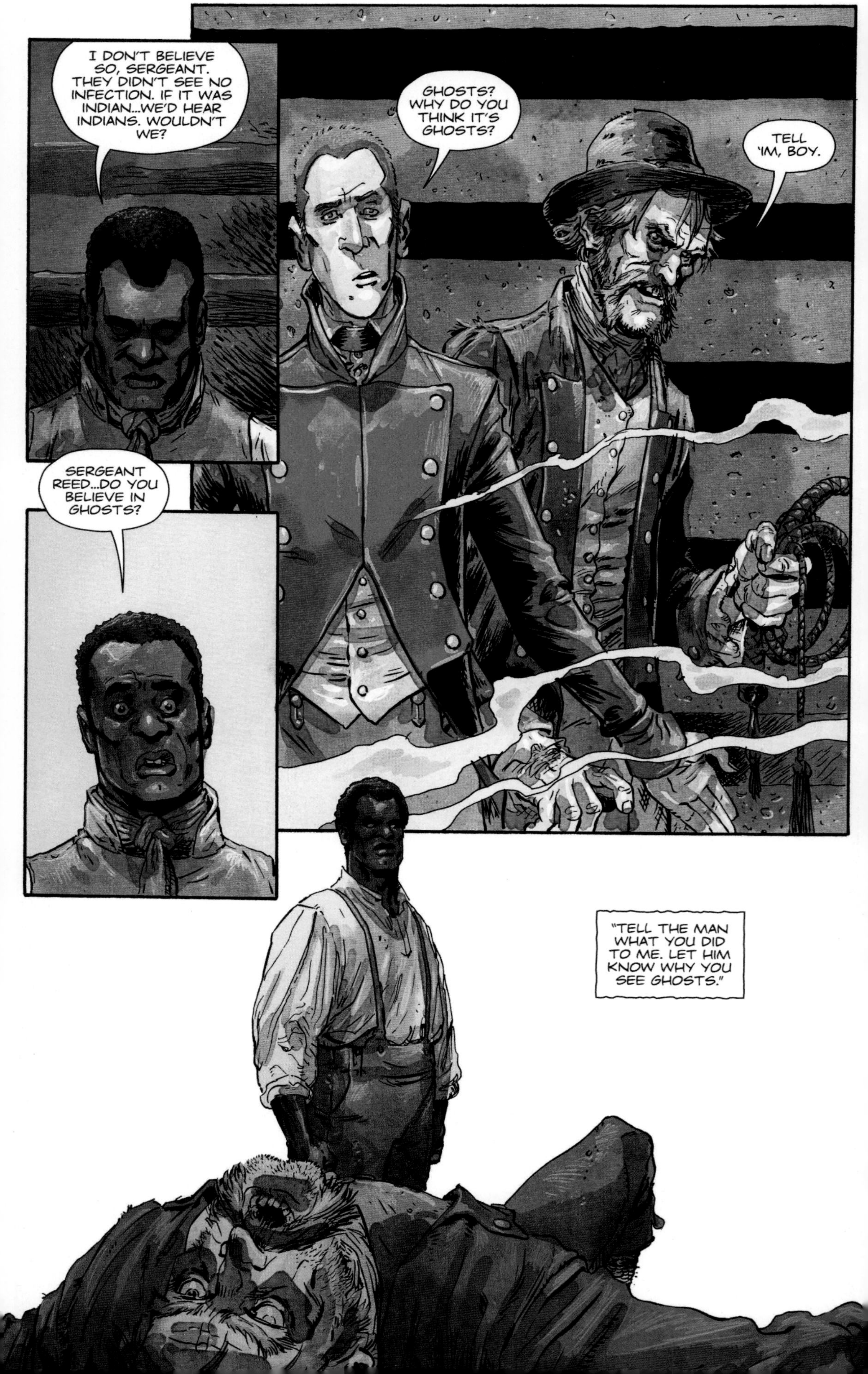
I DON'T BELIEVE SO, SERGEANT. THEY DIDN'T SEE NO INFECTION. IF IT WAS INDIAN...WE'D HEAR INDIANS. WOULDN'T WE?
SERGEANT REED...DO YOU BELIEVE IN GHOSTS?
GHOSTS? WHY DO YOU THINK IT'S GHOSTS?
TELL 'IM, BOY.
"TELL THE MAN WHAT YOU DID TO ME. LET HIM KNOW WHY YOU SEE GHOSTS."

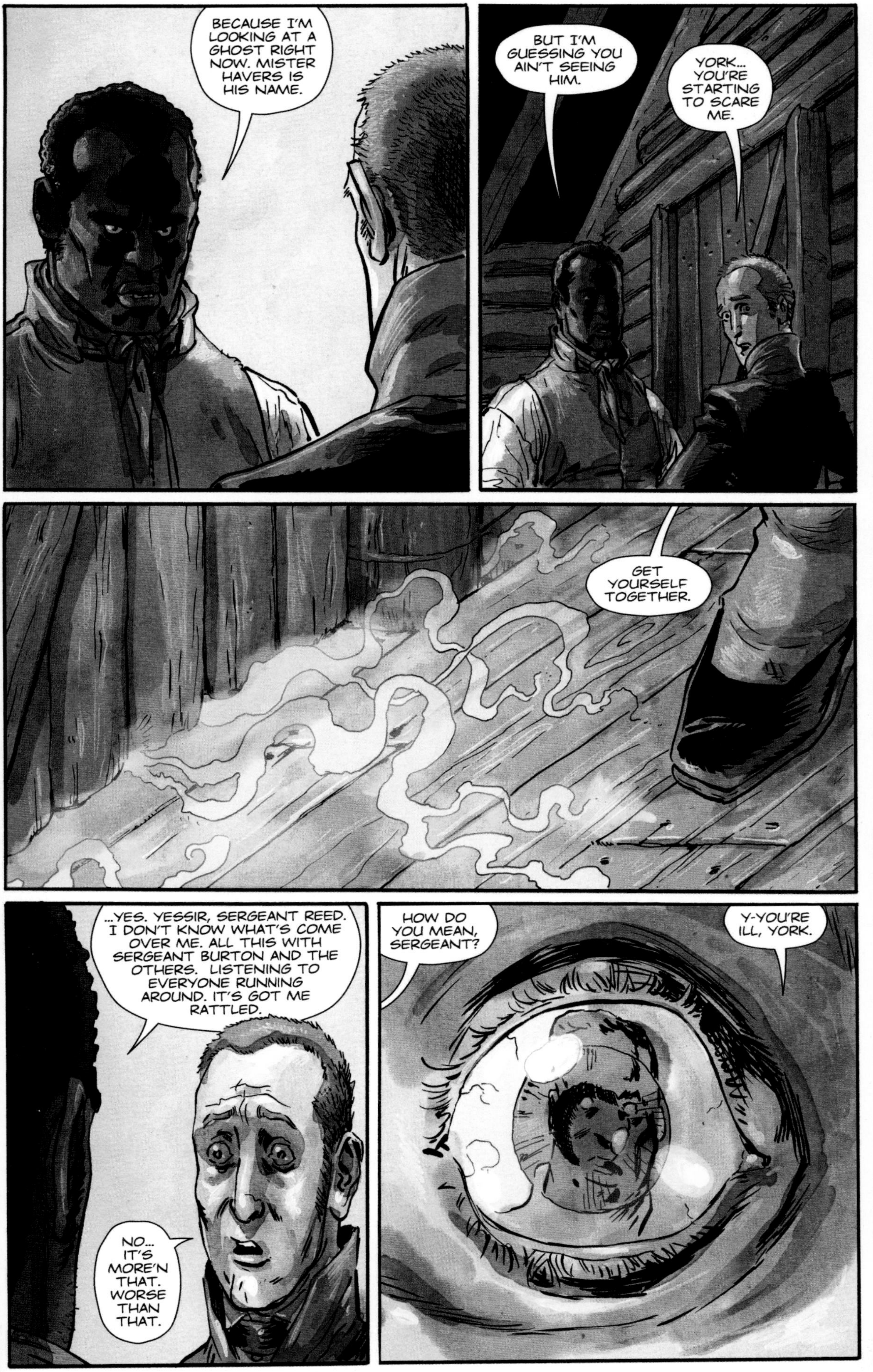
BECAUSE I'M LOOKING AT A GHOST RIGHT NOW. MISTER HAVERS IS HIS NAME.
BUT I'M GUESSING YOU AIN'T SEEING HIM.
YORK... YOU'RE STARTING TO SCARE ME.
GET YOURSELF TOGETHER.
...YES. YESSIR, SERGEANT REED. I DON'T KNOW WHAT'S COME OVER ME. ALL THIS WITH SERGEANT BURTON AND THE OTHERS. LISTENING TO EVERYONE RUNNING AROUND. IT'S GOT ME RATTLED.
NO... IT'S MORE'N THAT. WORSE THAN THAT.
Y-YOU'RE ILL, YORK.
HOW DO YOU MEAN, SERGEANT?

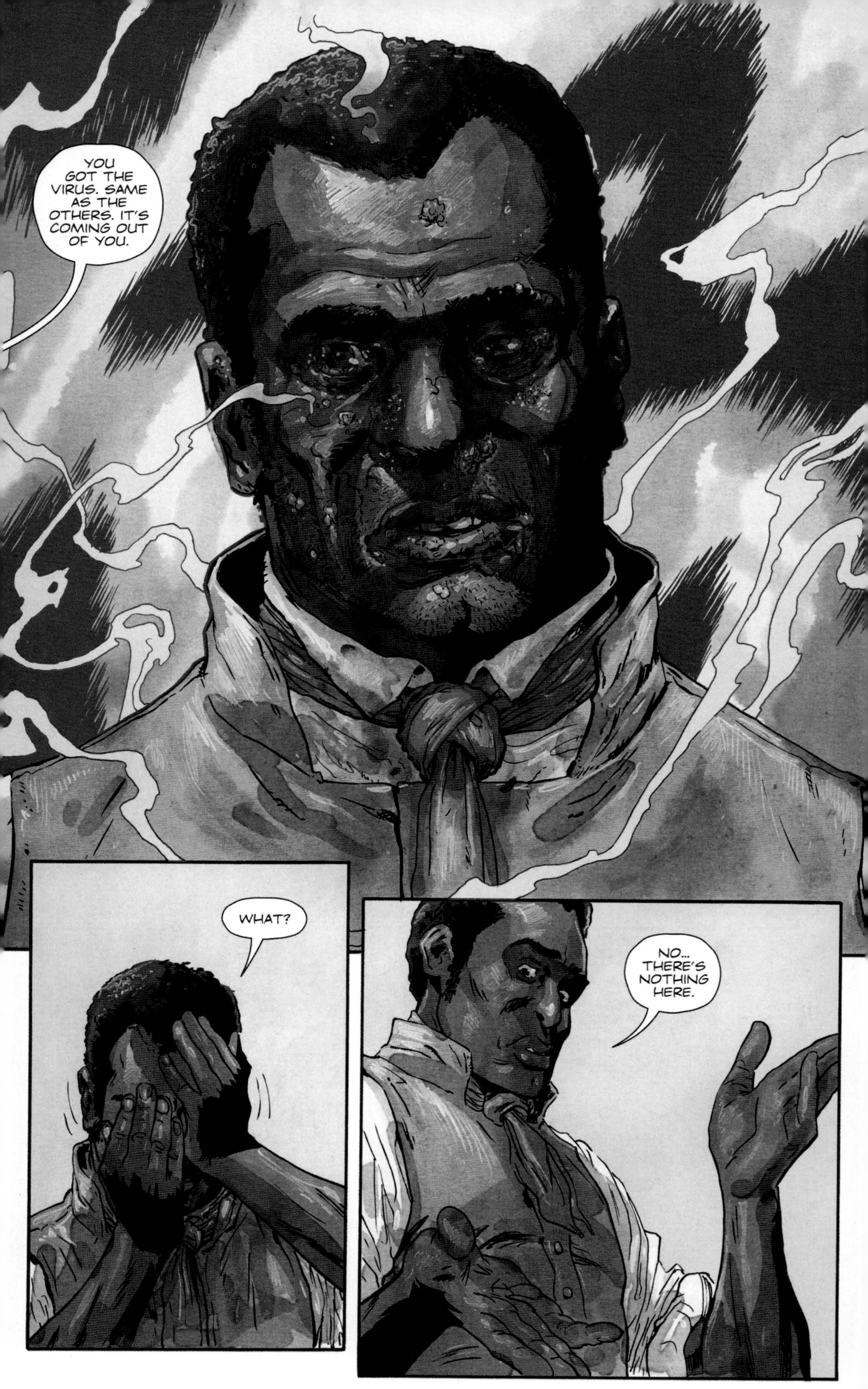
YOU GOT THE VIRUS. SAME AS THE OTHERS. IT'S COMING OUT OF YOU.
WHAT?
NO... THERE'S NOTHING HERE.

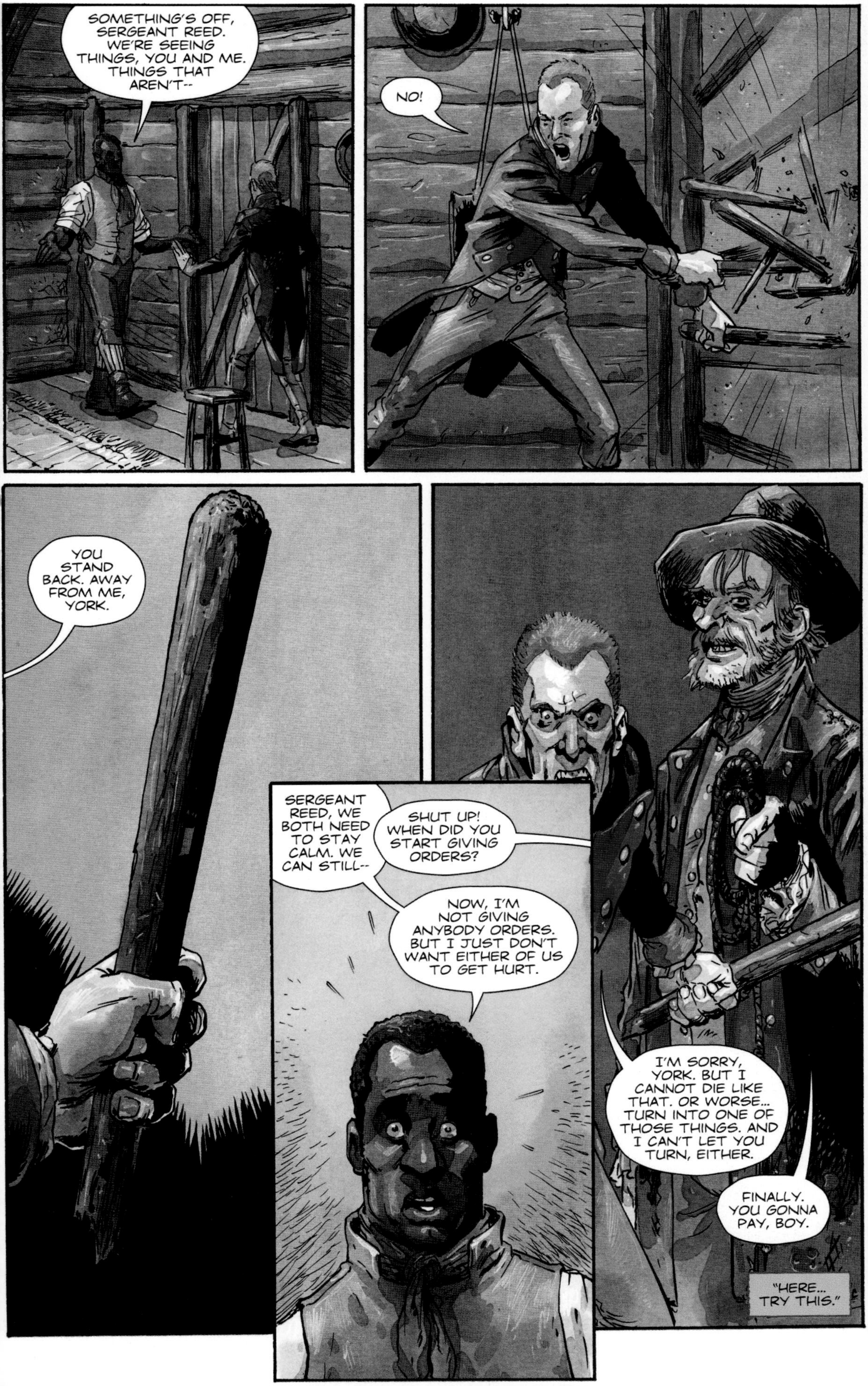
SOMETHING'S OFF, SERGEANT REED. WE'RE SEEING THINGS, YOU AND ME. THINGS THAT AREN'T--
NO!
YOU STAND BACK. AWAY FROM ME, YORK.
SERGEANT REED, WE BOTH NEED TO STAY CALM. WE CAN STILL--
SHUT UP! WHEN DID YOU START GIVING ORDERS?
NOW, I'M NOT GIVING ANYBODY ORDERS. BUT I JUST DON'T WANT EITHER OF US TO GET HURT.
I'M SORRY, YORK. BUT I CANNOT DIE LIKE THAT. OR WORSE... TURN INTO ONE OF THOSE THINGS. AND I CAN'T LET YOU TURN, EITHER.
FINALLY. YOU GONNA PAY, BOY.
"HERE... TRY THIS."

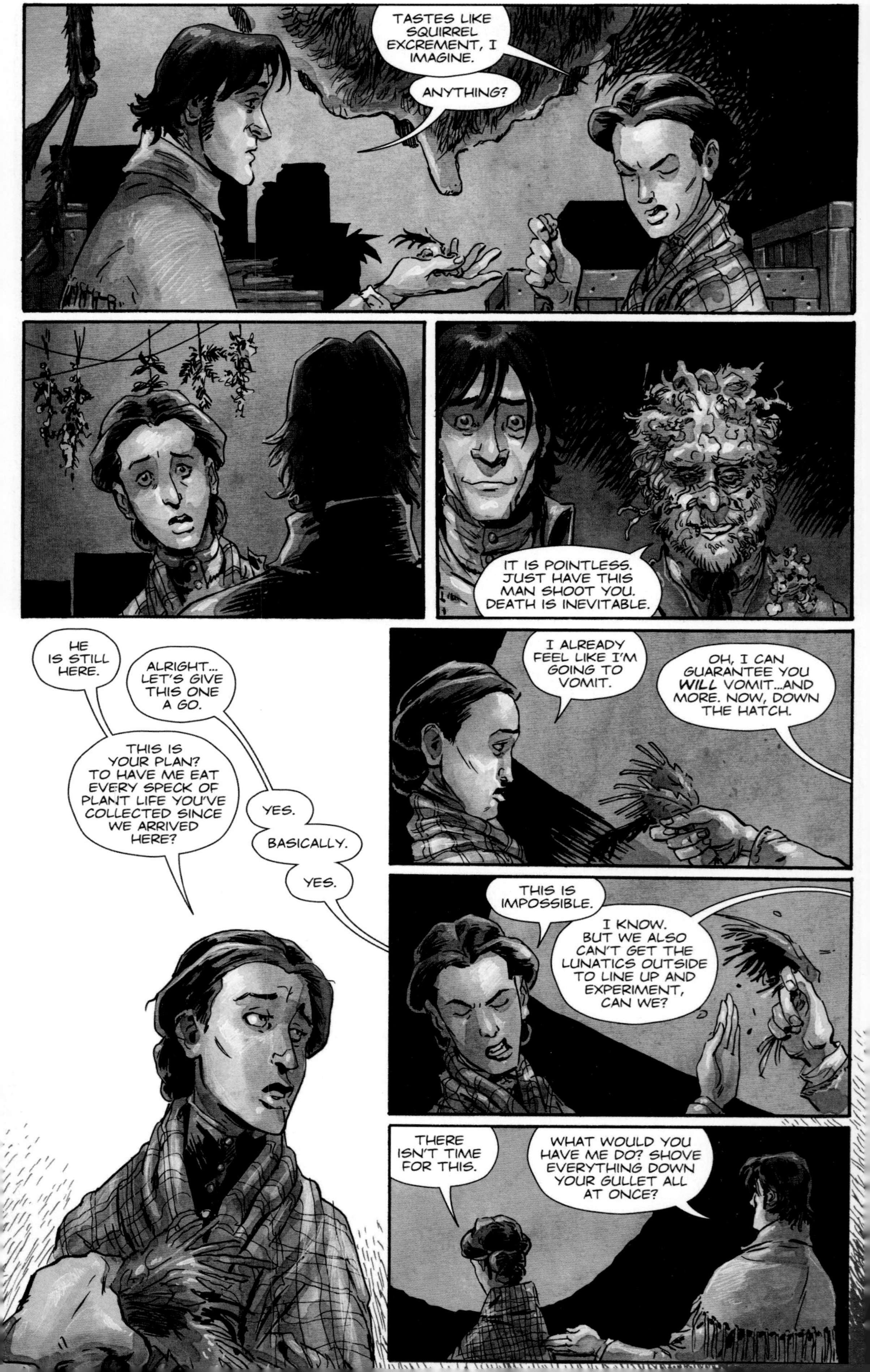
TASTES LIKE SQUIRREL EXCREMENT, I IMAGINE.
ANYTHING?
IT IS POINTLESS. JUST HAVE THIS MAN SHOOT YOU. DEATH IS INEVITABLE.
HE IS STILL HERE.
ALRIGHT... LET'S GIVE THIS ONE A GO.
THIS IS YOUR PLAN? TO HAVE ME EAT EVERY SPECK OF PLANT LIFE YOU'VE COLLECTED SINCE WE ARRIVED HERE?
YES.
BASICALLY.
YES.
I ALREADY FEEL LIKE I'M GOING TO VOMIT.
OH, I CAN GUARANTEE YOU WILL VOMIT...AND MORE. NOW, DOWN THE HATCH.
THIS IS IMPOSSIBLE.
I KNOW. BUT WE ALSO CAN'T GET THE LUNATICS OUTSIDE TO LINE UP AND EXPERIMENT, CAN WE?
THERE ISN'T TIME FOR THIS.
WHAT WOULD YOU HAVE ME DO? SHOVE EVERYTHING DOWN YOUR GULLET ALL AT ONCE?

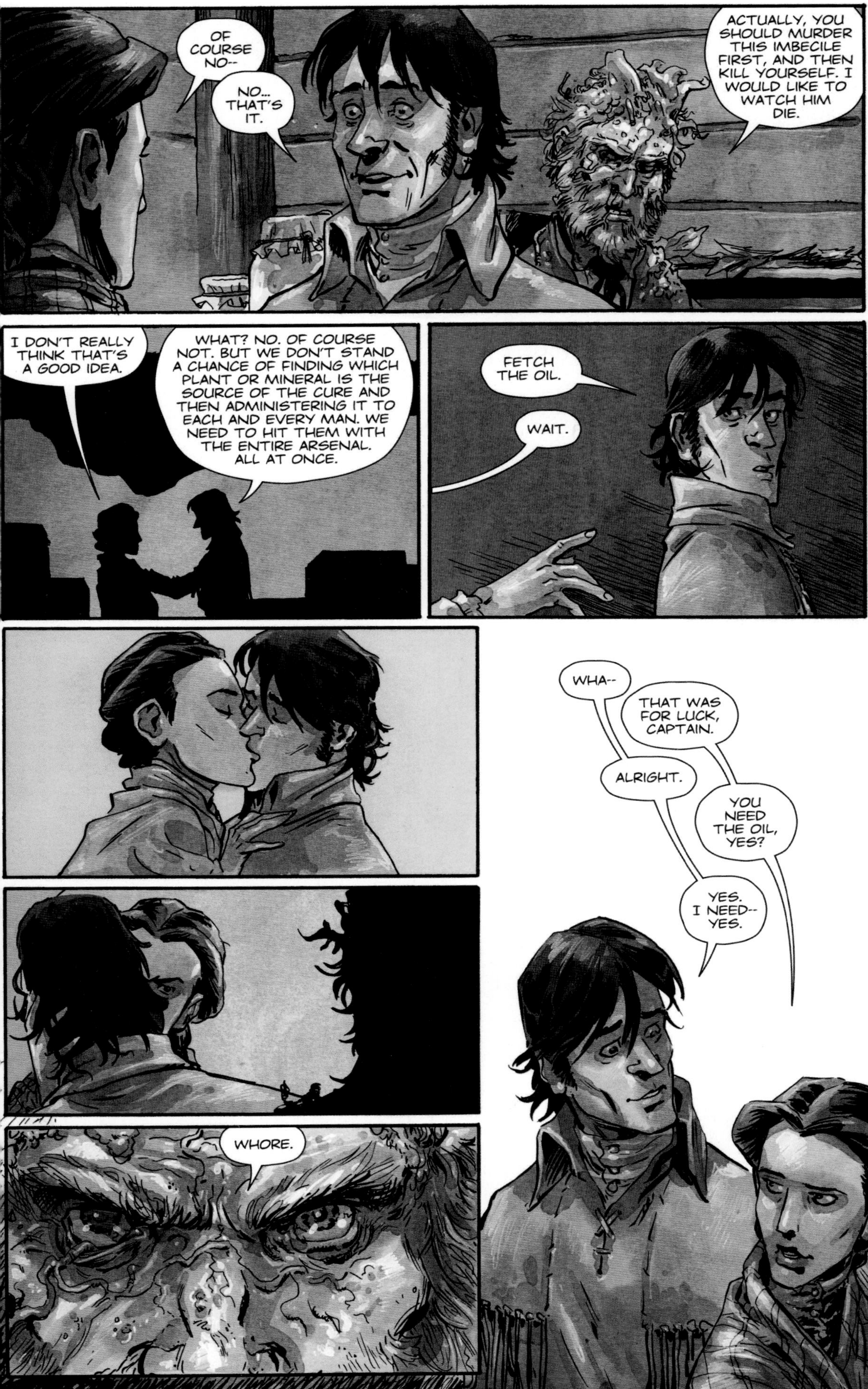
OF COURSE NO--
NO... THAT'S IT.
ACTUALLY, YOU SHOULD MURDER THIS IMBECILE FIRST, AND THEN KILL YOURSELF. I WOULD LIKE TO WATCH HIM DIE.
I DON'T REALLY THINK THAT'S A GOOD IDEA.
WHAT? NO. OF COURSE NOT. BUT WE DON'T STAND A CHANCE OF FINDING WHICH PLANT OR MINERAL IS THE SOURCE OF THE CURE AND THEN ADMINISTERING IT TO EACH AND EVERY MAN. WE NEED TO HIT THEM WITH THE ENTIRE ARSENAL. ALL AT ONCE.
FETCH THE OIL.
WAIT.
WHA--
THAT WAS FOR LUCK, CAPTAIN.
ALRIGHT.
YOU NEED THE OIL, YES?
YES. I NEED-- YES.
WHORE.

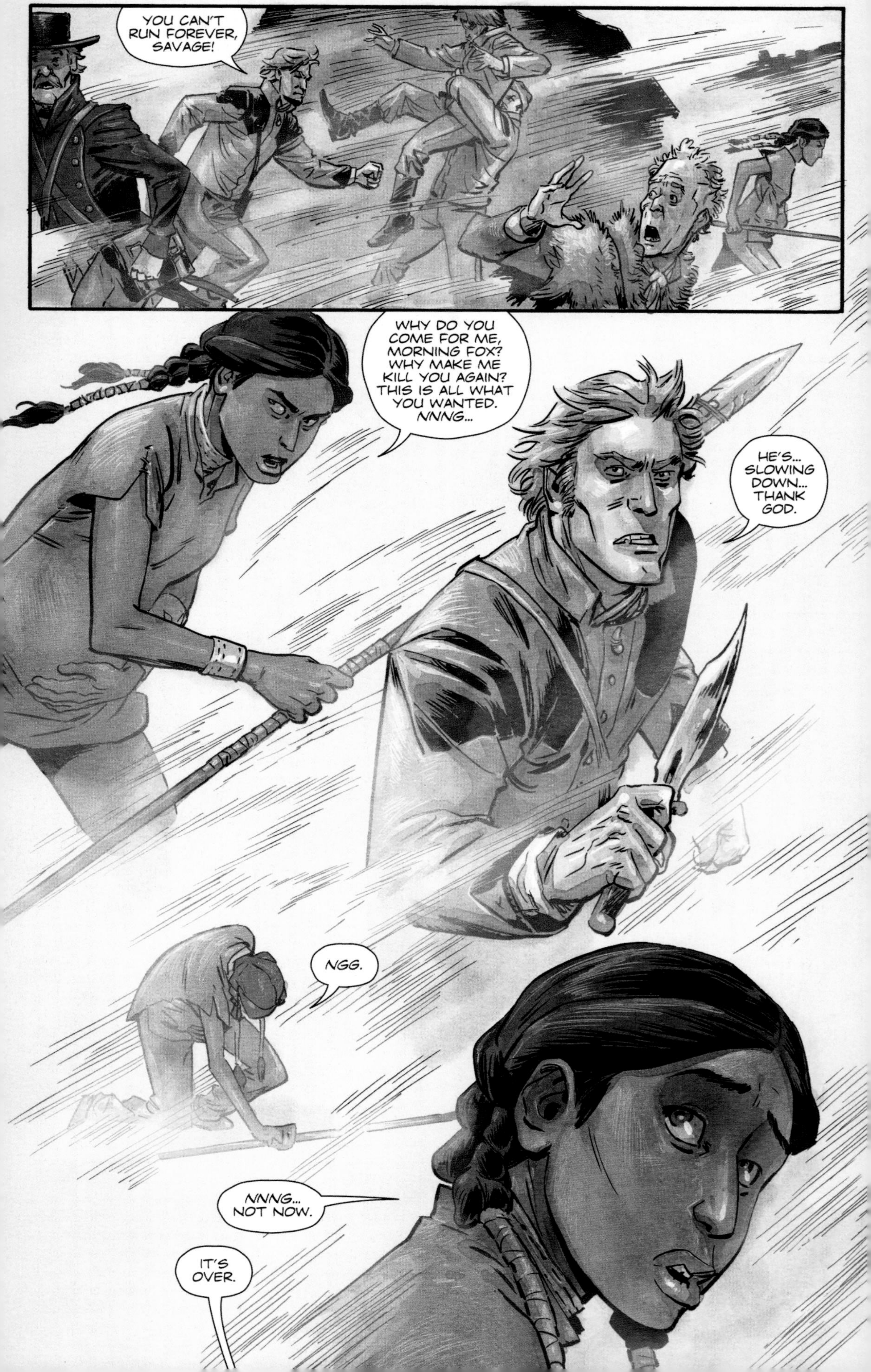
YOU CAN'T RUN FOREVER, SAVAGE!
WHY DO YOU COME FOR ME, MORNING FOX? WHY MAKE ME KILL YOU AGAIN? THIS IS ALL WHAT YOU WANTED. NNNG...
HE'S... SLOWING DOWN... THANK GOD.
NGG.
NNNG... NOT NOW.
IT'S OVER.

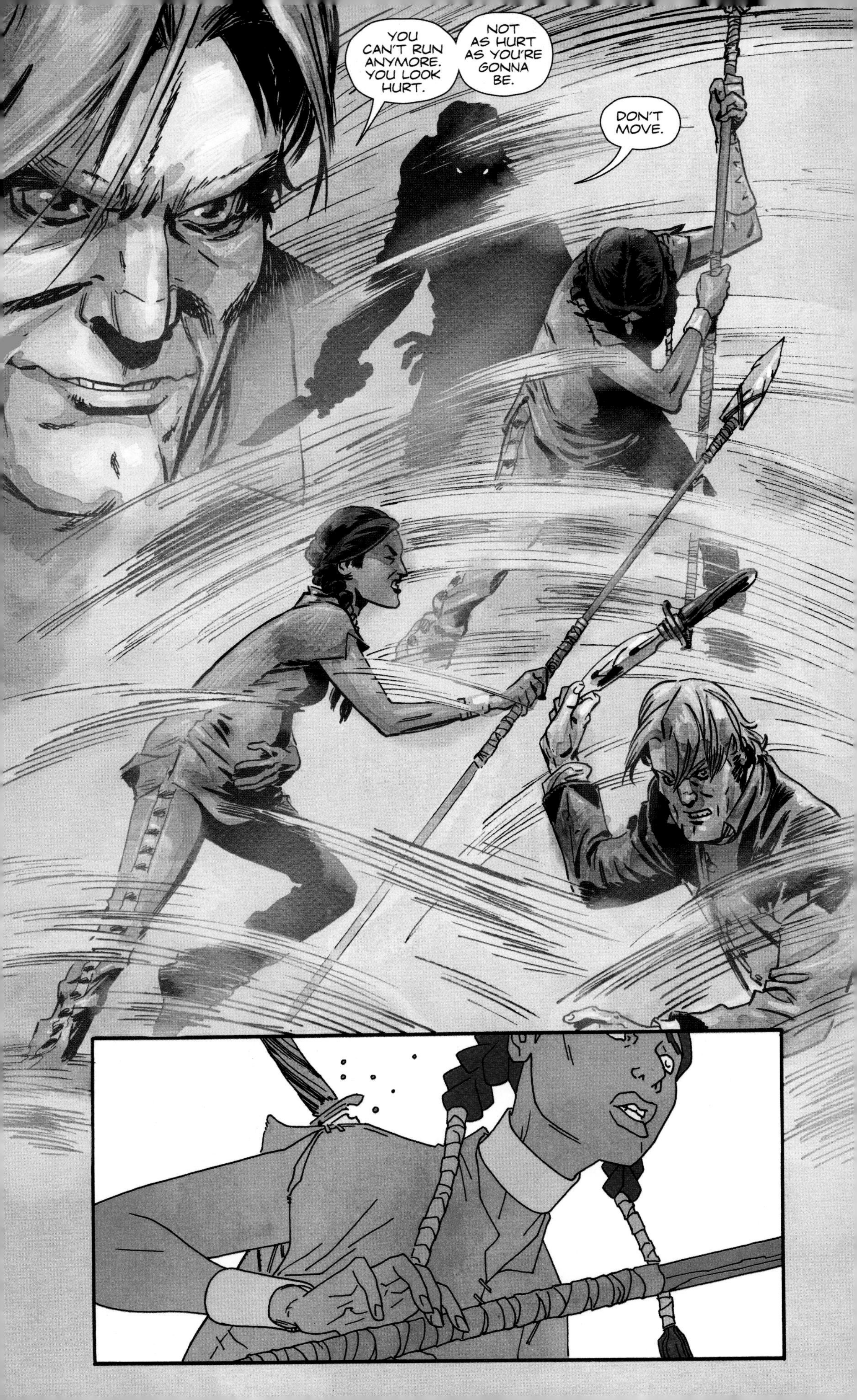
YOU CAN'T RUN ANYMORE. YOU LOOK HURT.
NOT AS HURT AS YOU'RE GONNA BE.
DON'T MOVE.

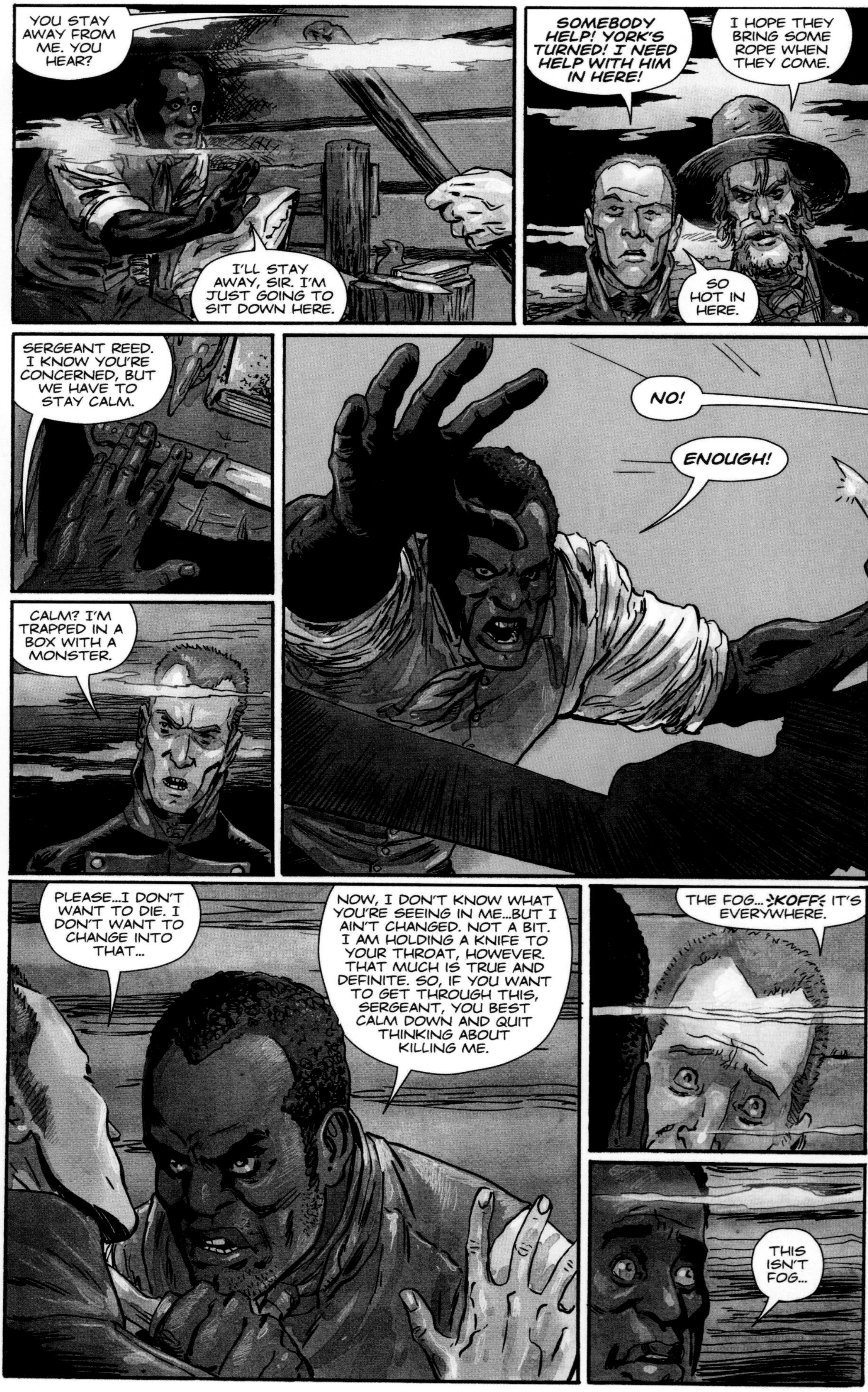
YOU STAY AWAY FROM ME. YOU HEAR?
I'LL STAY AWAY, SIR. I'M JUST GOING TO SIT DOWN HERE.
SOMEBODY HELP! YORK'S TURNED! I NEED HELP WITH HIM IN HERE!
I HOPE THEY BRING SOME ROPE WHEN THEY COME.
SO HOT IN HERE.
SERGEANT REED. I KNOW YOU'RE CONCERNED, BUT WE HAVE TO STAY CALM.
NO!
ENOUGH!
CALM? I'M TRAPPED IN A BOX WITH A MONSTER.
PLEASE...I DON'T WANT TO DIE. I DON'T WANT TO CHANGE INTO THAT...
NOW, I DON'T KNOW WHAT YOU'RE SEEING IN ME...BUT I AIN'T CHANGED. NOT A BIT. I AM HOLDING A KNIFE TO YOUR THROAT, HOWEVER. THAT MUCH IS TRUE AND DEFINITE. SO, IF YOU WANT TO GET THROUGH THIS, SERGEANT, YOU BEST CALM DOWN AND QUIT THINKING ABOUT KILLING ME.
THE FOG... KOFF IT'S EVERYWHERE.
THIS ISN'T FOG...

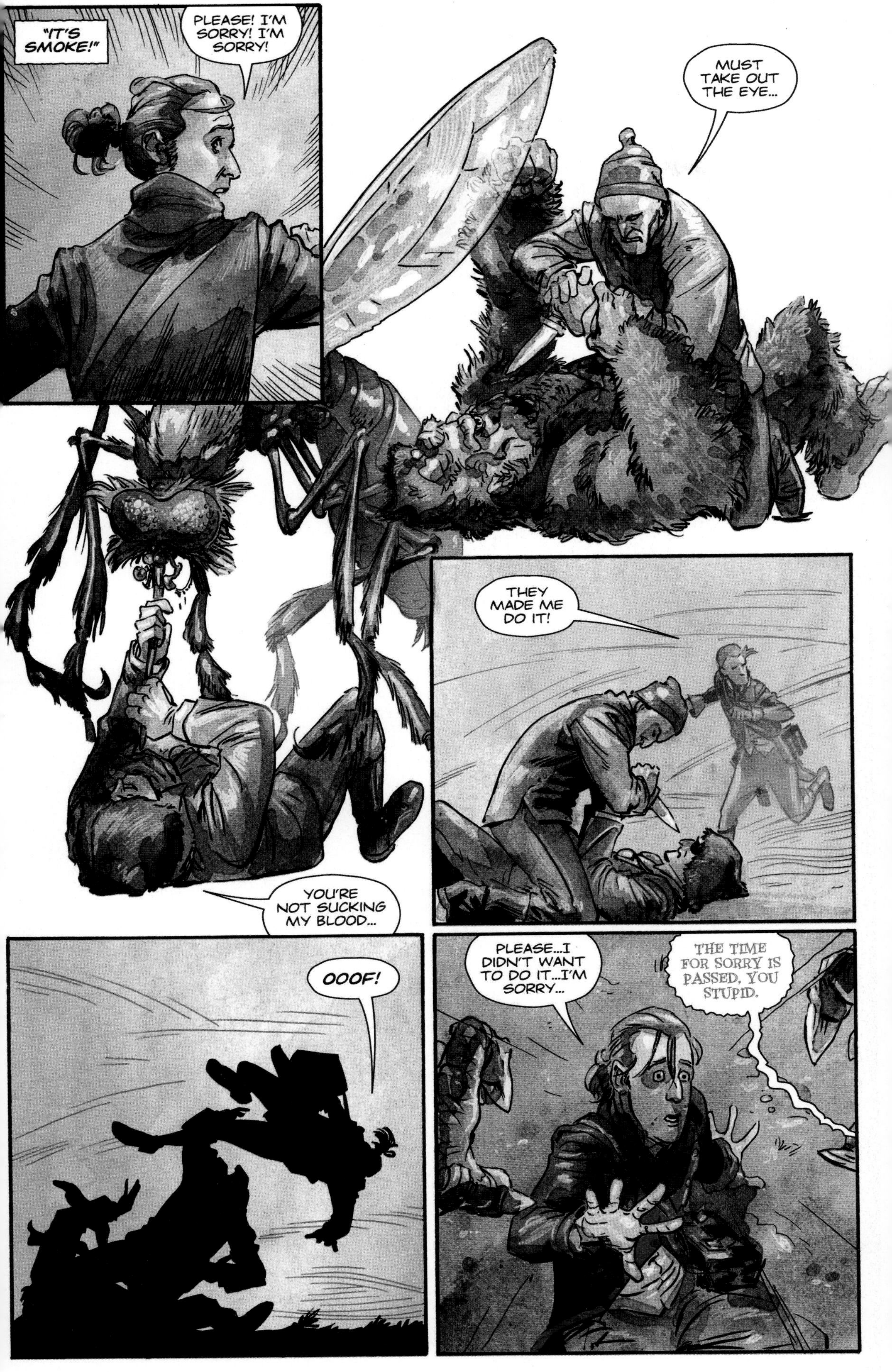
"IT'S SMOKE!"
PLEASE! I'M SORRY! I'M SORRY!
MUST TAKE OUT THE EYE...
YOU'RE NOT SUCKING MY BLOOD...
THEY MADE ME DO IT!
OOOF!
PLEASE...I DIDN'T WANT TO DO IT...I'M SORRY...
THE TIME FOR SORRY IS PASSED, YOU STUPID.

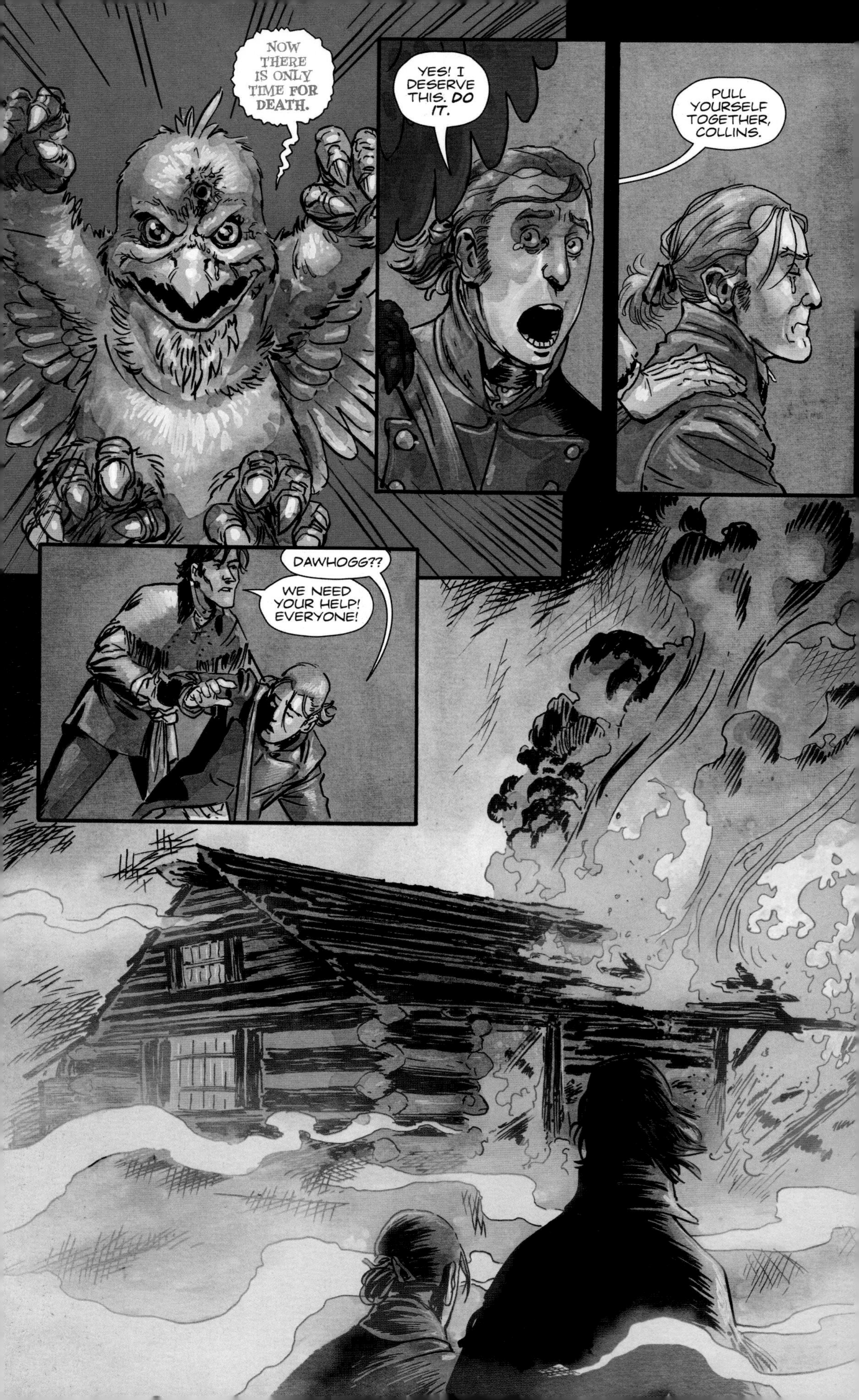
NOW THERE IS ONLY TIME FOR DEATH.
YES! I DESERVE THIS. DO IT.
PULL YOURSELF TOGETHER, COLLINS.
DAWHOGG??
WE NEED YOUR HELP! EVERYONE!

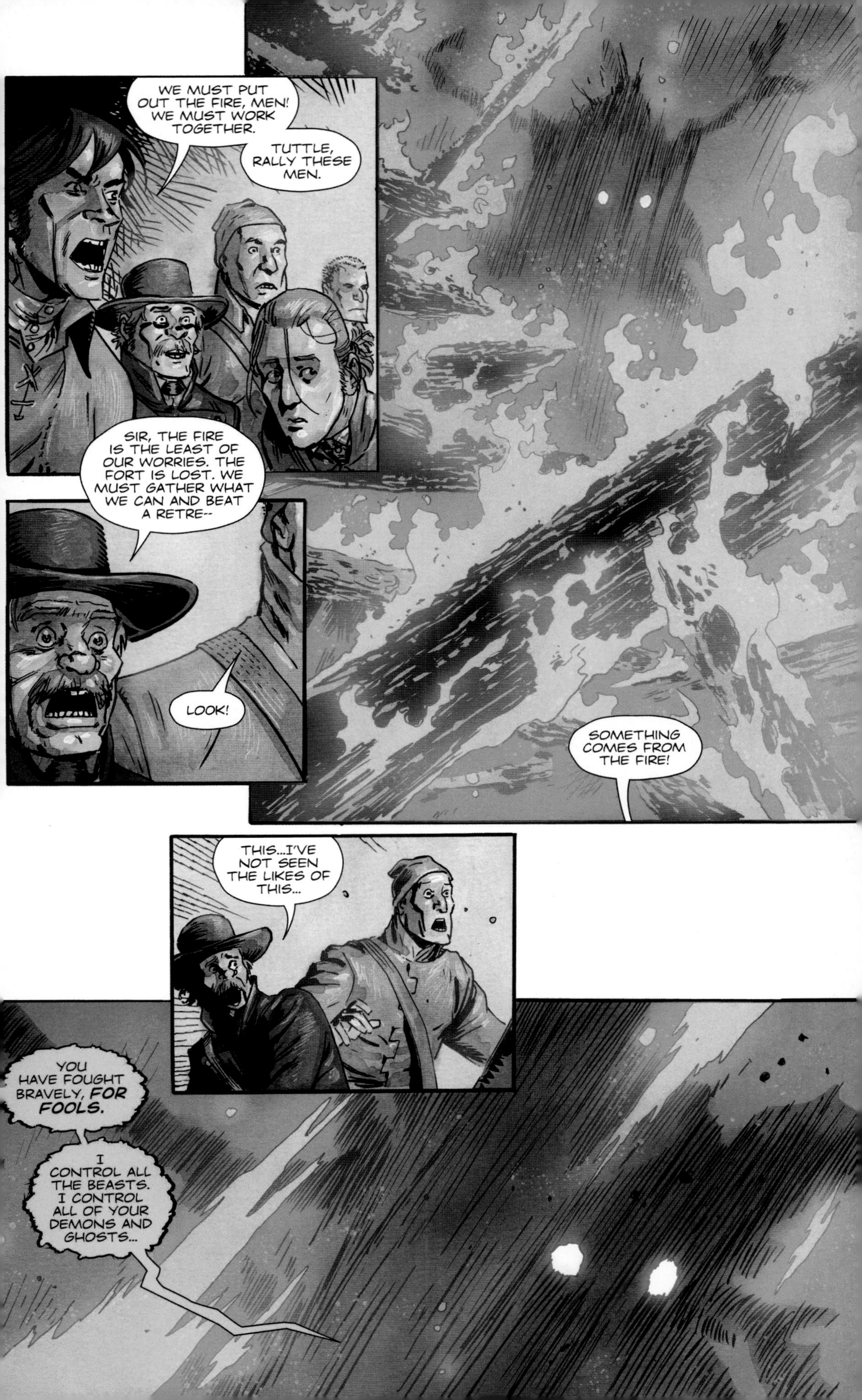
WE MUST PUT OUT THE FIRE, MEN! WE MUST WORK TOGETHER.
TUTTLE, RALLY THESE MEN.
SIR, THE FIRE IS THE LEAST OF OUR WORRIES. THE FORT IS LOST. WE MUST GATHER WHAT WE CAN AND BEAT A RETRE--
LOOK!
SOMETHING COMES FROM THE FIRE!
THIS...I'VE NOT SEEN THE LIKES OF THIS...
YOU HAVE FOUGHT BRAVELY, **FOR FOOLS.**
I CONTROL ALL THE BEASTS. I CONTROL ALL OF YOUR DEMONS AND GHOSTS...

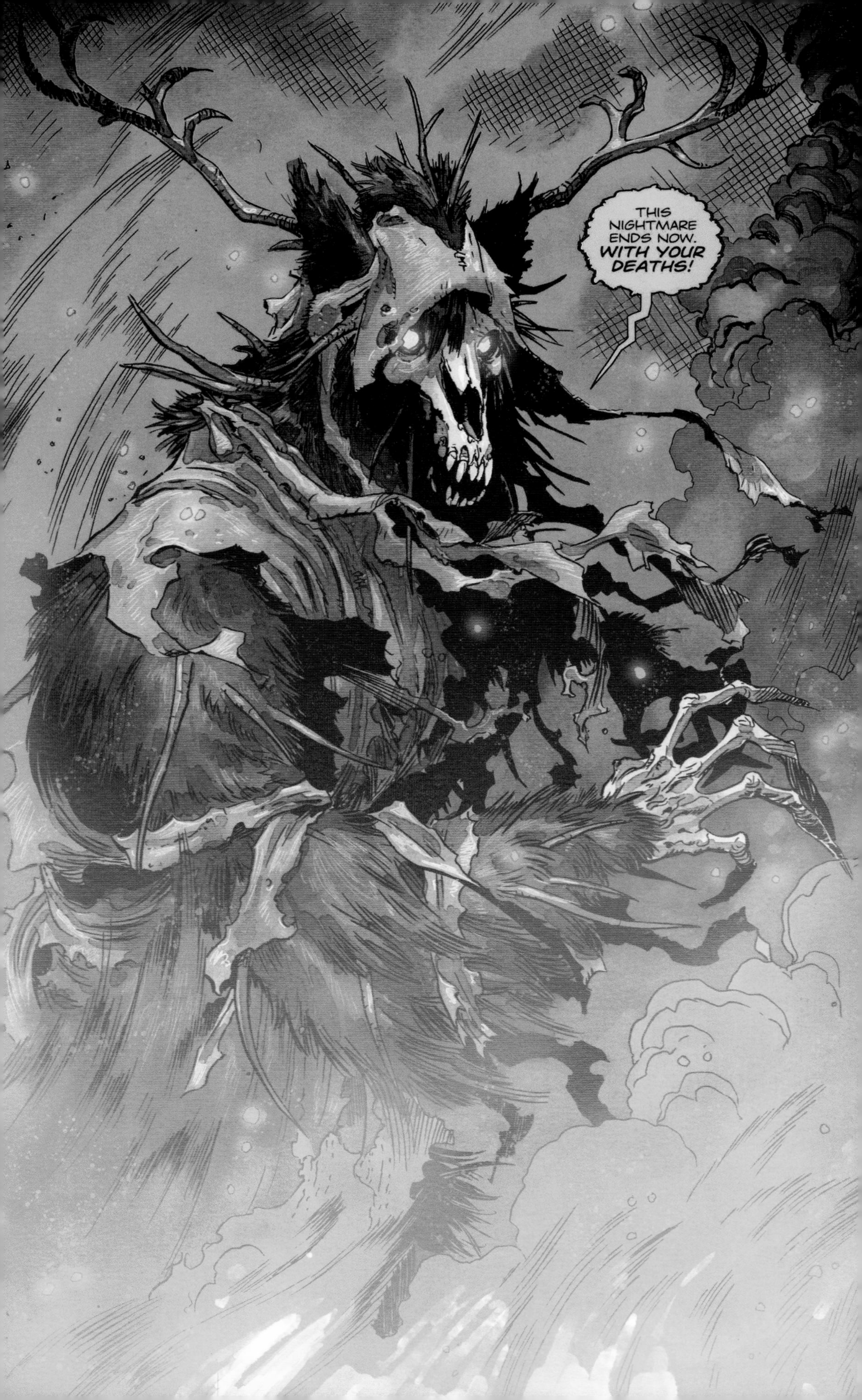
THIS NIGHTMARE ENDS NOW. WITH YOUR DEATHS!

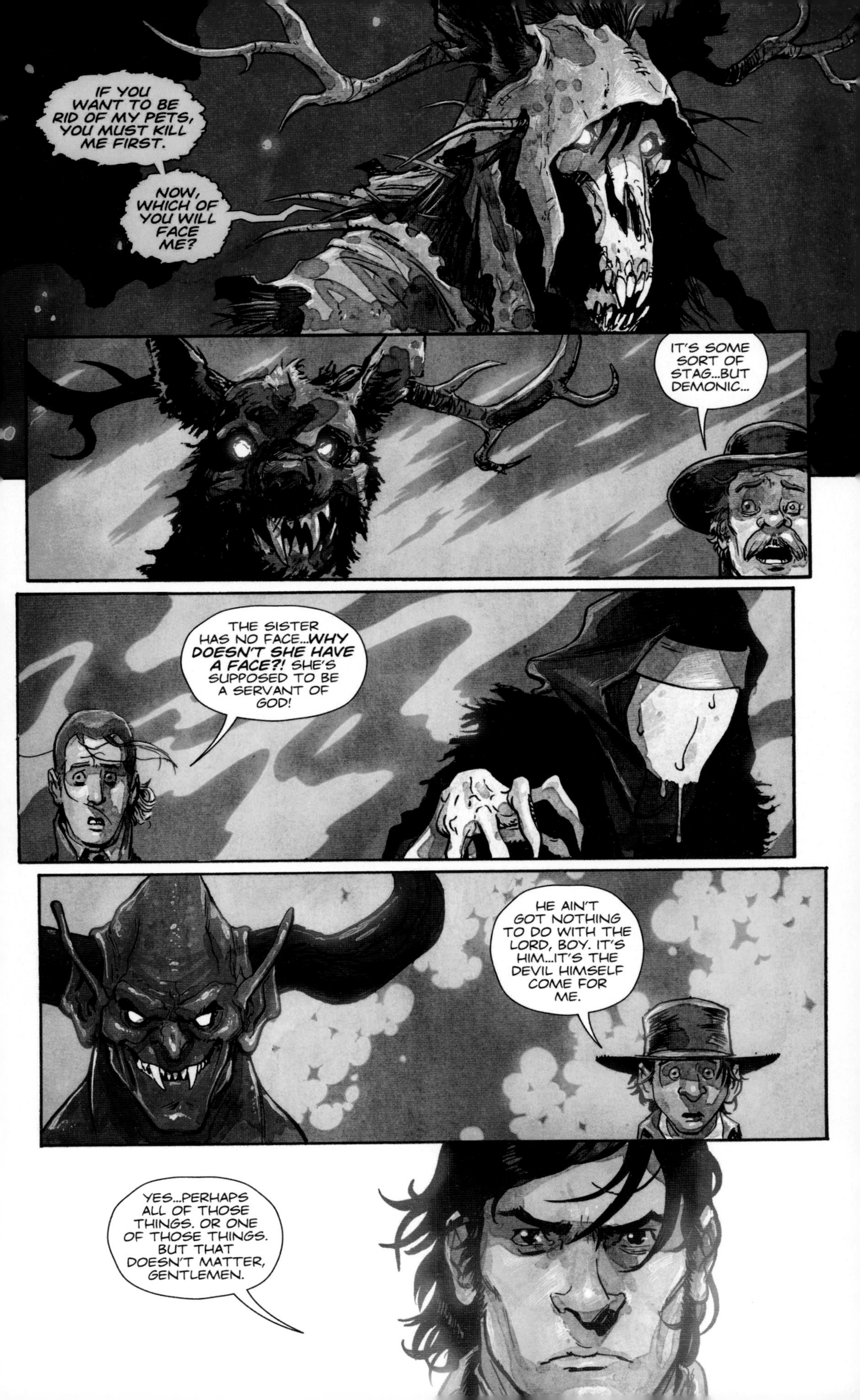
IF YOU WANT TO BE RID OF MY PETS, YOU MUST KILL ME FIRST.
NOW, WHICH OF YOU WILL FACE ME?
IT'S SOME SORT OF STAG...BUT DEMONIC...
THE SISTER HAS NO FACE...WHY DOESN'T SHE HAVE A FACE?! SHE'S SUPPOSED TO BE A SERVANT OF GOD!
HE AIN'T GOT NOTHING TO DO WITH THE LORD, BOY. IT'S HIM...IT'S THE DEVIL HIMSELF COME FOR ME.
YES...PERHAPS ALL OF THOSE THINGS. OR ONE OF THOSE THINGS. BUT THAT DOESN'T MATTER, GENTLEMEN.

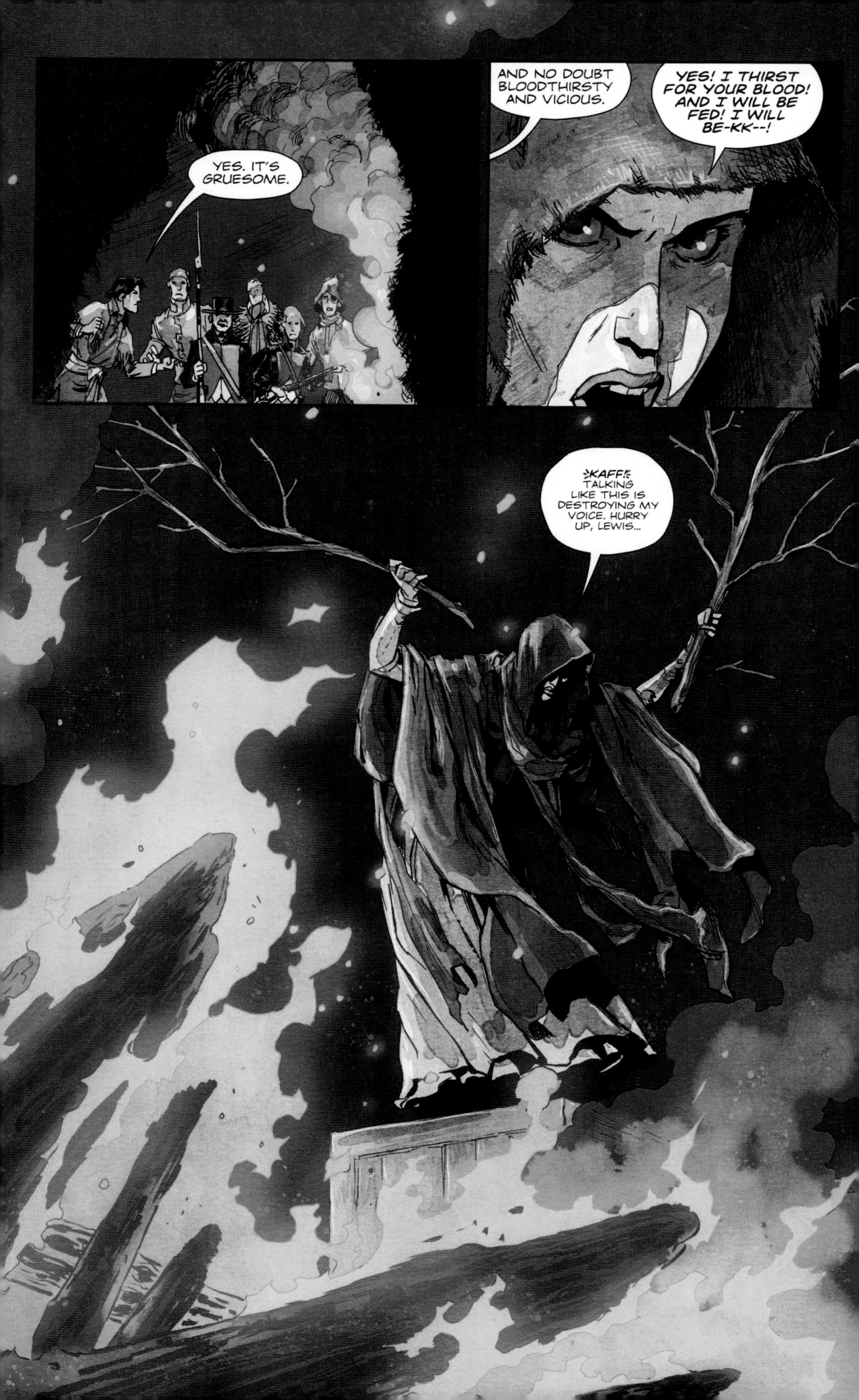
YES. IT'S GRUESOME.
AND NO DOUBT BLOODTHIRSTY AND VICIOUS.
YES! I THIRST FOR YOUR BLOOD! AND I WILL BE FED! I WILL BE-KK--!
*KAFF* TALKING LIKE THIS IS DESTROYING MY VOICE. HURRY UP, LEWIS...

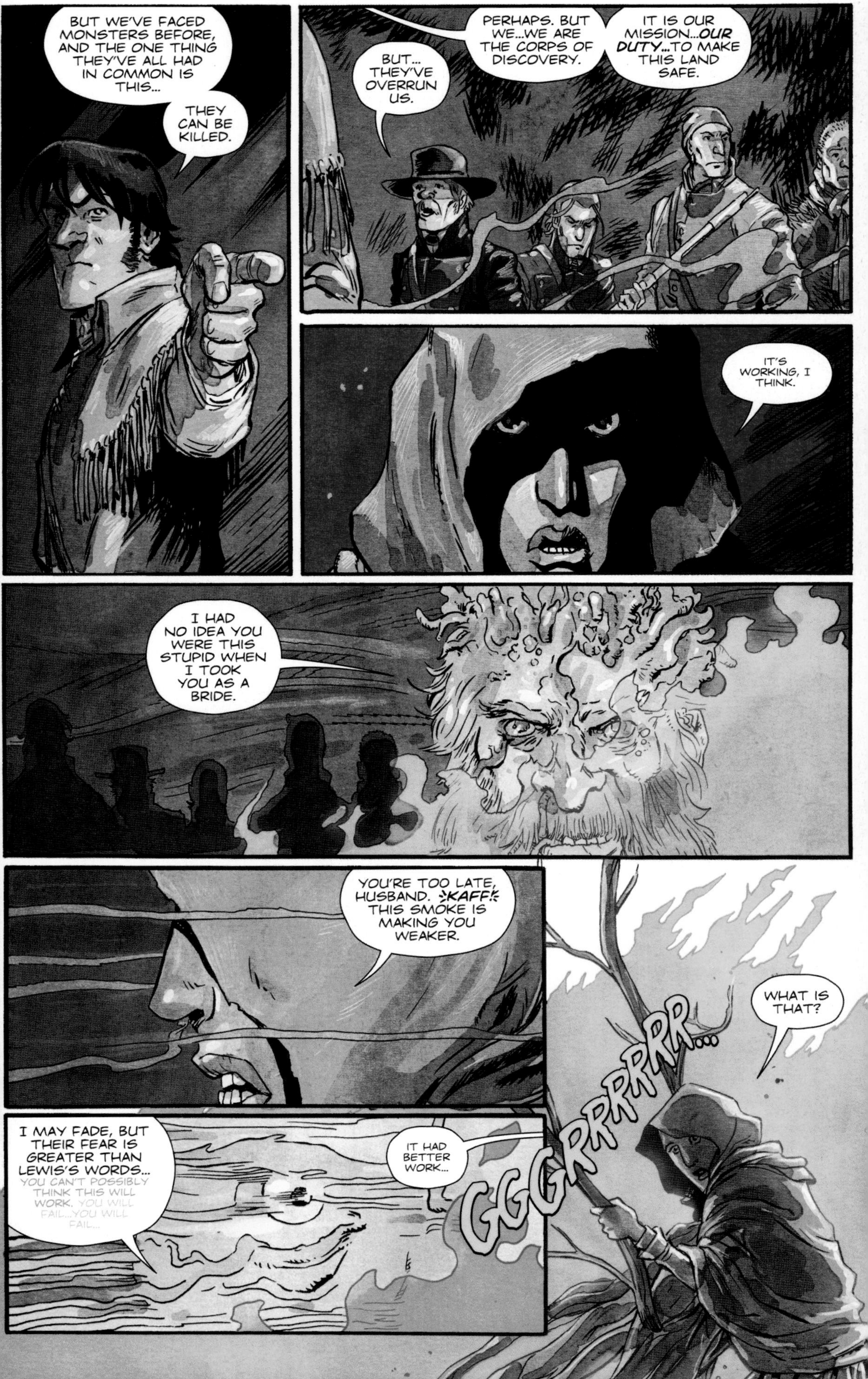
BUT WE'VE FACED MONSTERS BEFORE, AND THE ONE THING THEY'VE ALL HAD IN COMMON IS THIS...
THEY CAN BE KILLED.
BUT... THEY'VE OVERRUN US.
PERHAPS. BUT WE...WE ARE THE CORPS OF DISCOVERY.
IT IS OUR MISSION...OUR DUTY...TO MAKE THIS LAND SAFE.
IT'S WORKING, I THINK.
I HAD NO IDEA YOU WERE THIS STUPID WHEN I TOOK YOU AS A BRIDE.
YOU'RE TOO LATE, HUSBAND. KAFF! THIS SMOKE IS MAKING YOU WEAKER.
I MAY FADE, BUT THEIR FEAR IS GREATER THAN LEWIS'S WORDS... YOU CAN'T POSSIBLY THINK THIS WILL WORK. YOU WILL FAIL...YOU WILL FAIL...
IT HAD BETTER WORK...
WHAT IS THAT?
GGGRRRRRRR...

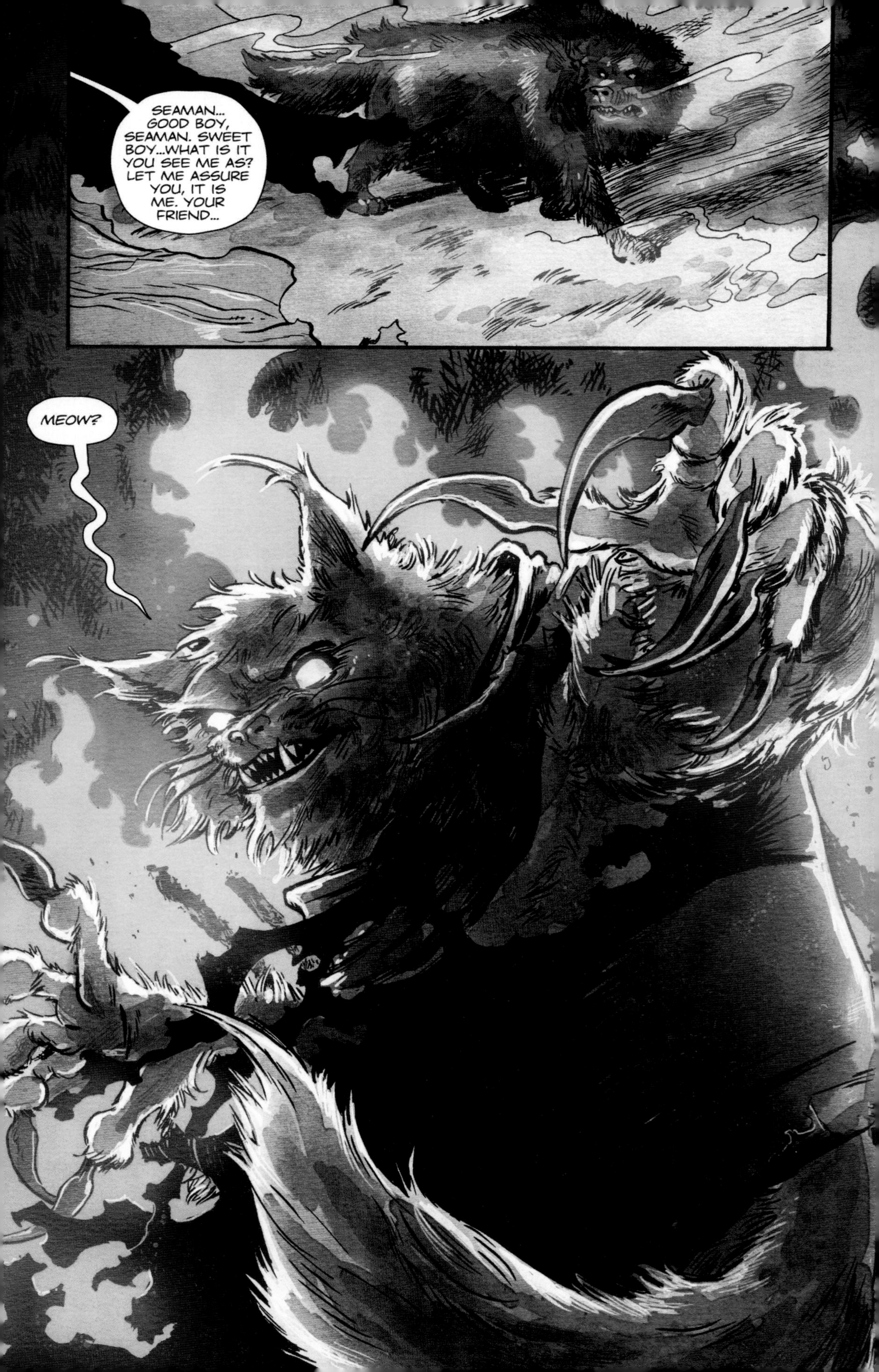
SEAMAN... GOOD BOY, SEAMAN. SWEET BOY...WHAT IS IT YOU SEE ME AS? LET ME ASSURE YOU, IT IS ME. YOUR FRIEND...
MEOW?

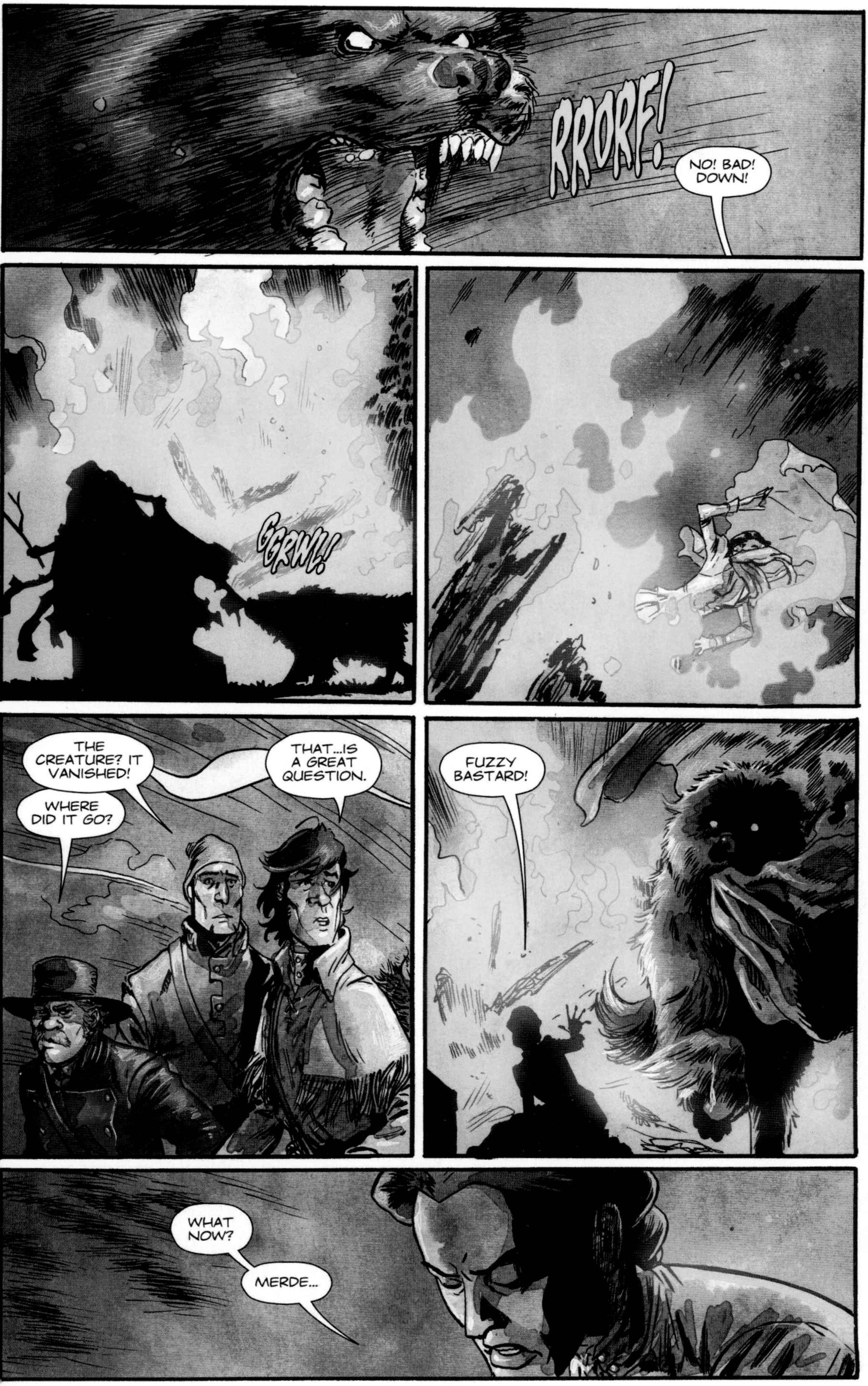
RRORF!
NO! BAD! DOWN!
GGRWL!
THE CREATURE? IT VANISHED!
THAT...IS A GREAT QUESTION.
WHERE DID IT GO?
FUZZY BASTARD!
WHAT NOW?
MERDE...

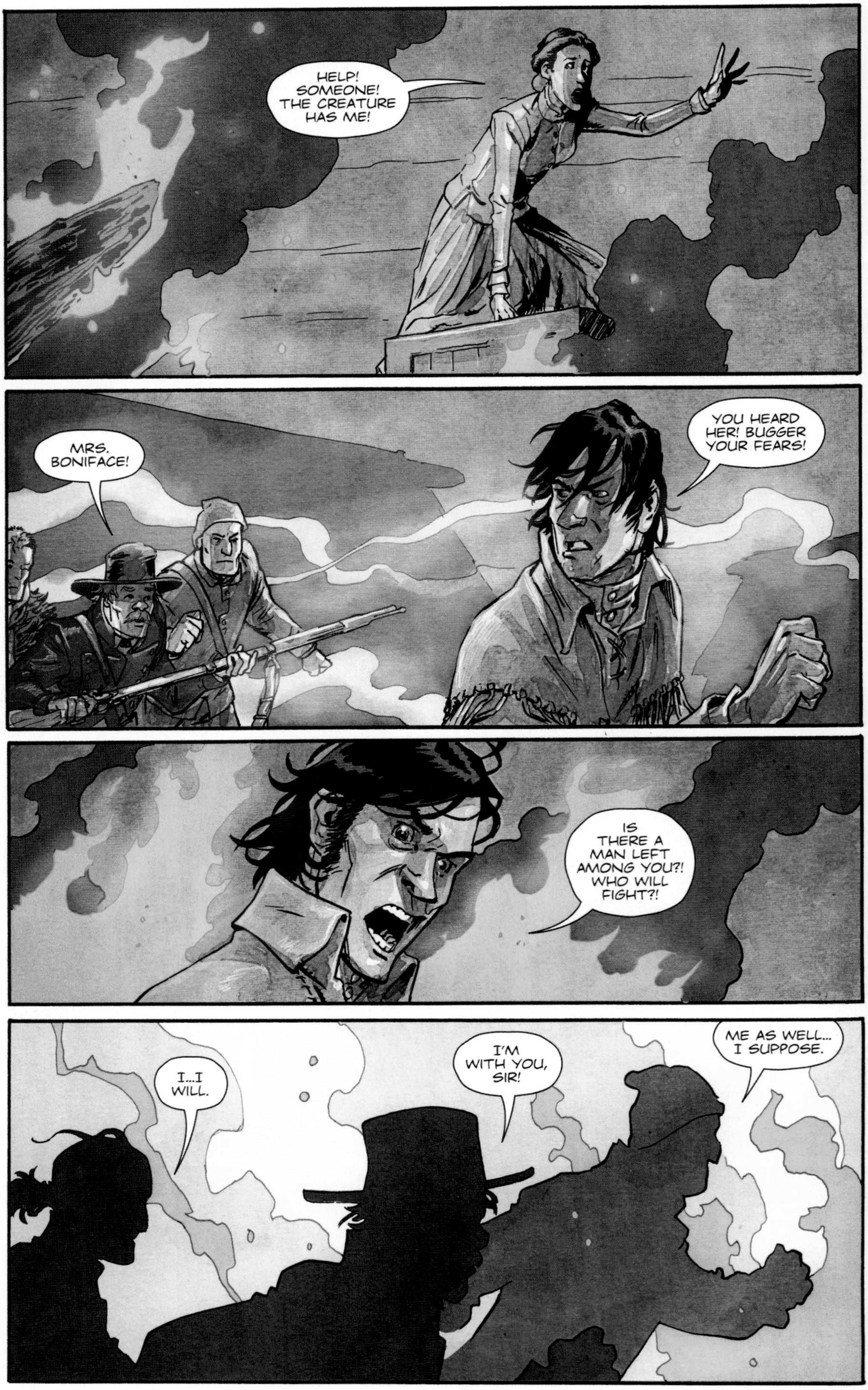
HELP! SOMEONE! THE CREATURE HAS ME!
MRS. BONIFACE!
YOU HEARD HER! BUGGER YOUR FEARS!
IS THERE A MAN LEFT AMONG YOU?! WHO WILL FIGHT?!
I...I WILL.
I'M WITH YOU, SIR!
ME AS WELL... I SUPPOSE.

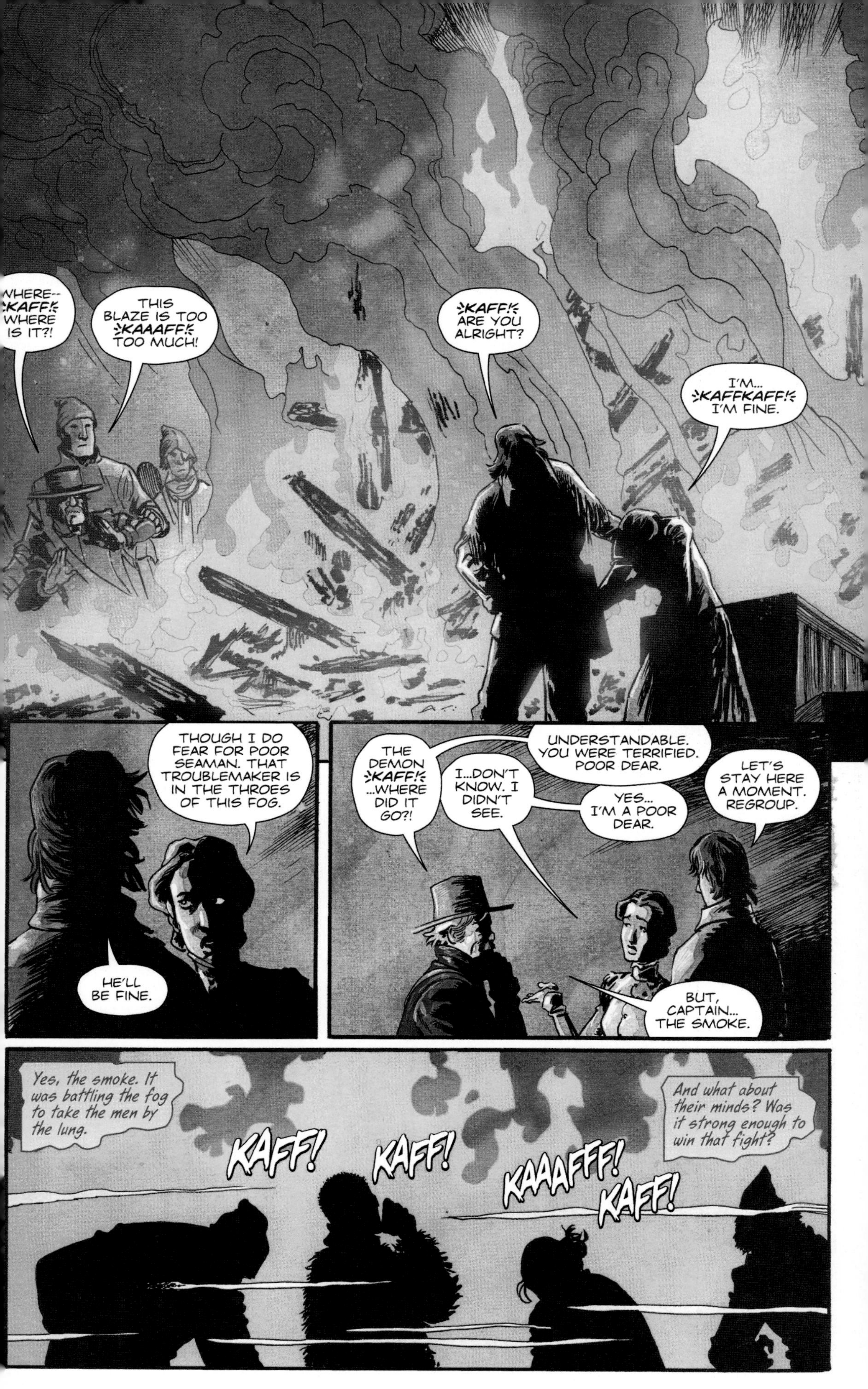

WHERE-- KAFF! WHERE IS IT?!
THIS BLAZE IS TOO KAAAFF! TOO MUCH!
KAFF! ARE YOU ALRIGHT?
I'M... KAFFKAFF! I'M FINE.
THOUGH I DO FEAR FOR POOR SEAMAN. THAT TROUBLEMAKER IS IN THE THROES OF THIS FOG.
HE'LL BE FINE.
THE DEMON KAFF! ...WHERE DID IT GO?!
UNDERSTANDABLE. YOU WERE TERRIFIED. POOR DEAR.
I...DON'T KNOW. I DIDN'T SEE.
YES... I'M A POOR DEAR.
LET'S STAY HERE A MOMENT. REGROUP.
BUT, CAPTAIN... THE SMOKE.
Yes, the smoke. It was battling the fog to take the men by the lung.
And what about their minds? Was it strong enough to win that fight?
KAFF!
KAFF!
KAAAFFF!
KAFF!

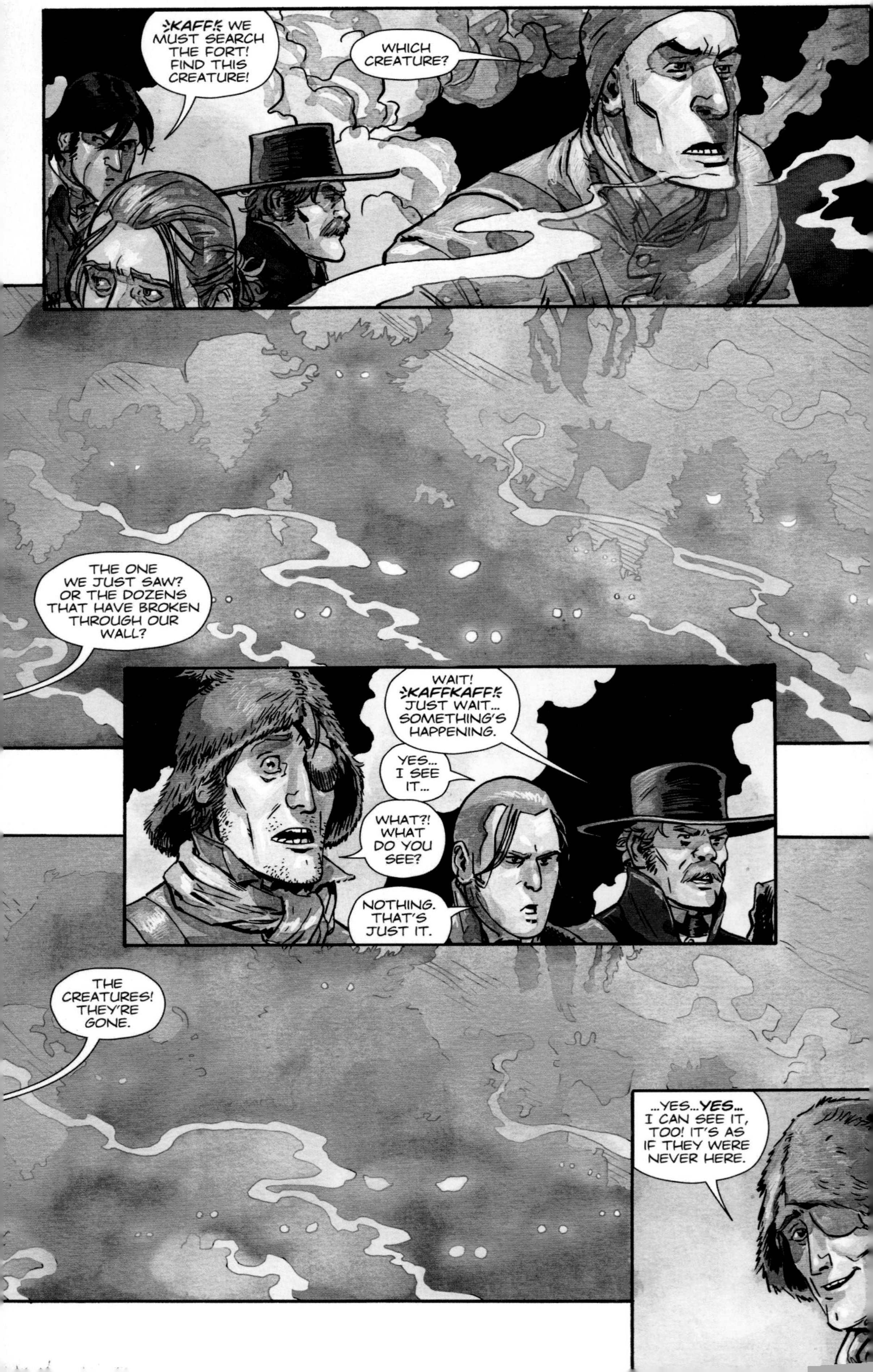
*KAFF!* WE MUST SEARCH THE FORT! FIND THIS CREATURE!
WHICH CREATURE?
THE ONE WE JUST SAW? OR THE DOZENS THAT HAVE BROKEN THROUGH OUR WALL?
WAIT! *KAFFKAFF!* JUST WAIT... SOMETHING'S HAPPENING.
YES... I SEE IT...
WHAT?! WHAT DO YOU SEE?
NOTHING. THAT'S JUST IT.
THE CREATURES! THEY'RE GONE.
...YES...YES... I CAN SEE IT, TOO! IT'S AS IF THEY WERE NEVER HERE.

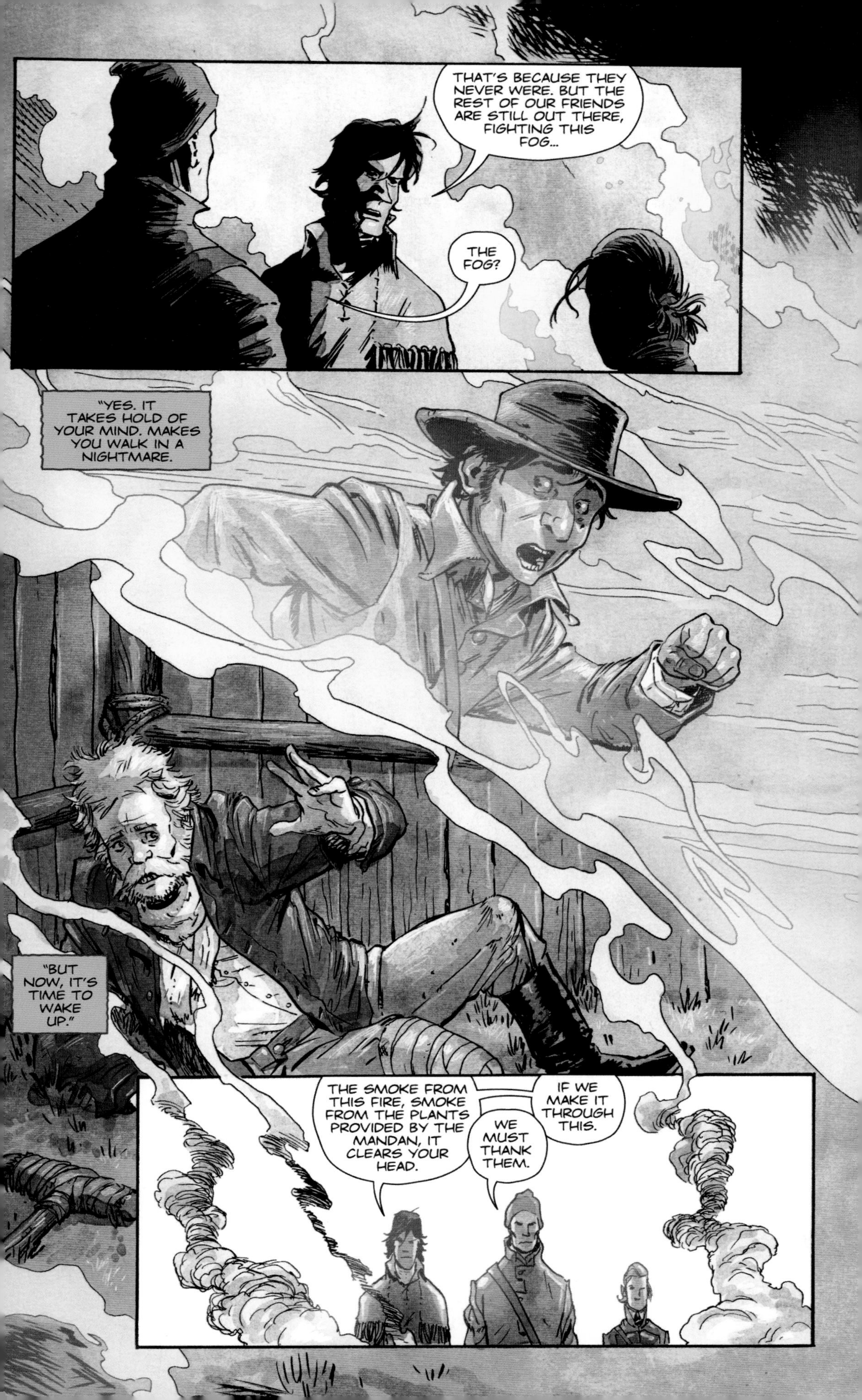
THAT'S BECAUSE THEY NEVER WERE. BUT THE REST OF OUR FRIENDS ARE STILL OUT THERE, FIGHTING THIS FOG...
THE FOG?
"YES. IT TAKES HOLD OF YOUR MIND. MAKES YOU WALK IN A NIGHTMARE.
"BUT NOW, IT'S TIME TO WAKE UP."
THE SMOKE FROM THIS FIRE, SMOKE FROM THE PLANTS PROVIDED BY THE MANDAN, IT CLEARS YOUR HEAD.
IF WE MAKE IT THROUGH THIS.
WE MUST THANK THEM.

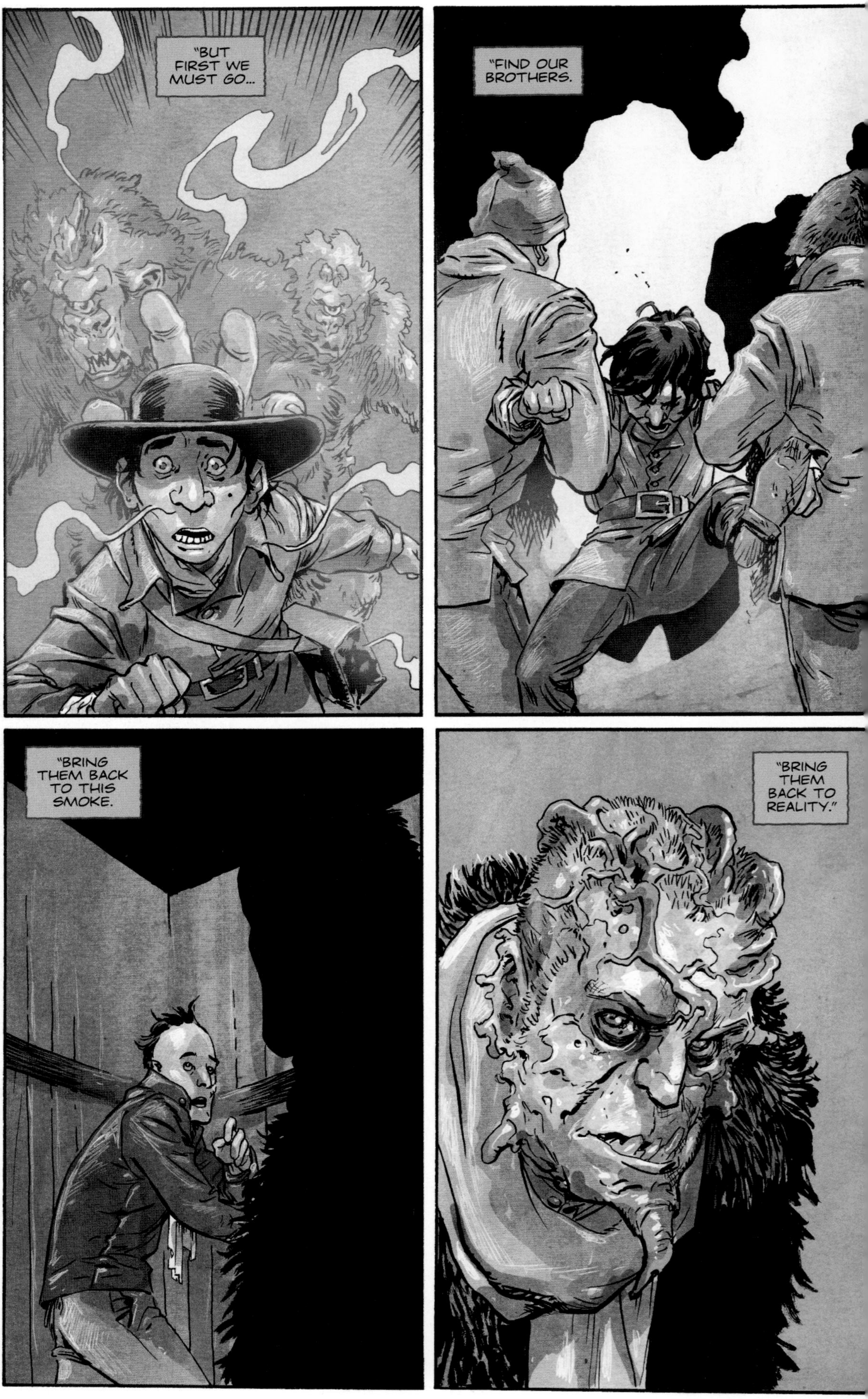
"BUT FIRST WE MUST GO...
"FIND OUR BROTHERS.
"BRING THEM BACK TO THIS SMOKE.
"BRING THEM BACK TO REALITY."

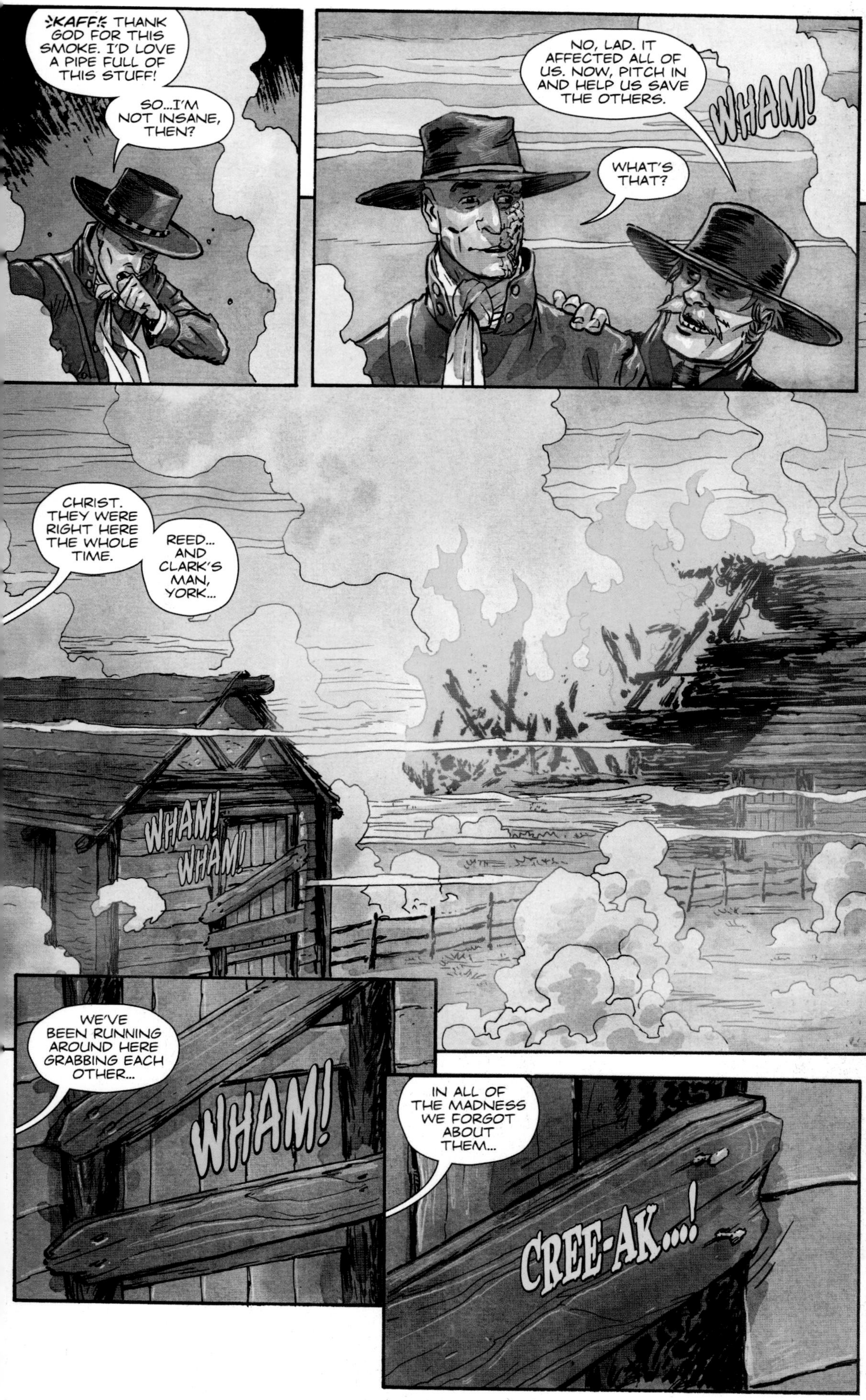
*KAFF!* THANK GOD FOR THIS SMOKE. I'D LOVE A PIPE FULL OF THIS STUFF!
SO...I'M NOT INSANE, THEN?
NO, LAD. IT AFFECTED ALL OF US. NOW, PITCH IN AND HELP US SAVE THE OTHERS.
WHAM!
WHAT'S THAT?
CHRIST. THEY WERE RIGHT HERE THE WHOLE TIME.
REED... AND CLARK'S MAN, YORK...
WHAM! WHAM!
WE'VE BEEN RUNNING AROUND HERE GRABBING EACH OTHER...
WHAM!
IN ALL OF THE MADNESS WE FORGOT ABOUT THEM...
CREE-AK...!

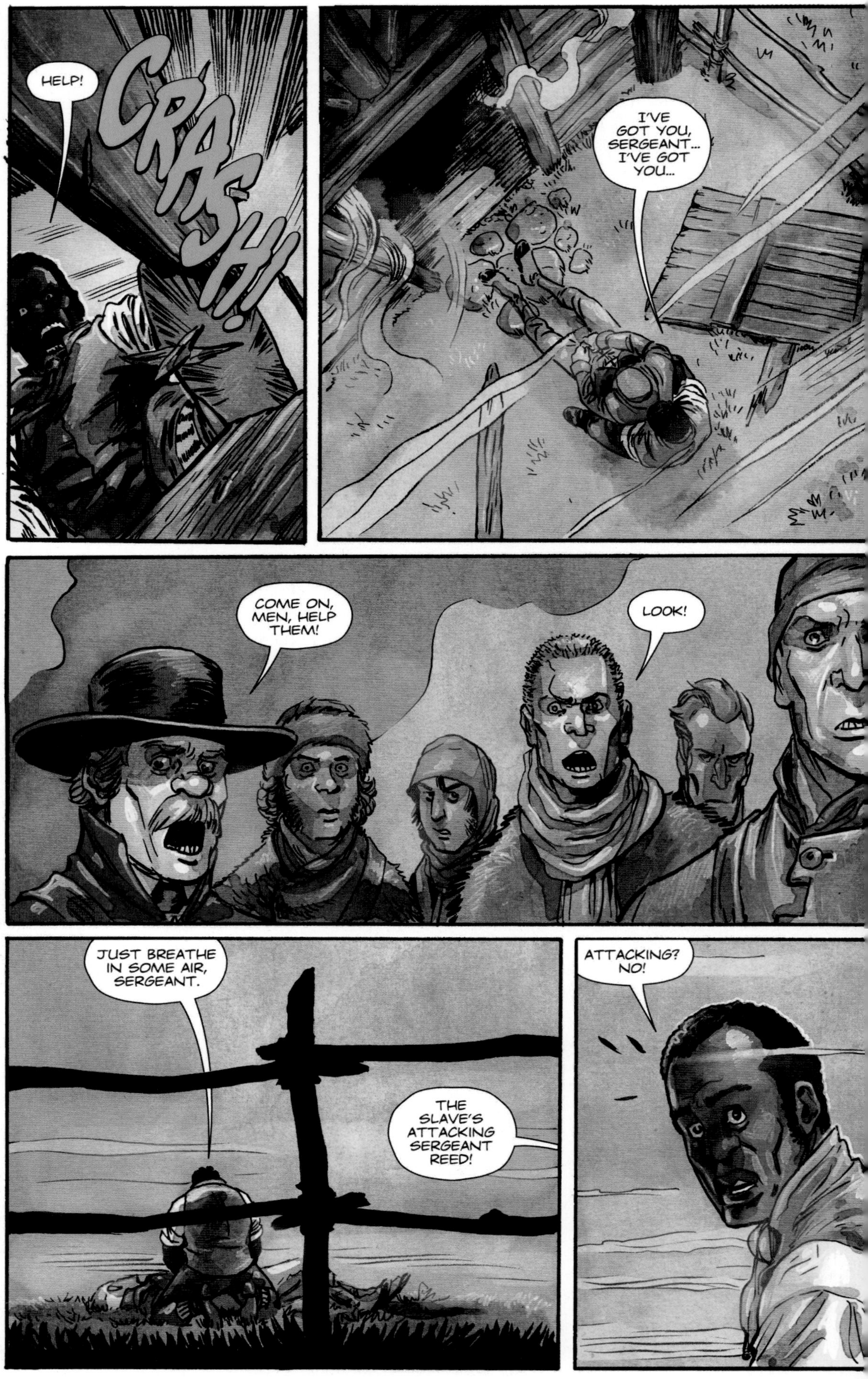
HELP!
CRASH!
I'VE GOT YOU, SERGEANT... I'VE GOT YOU...
COME ON, MEN, HELP THEM!
LOOK!
JUST BREATHE IN SOME AIR, SERGEANT.
THE SLAVE'S ATTACKING SERGEANT REED!
ATTACKING? NO!

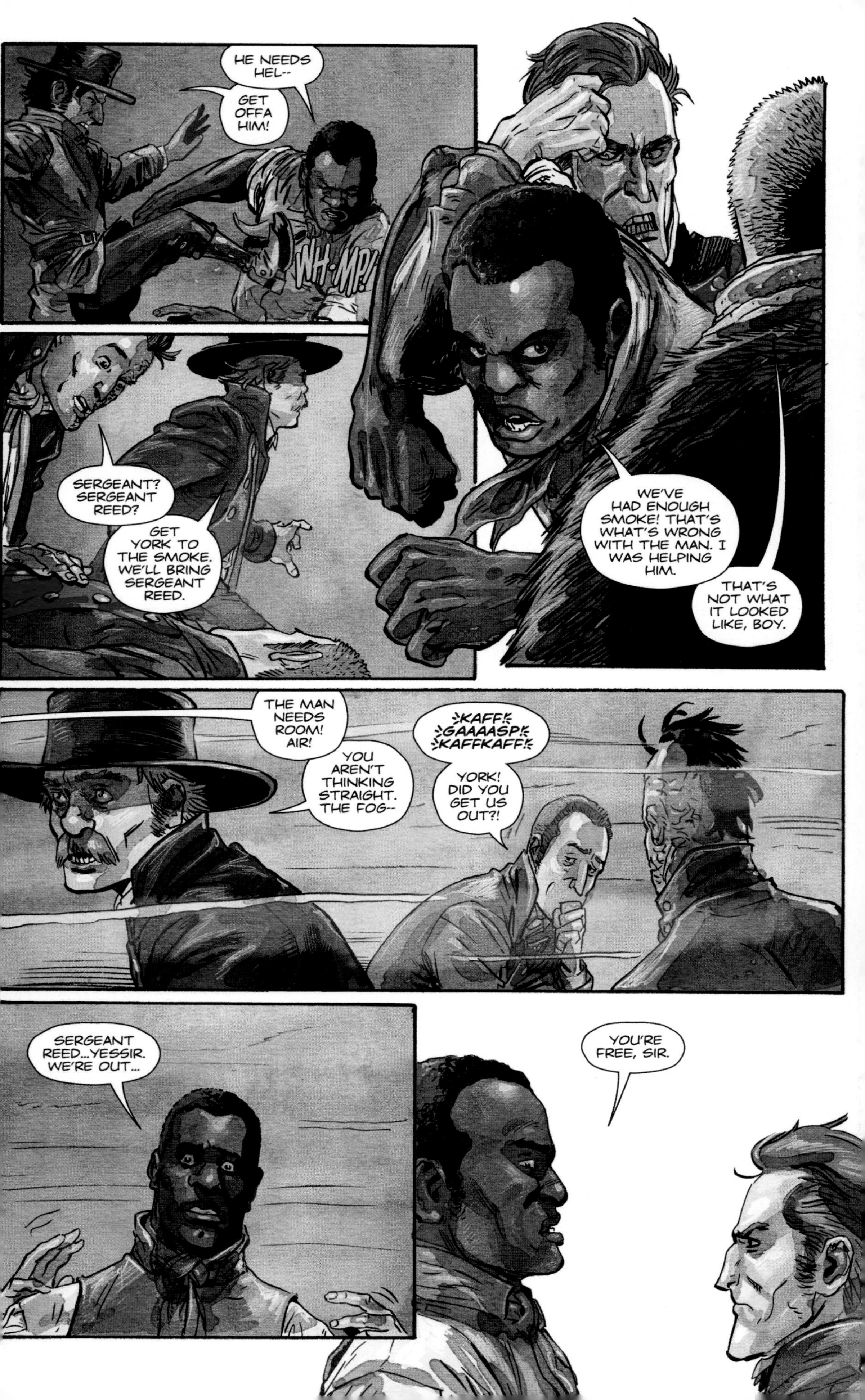
HE NEEDS HEL--
GET OFFA HIM!
WH-MP!
WE'VE HAD ENOUGH SMOKE! THAT'S WHAT'S WRONG WITH THE MAN. I WAS HELPING HIM.
THAT'S NOT WHAT IT LOOKED LIKE, BOY.
SERGEANT? SERGEANT REED?
GET YORK TO THE SMOKE. WE'LL BRING SERGEANT REED.
THE MAN NEEDS ROOM! AIR!
YOU AREN'T THINKING STRAIGHT. THE FOG--
KAFF! GAAAASP! KAFFKAFF!
YORK! DID YOU GET US OUT?!
SERGEANT REED...YESSIR. WE'RE OUT...
YOU'RE FREE, SIR.

As the men gathered their senses, I searched for two of the most senseless creatures I know.

CLARK? CLARK?

NOTHING.

WE'LL FIND THEM.

THIS IS BAD. I CAN FEEL IT.

THEY COULD'VE KILLED EACH OTHER BY NOW.

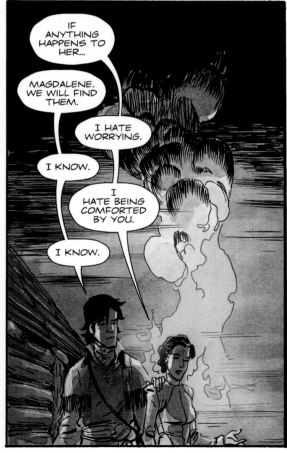

IF ANYTHING HAPPENS TO HER...

MAGDALENE. WE WILL FIND THEM.

I HATE WORRYING.

I KNOW.

I HATE BEING COMFORTED BY YOU.

I KNOW.

LEWIS!

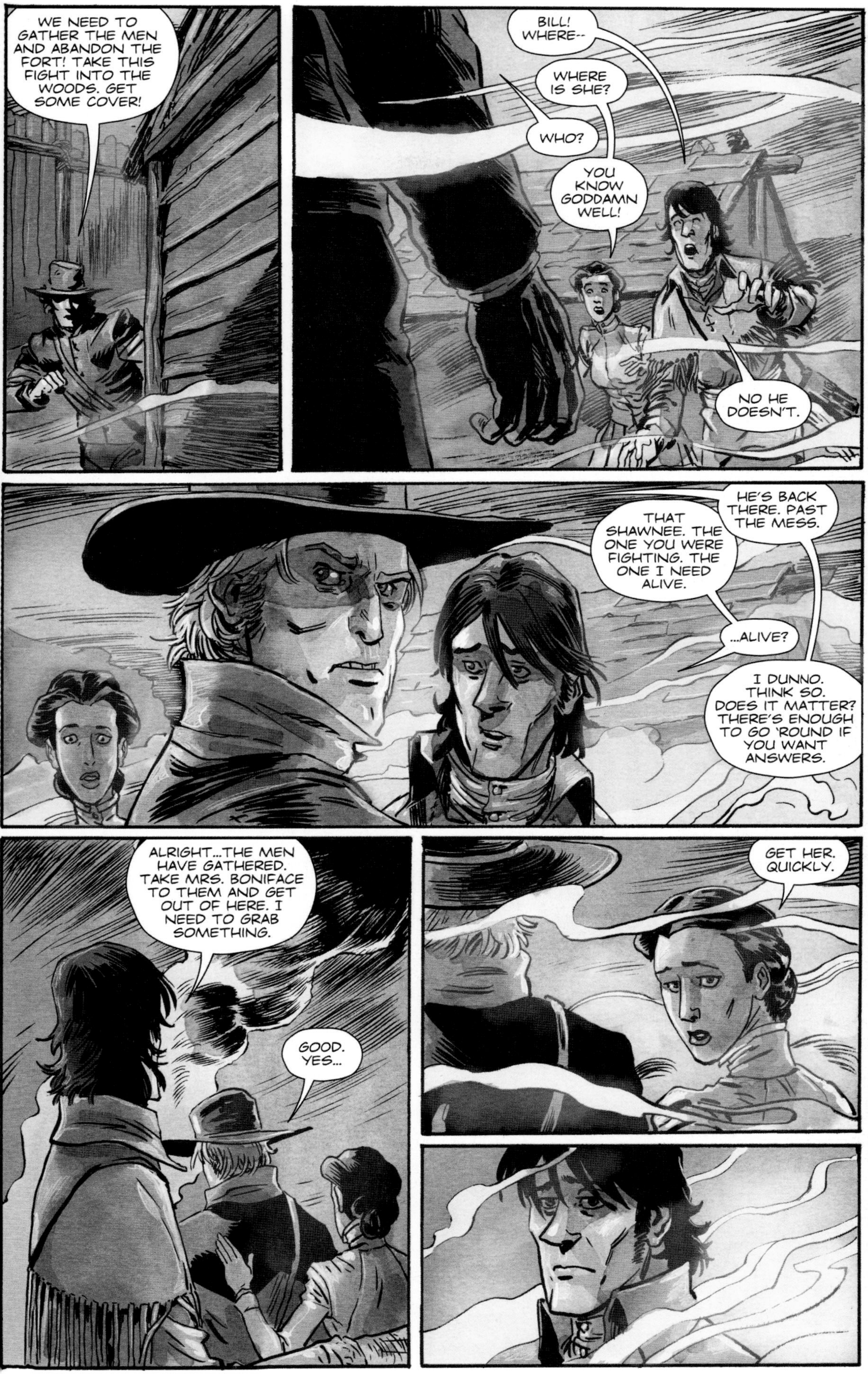
WE NEED TO GATHER THE MEN AND ABANDON THE FORT! TAKE THIS FIGHT INTO THE WOODS. GET SOME COVER!
BILL! WHERE--
WHERE IS SHE?
WHO?
YOU KNOW GODDAMN WELL!
NO HE DOESN'T.
THAT SHAWNEE. THE ONE YOU WERE FIGHTING. THE ONE I NEED ALIVE.
HE'S BACK THERE. PAST THE MESS.
...ALIVE?
I DUNNO. THINK SO. DOES IT MATTER? THERE'S ENOUGH TO GO 'ROUND IF YOU WANT ANSWERS.
ALRIGHT...THE MEN HAVE GATHERED. TAKE MRS. BONIFACE TO THEM AND GET OUT OF HERE. I NEED TO GRAB SOMETHING.
GOOD. YES...
GET HER. QUICKLY.

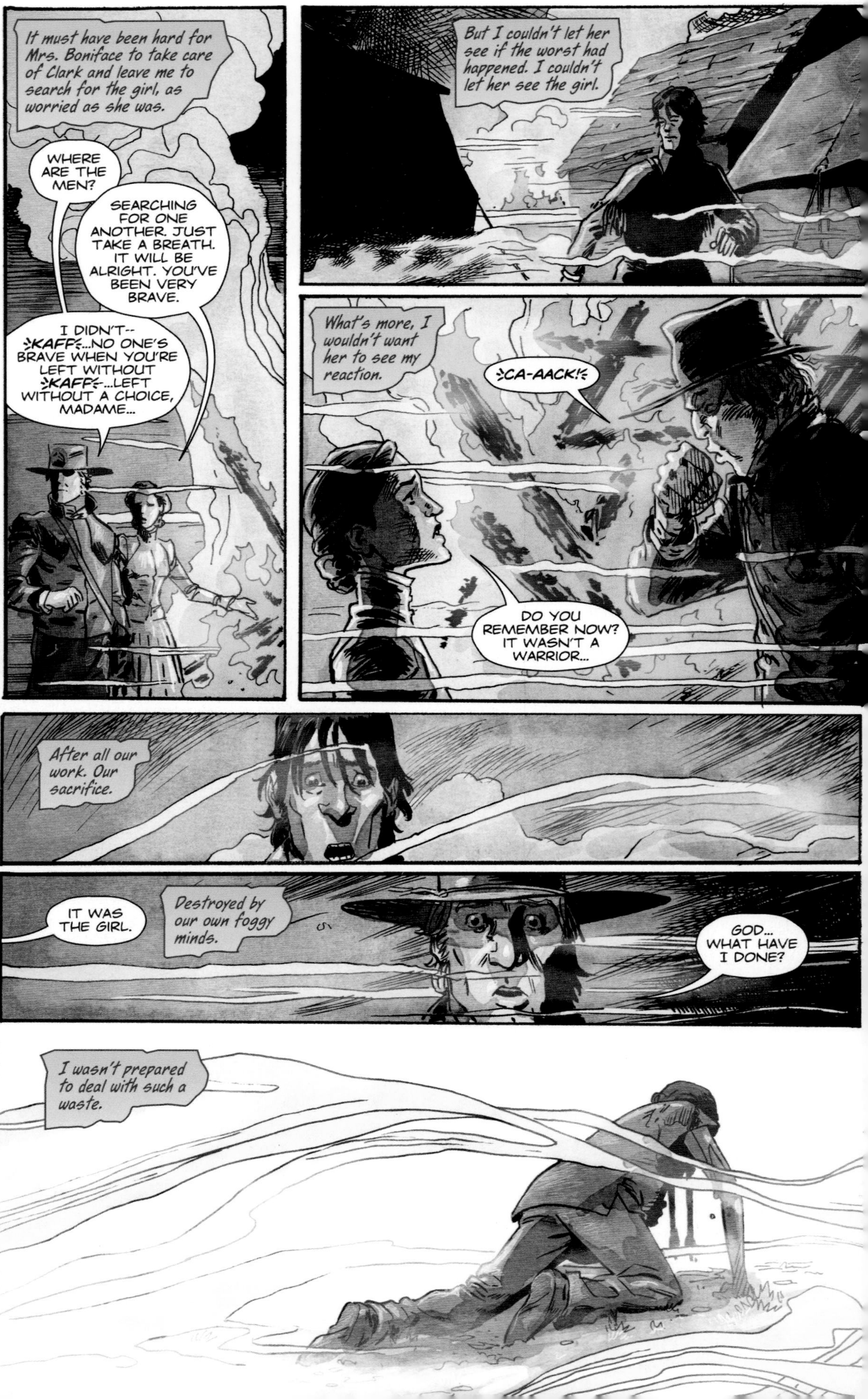

It must have been hard for Mrs. Boniface to take care of Clark and leave me to search for the girl, as worried as she was.
WHERE ARE THE MEN?
SEARCHING FOR ONE ANOTHER. JUST TAKE A BREATH. IT WILL BE ALRIGHT. YOU'VE BEEN VERY BRAVE.
I DIDN'T-- KAFF ...NO ONE'S BRAVE WHEN YOU'RE LEFT WITHOUT KAFF ...LEFT WITHOUT A CHOICE, MADAME...
But I couldn't let her see if the worst had happened. I couldn't let her see the girl.
What's more, I wouldn't want her to see my reaction.
CA-AACK!
DO YOU REMEMBER NOW? IT WASN'T A WARRIOR...
After all our work. Our sacrifice.
IT WAS THE GIRL.
Destroyed by our own foggy minds.
GOD... WHAT HAVE I DONE?
I wasn't prepared to deal with such a waste.

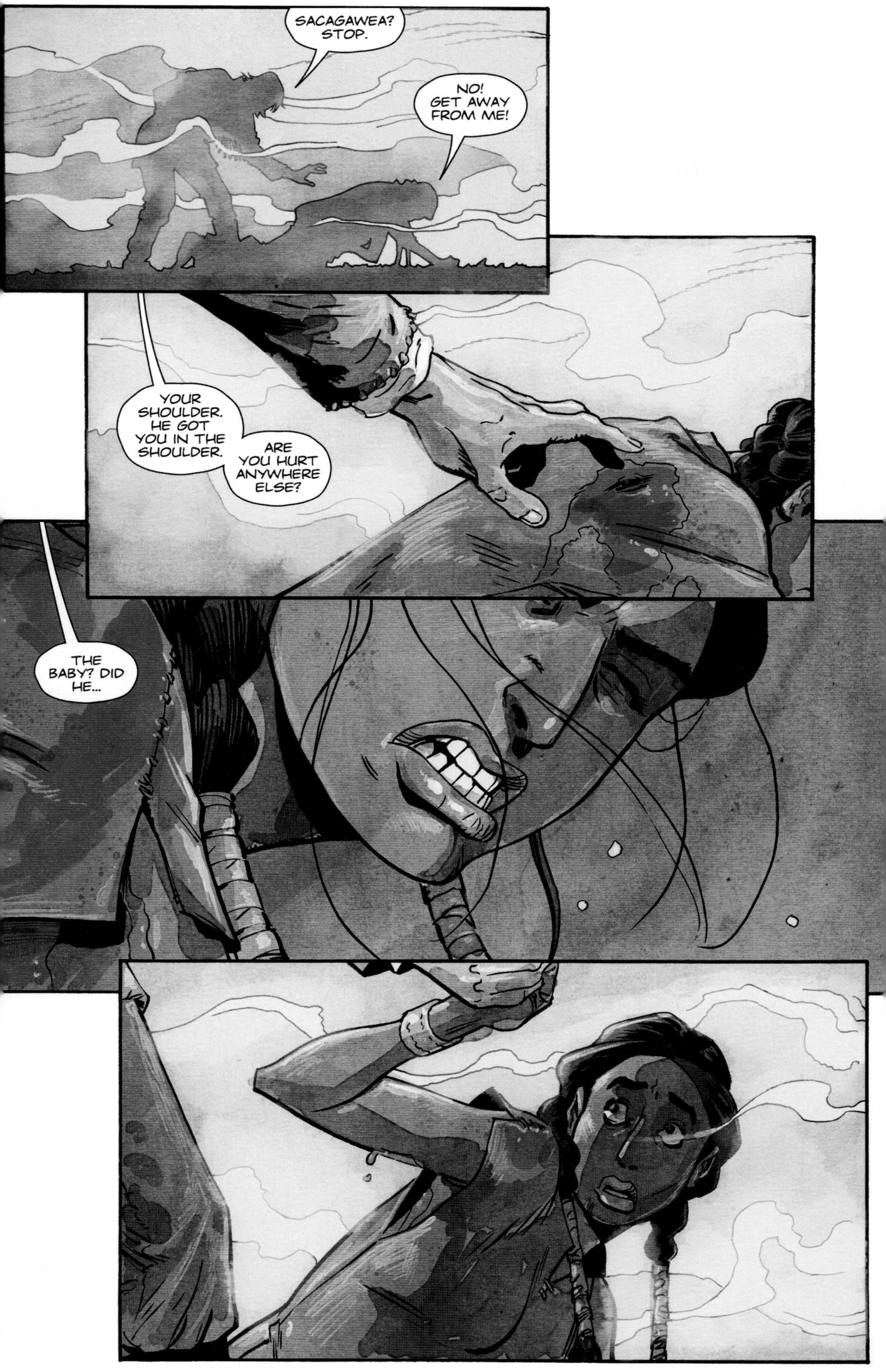
SACAGAWEA? STOP.
NO! GET AWAY FROM ME!
YOUR SHOULDER. HE GOT YOU IN THE SHOULDER.
ARE YOU HURT ANYWHERE ELSE?
THE BABY? DID HE...

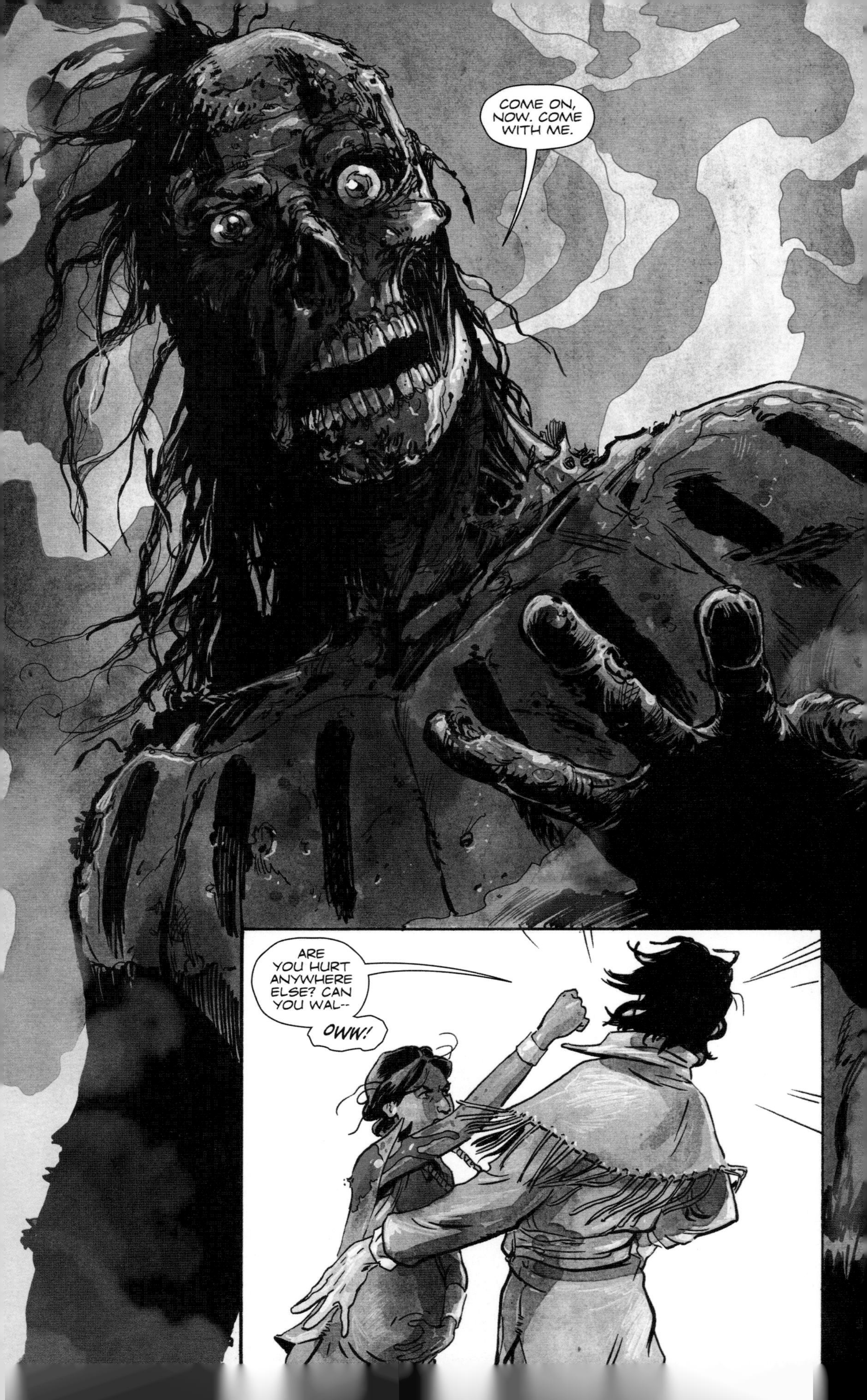
COME ON, NOW. COME WITH ME.
ARE YOU HURT ANYWHERE ELSE? CAN YOU WAL--
OWW!

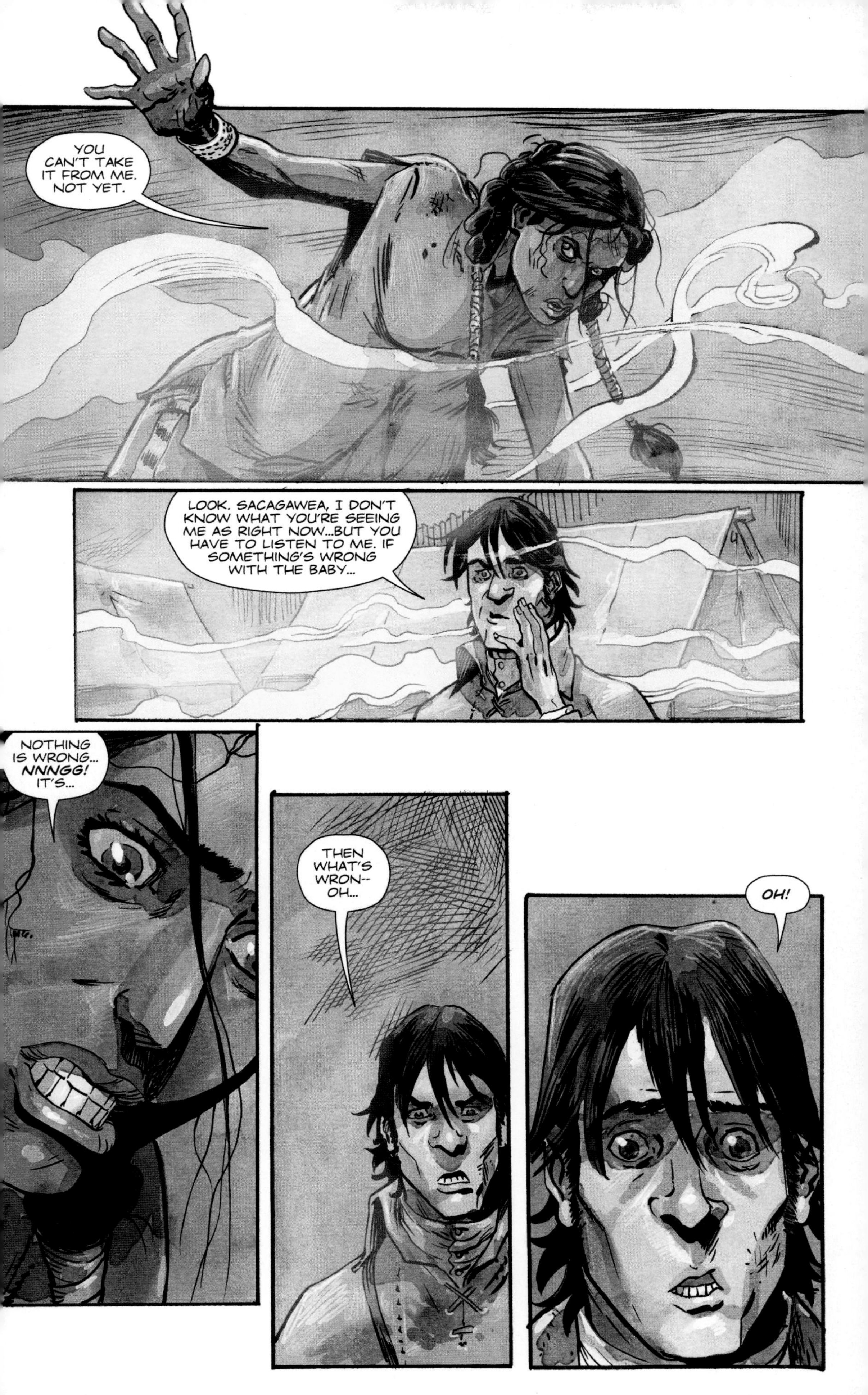
YOU CAN'T TAKE IT FROM ME. NOT YET.
LOOK. SACAGAWEA, I DON'T KNOW WHAT YOU'RE SEEING ME AS RIGHT NOW...BUT YOU HAVE TO LISTEN TO ME. IF SOMETHING'S WRONG WITH THE BABY...
NOTHING IS WRONG... ***NNNGG!*** IT'S...
THEN WHAT'S WRON-- OH...
*OH!*

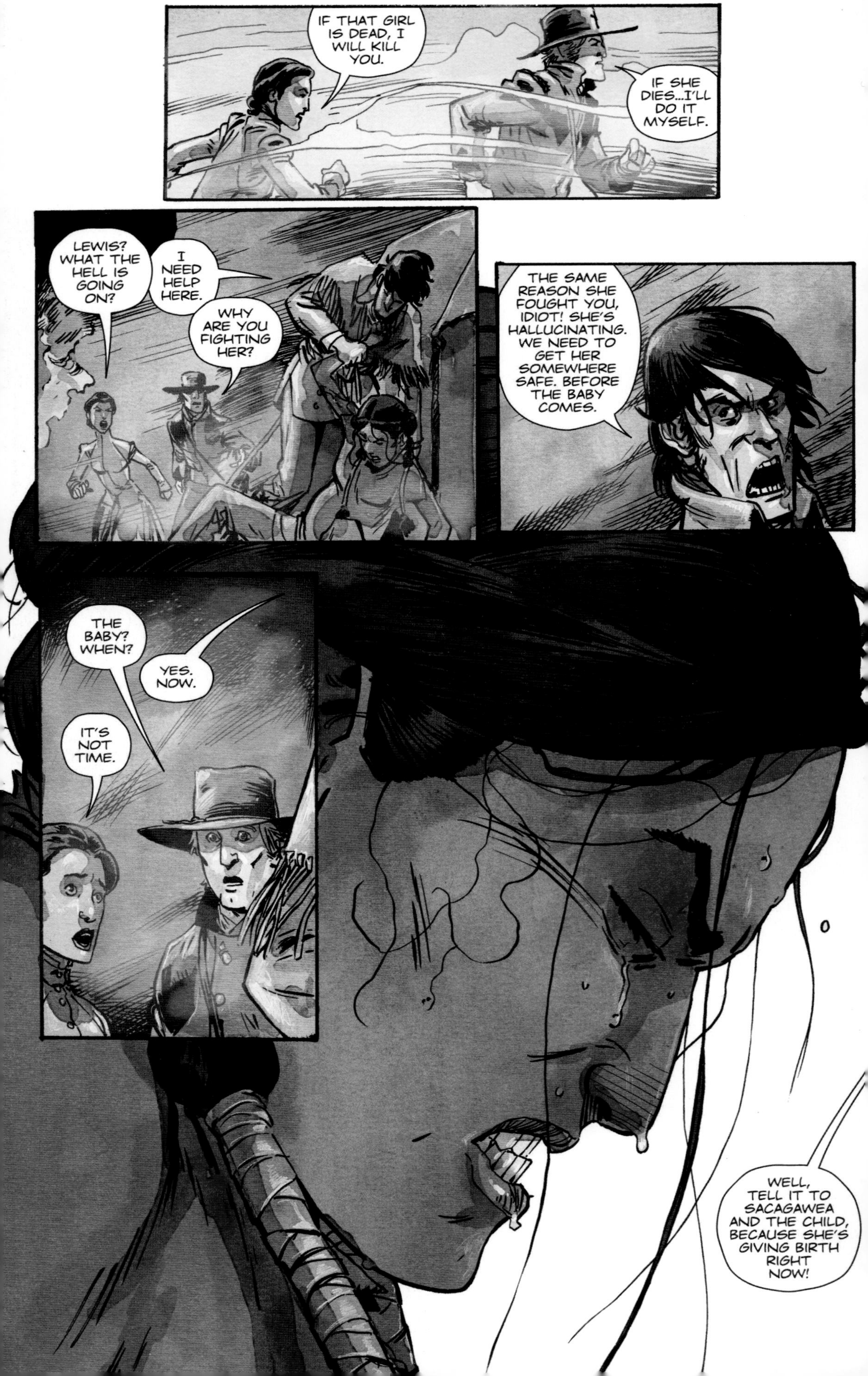
IF THAT GIRL IS DEAD, I WILL KILL YOU.
IF SHE DIES...I'LL DO IT MYSELF.
LEWIS? WHAT THE HELL IS GOING ON?
I NEED HELP HERE.
WHY ARE YOU FIGHTING HER?
THE SAME REASON SHE FOUGHT YOU, IDIOT! SHE'S HALLUCINATING. WE NEED TO GET HER SOMEWHERE SAFE. BEFORE THE BABY COMES.
THE BABY? WHEN?
YES. NOW.
IT'S NOT TIME.
WELL, TELL IT TO SACAGAWEA AND THE CHILD, BECAUSE SHE'S GIVING BIRTH RIGHT NOW!

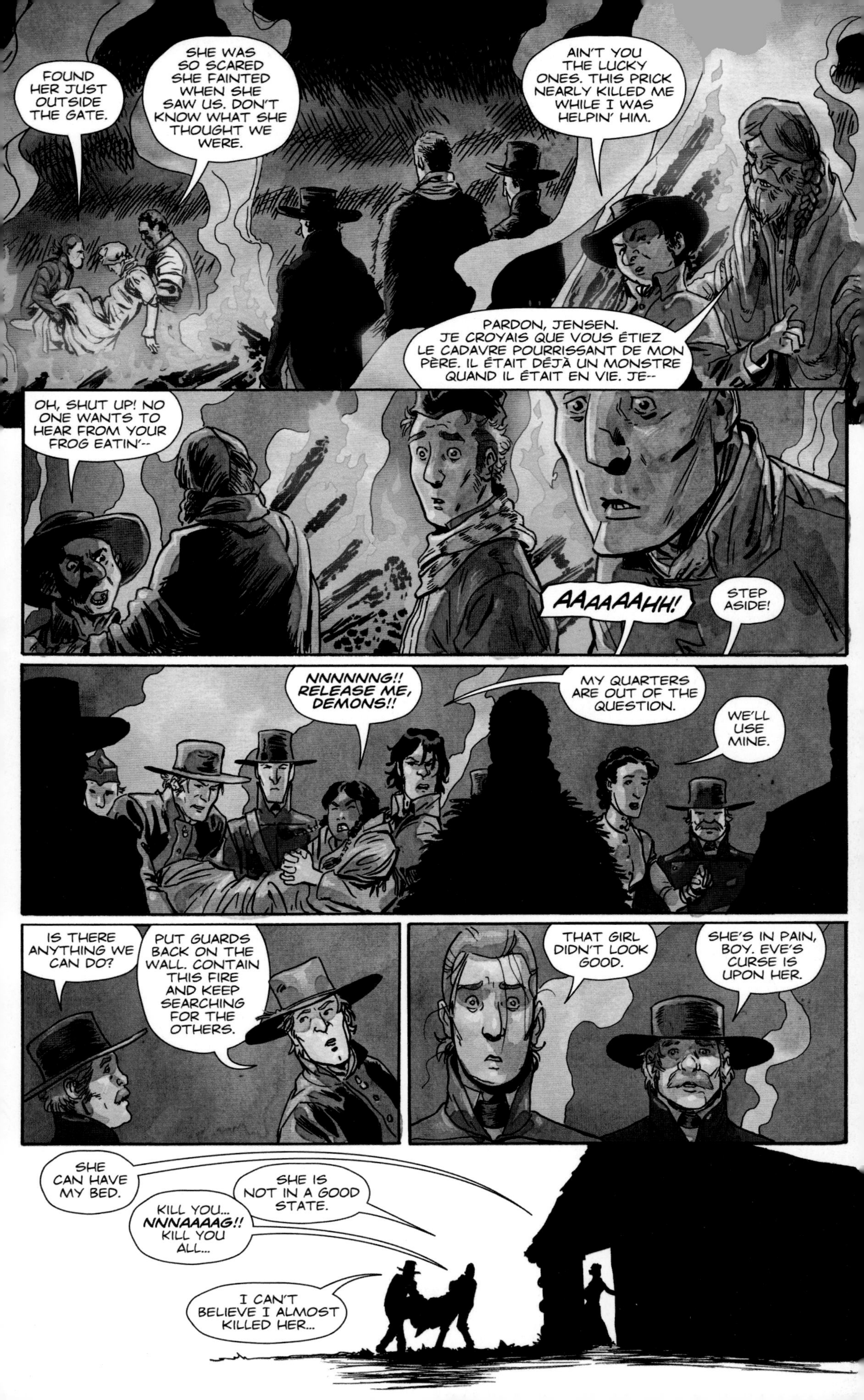
FOUND HER JUST OUTSIDE THE GATE.
SHE WAS SO SCARED SHE FAINTED WHEN SHE SAW US. DON'T KNOW WHAT SHE THOUGHT WE WERE.
AIN'T YOU THE LUCKY ONES. THIS PRICK NEARLY KILLED ME WHILE I WAS HELPIN' HIM.
PARDON, JENSEN. JE CROYAIS QUE VOUS ÉTIEZ LE CADAVRE POURRISSANT DE MON PÈRE. IL ÉTAIT DÉJÀ UN MONSTRE QUAND IL ÉTAIT EN VIE. JE--
OH, SHUT UP! NO ONE WANTS TO HEAR FROM YOUR FROG EATIN'--
AAAAAAHH!
STEP ASIDE!
NNNNNNG!! RELEASE ME, DEMONS!!
MY QUARTERS ARE OUT OF THE QUESTION.
WE'LL USE MINE.
IS THERE ANYTHING WE CAN DO?
PUT GUARDS BACK ON THE WALL. CONTAIN THIS FIRE AND KEEP SEARCHING FOR THE OTHERS.
THAT GIRL DIDN'T LOOK GOOD.
SHE'S IN PAIN, BOY. EVE'S CURSE IS UPON HER.
SHE CAN HAVE MY BED.
SHE IS NOT IN A GOOD STATE.
KILL YOU... NNNAAAAG!! KILL YOU ALL...
I CAN'T BELIEVE I ALMOST KILLED HER...

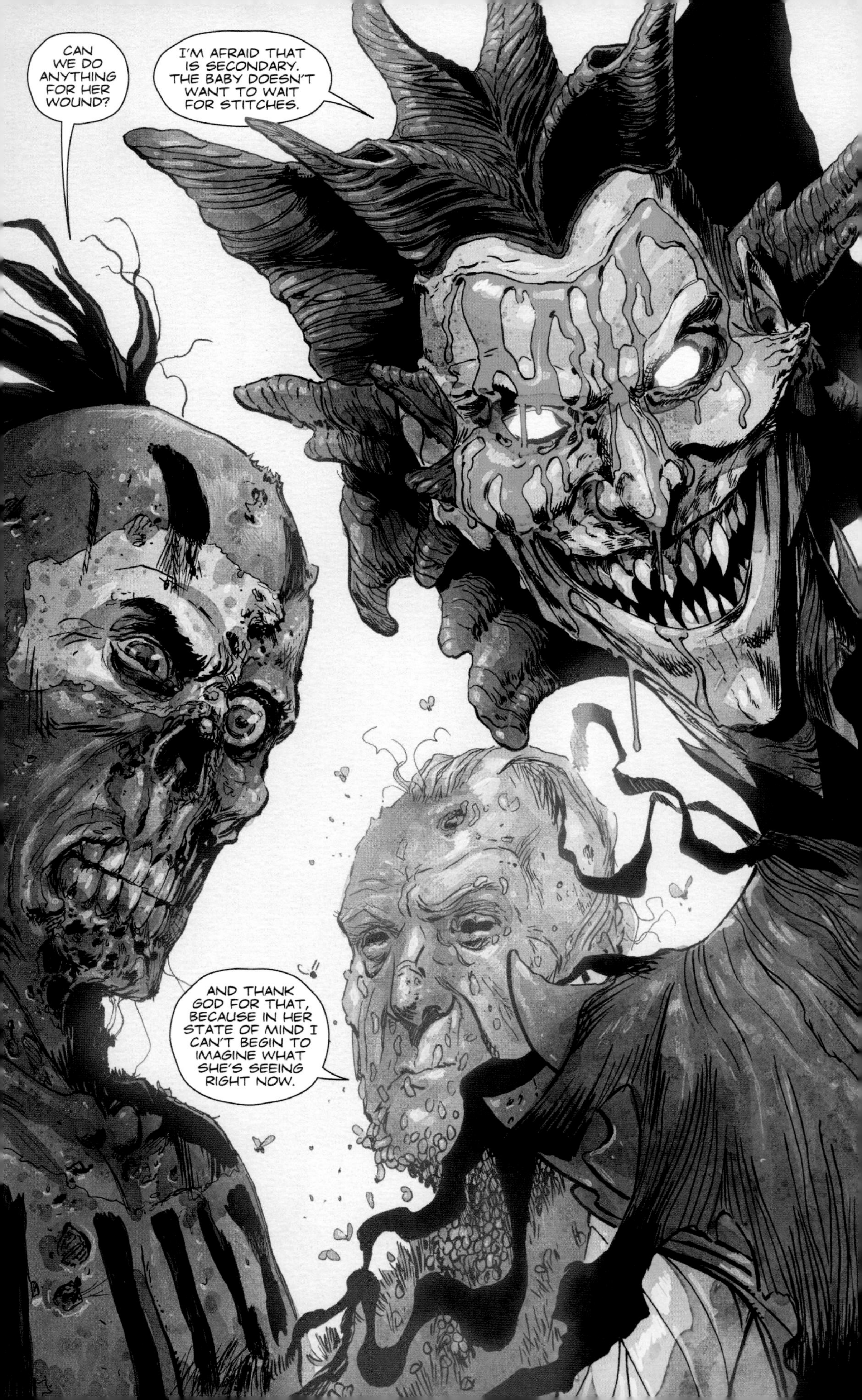
CAN WE DO ANYTHING FOR HER WOUND?
I'M AFRAID THAT IS SECONDARY. THE BABY DOESN'T WANT TO WAIT FOR STITCHES.
AND THANK GOD FOR THAT, BECAUSE IN HER STATE OF MIND I CAN'T BEGIN TO IMAGINE WHAT SHE'S SEEING RIGHT NOW.

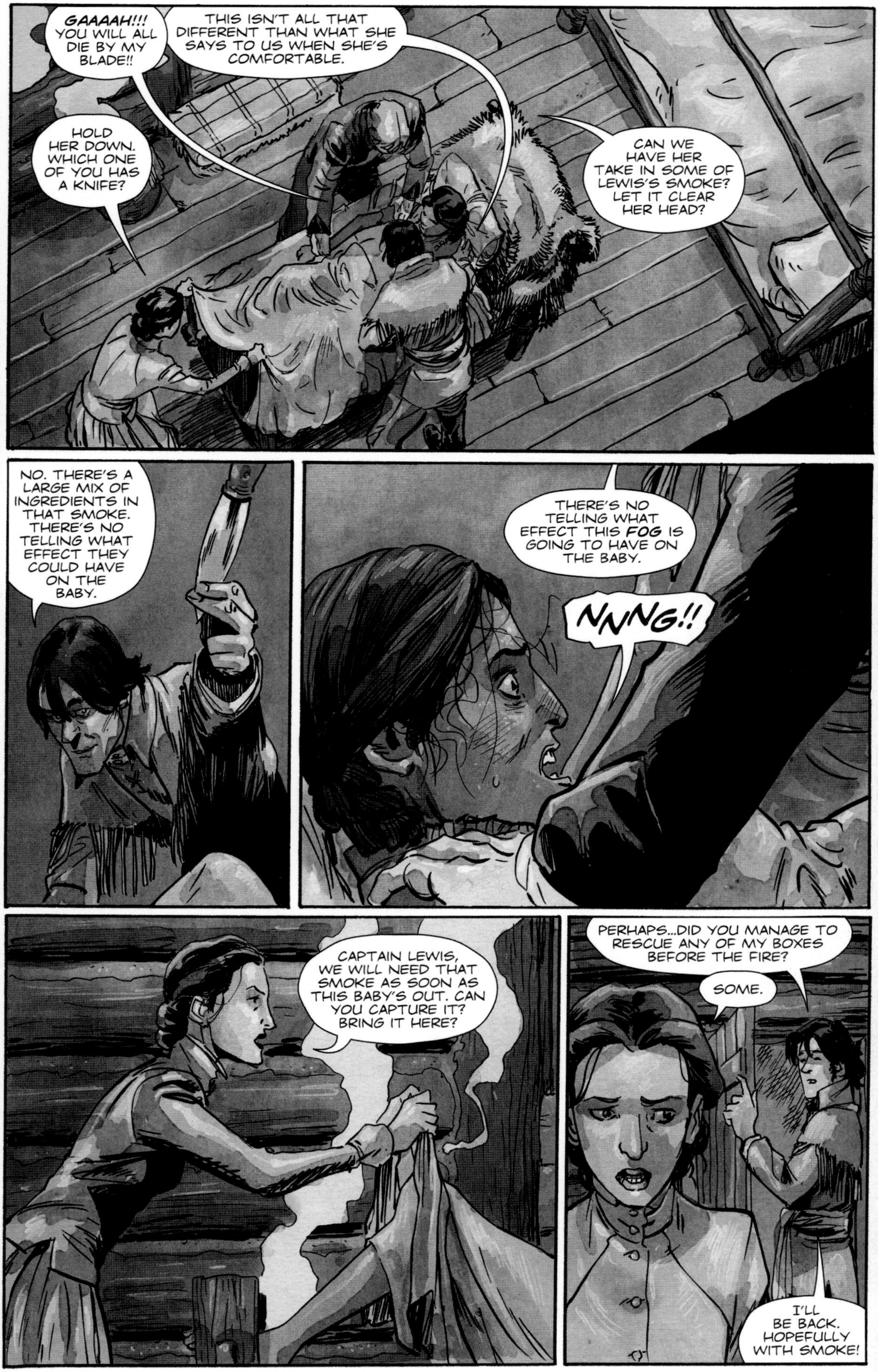
GAAAAH!!! YOU WILL ALL DIE BY MY BLADE!!
THIS ISN'T ALL THAT DIFFERENT THAN WHAT SHE SAYS TO US WHEN SHE'S COMFORTABLE.
HOLD HER DOWN. WHICH ONE OF YOU HAS A KNIFE?
CAN WE HAVE HER TAKE IN SOME OF LEWIS'S SMOKE? LET IT CLEAR HER HEAD?
NO. THERE'S A LARGE MIX OF INGREDIENTS IN THAT SMOKE. THERE'S NO TELLING WHAT EFFECT THEY COULD HAVE ON THE BABY.
THERE'S NO TELLING WHAT EFFECT THIS FOG IS GOING TO HAVE ON THE BABY.
NNNG!!
CAPTAIN LEWIS, WE WILL NEED THAT SMOKE AS SOON AS THIS BABY'S OUT. CAN YOU CAPTURE IT? BRING IT HERE?
PERHAPS...DID YOU MANAGE TO RESCUE ANY OF MY BOXES BEFORE THE FIRE?
SOME.
I'LL BE BACK. HOPEFULLY WITH SMOKE!

RIGHT. IT'S YOU AND I, THEN, CAPTAIN.

YES.

AAAHHHH!

CAN YOU HOLD HER BY YOURSELF?

I WILL.

DON'T SUPPOSE ANYONE KNOWS WHERE THE FATHER IS?

HE WAS OUT HUNTING WHEN THE FOG ROLLED IN. PROBABLY FOR THE BEST THAT HE ISN'T HERE FOR THIS. USELESS AS HE IS--

NO!!! AAAAAH!

WHAT ARE YOU DOING?

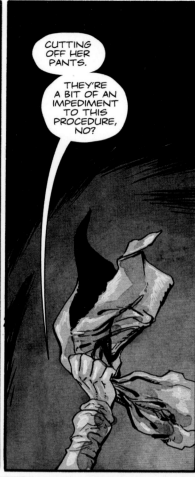

CUTTING OFF HER PANTS.

THEY'RE A BIT OF AN IMPEDIMENT TO THIS PROCEDURE, NO?

YOU CAN'T HAVE IT. YOU CAN'T TAKE IT FROM ME. NNNNNG! IT...IT'S NOT FOR YOU.

SACAGAWEA. CAN YOU HEAR ME? DO YOU KNOW WHO I AM?

YOU'RE A DEMON... AND SO IS HE. TRYING TO TRICK ME INTO THINKING YOU'RE THE WOMAN. MAGDA-- LAAAAAHH. BUT I SEE THROUGH YOU.

HERE... TAKE THIS.

NNNN WHAT?! WHAT IS THIS?

YES. WHAT IS THIS?

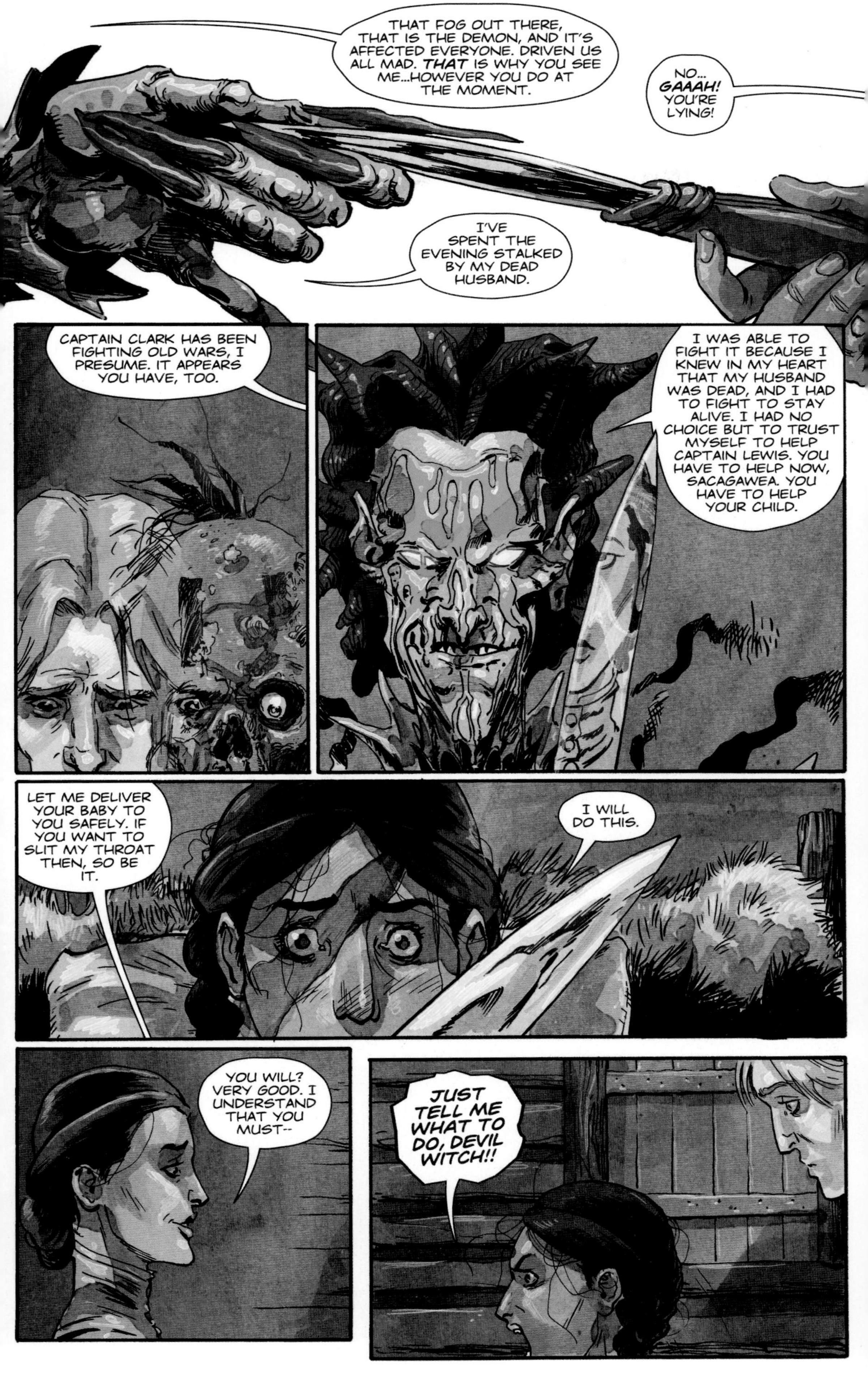

THAT FOG OUT THERE, THAT IS THE DEMON, AND IT'S AFFECTED EVERYONE. DRIVEN US ALL MAD. THAT IS WHY YOU SEE ME...HOWEVER YOU DO AT THE MOMENT.
NO... GAAAH! YOU'RE LYING!
I'VE SPENT THE EVENING STALKED BY MY DEAD HUSBAND.
CAPTAIN CLARK HAS BEEN FIGHTING OLD WARS, I PRESUME. IT APPEARS YOU HAVE, TOO.
I WAS ABLE TO FIGHT IT BECAUSE I KNEW IN MY HEART THAT MY HUSBAND WAS DEAD, AND I HAD TO FIGHT TO STAY ALIVE. I HAD NO CHOICE BUT TO TRUST MYSELF TO HELP CAPTAIN LEWIS. YOU HAVE TO HELP NOW, SACAGAWEA. YOU HAVE TO HELP YOUR CHILD.
LET ME DELIVER YOUR BABY TO YOU SAFELY. IF YOU WANT TO SLIT MY THROAT THEN, SO BE IT.
I WILL DO THIS.
YOU WILL? VERY GOOD. I UNDERSTAND THAT YOU MUST--
JUST TELL ME WHAT TO DO, DEVIL WITCH!!

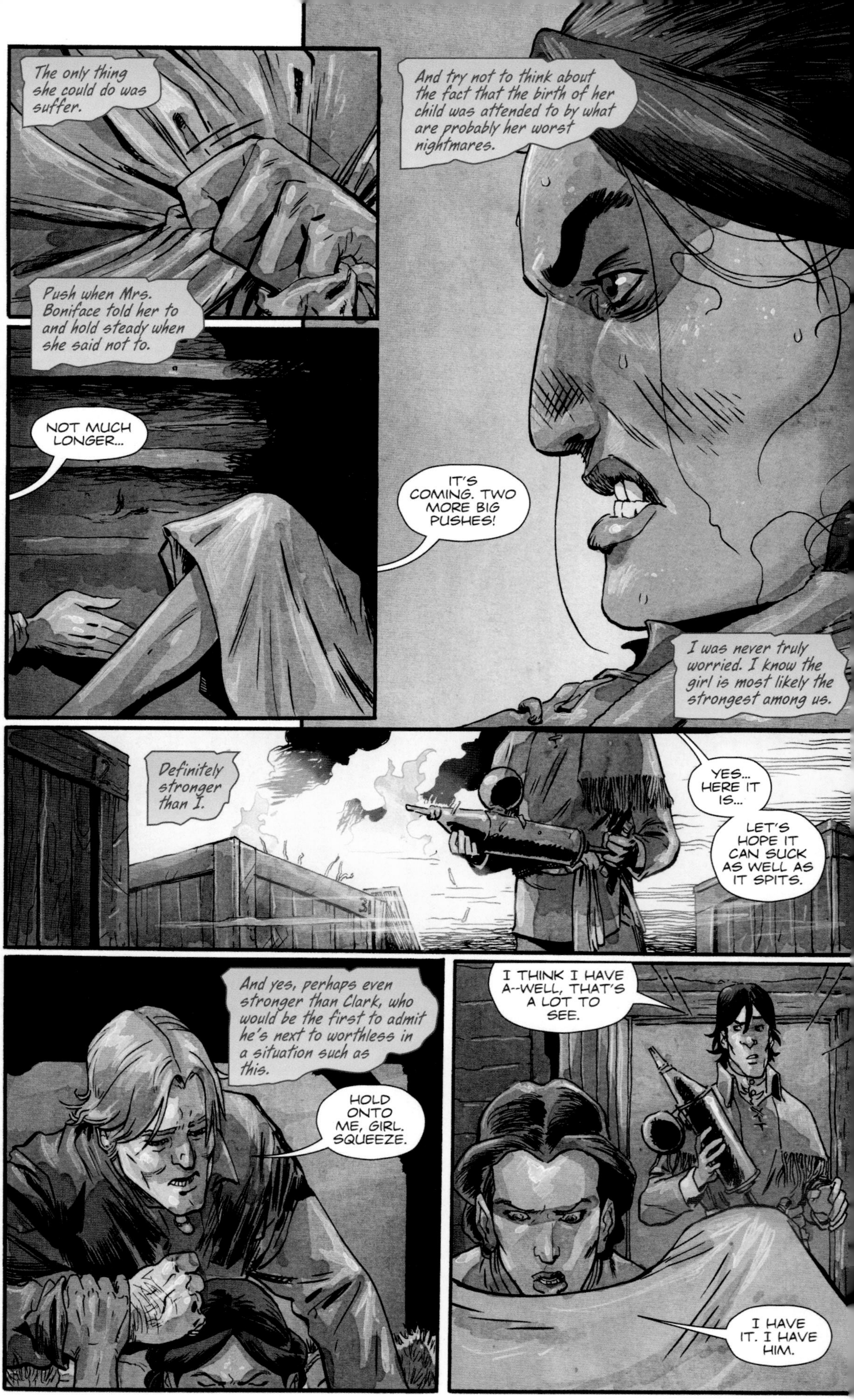
The only thing she could do was suffer.
And try not to think about the fact that the birth of her child was attended to by what are probably her worst nightmares.
Push when Mrs. Boniface told her to and hold steady when she said not to.
NOT MUCH LONGER...
IT'S COMING. TWO MORE BIG PUSHES!
I was never truly worried. I know the girl is most likely the strongest among us.
Definitely stronger than I.
YES... HERE IT IS...
LET'S HOPE IT CAN SUCK AS WELL AS IT SPITS.
And yes, perhaps even stronger than Clark, who would be the first to admit he's next to worthless in a situation such as this.
HOLD ONTO ME, GIRL. SQUEEZE.
I THINK I HAVE A--WELL, THAT'S A LOT TO SEE.
I HAVE IT. I HAVE HIM.

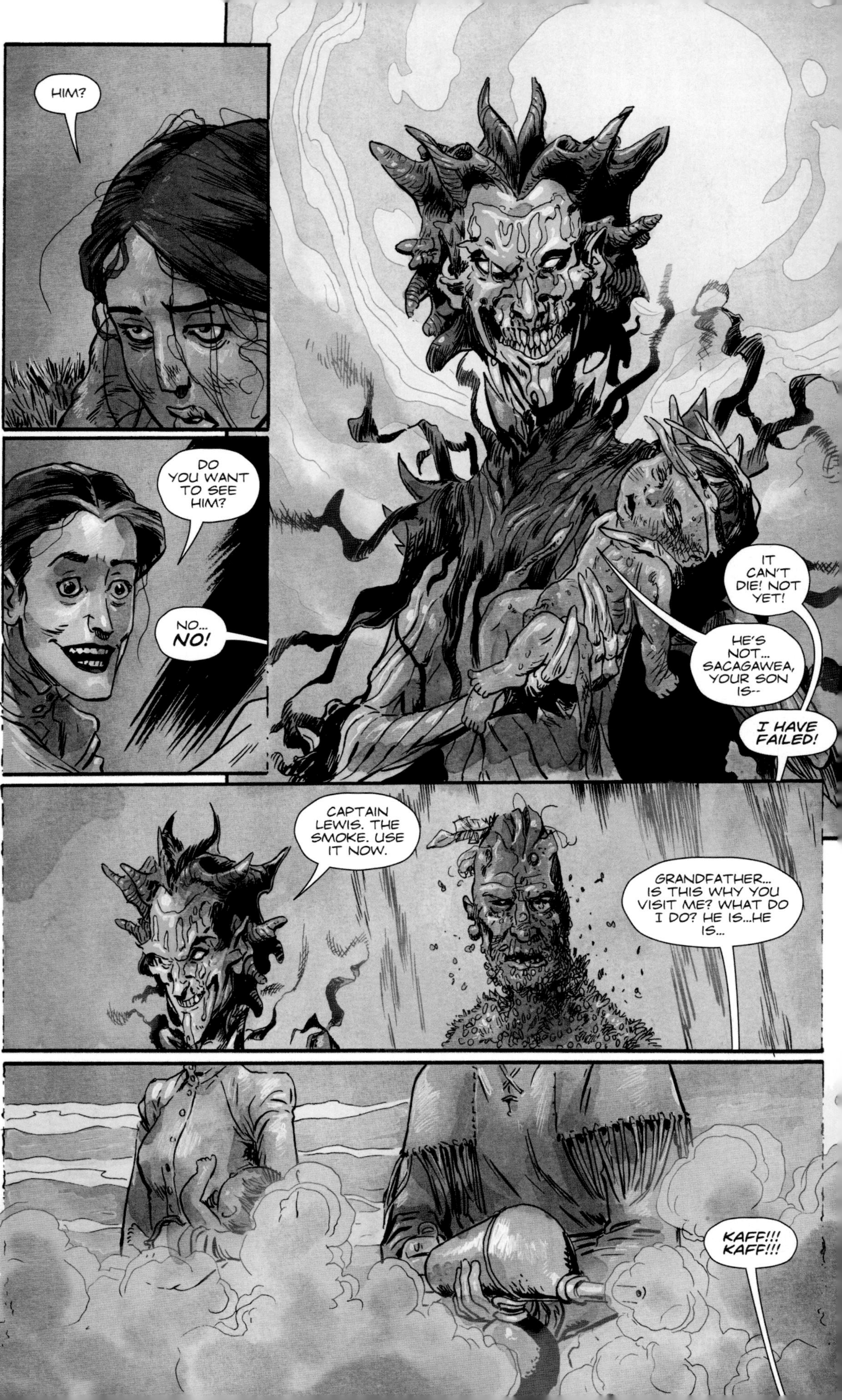
HIM?
DO YOU WANT TO SEE HIM?
NO... NO!
IT CAN'T DIE! NOT YET!
HE'S NOT... SACAGAWEA, YOUR SON IS--
I HAVE FAILED!
CAPTAIN LEWIS. THE SMOKE. USE IT NOW.
GRANDFATHER... IS THIS WHY YOU VISIT ME? WHAT DO I DO? HE IS...HE IS...
KAFF!!! KAFF!!!

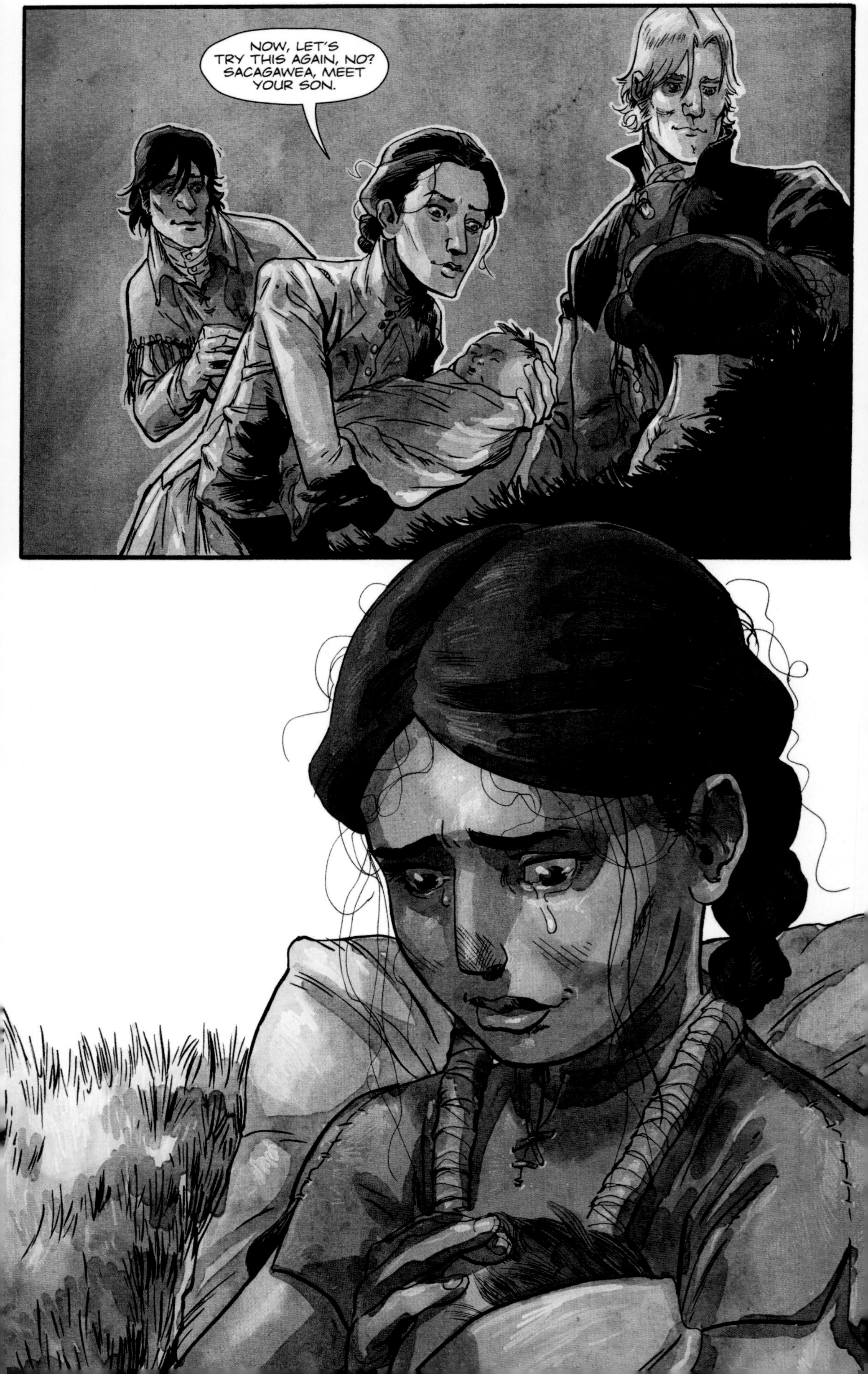
NOW, LET'S TRY THIS AGAIN, NO? SACAGAWEA, MEET YOUR SON.

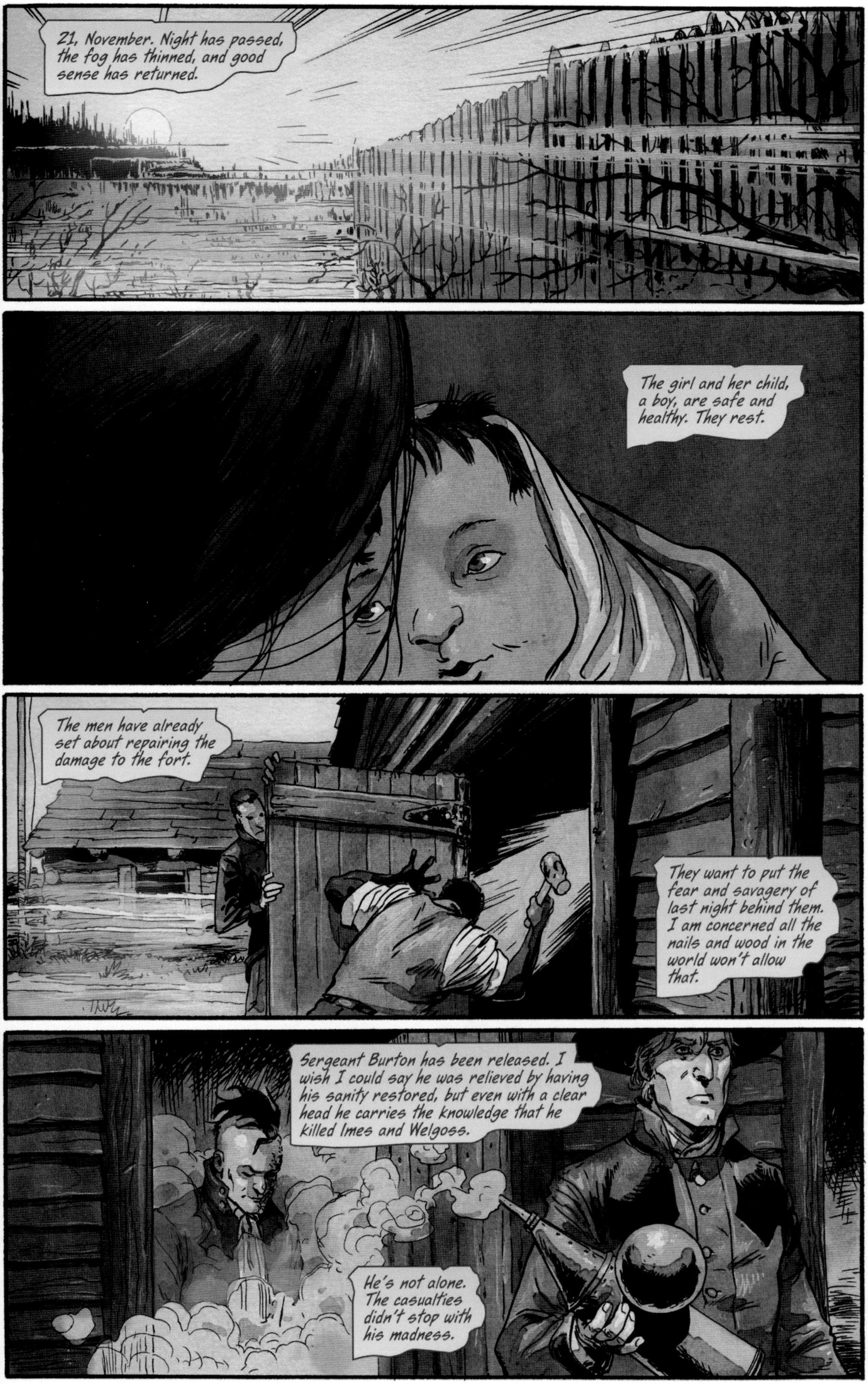
21, November. Night has passed, the fog has thinned, and good sense has returned.
The girl and her child, a boy, are safe and healthy. They rest.
The men have already set about repairing the damage to the fort.
They want to put the fear and savagery of last night behind them. I am concerned all the nails and wood in the world won't allow that.
Sergeant Burton has been released. I wish I could say he was relieved by having his sanity restored, but even with a clear head he carries the knowledge that he killed Imes and Welgoss.
He's not alone. The casualties didn't stop with his madness.

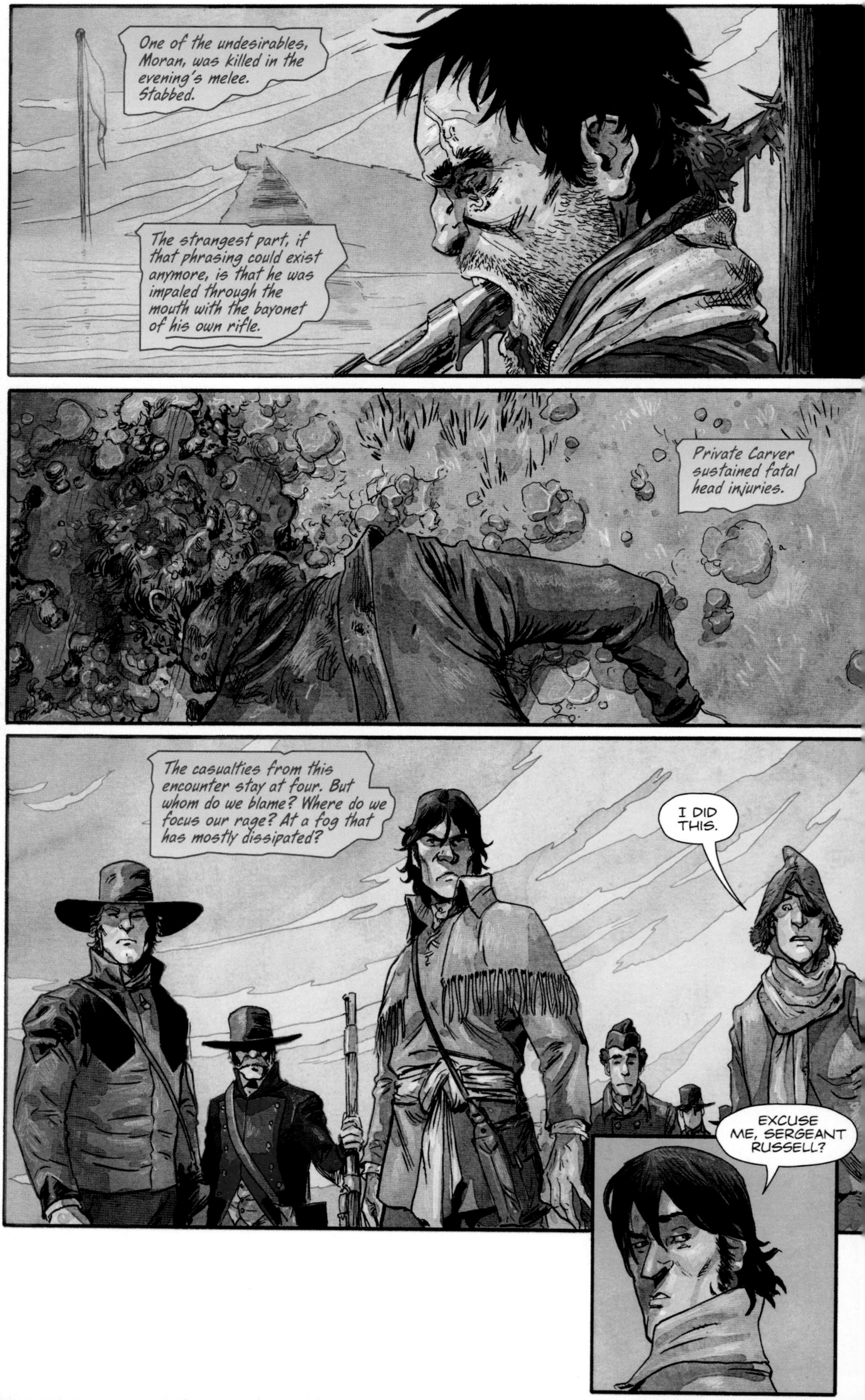
One of the undesirables, Moran, was killed in the evening's melee. Stabbed.
The strangest part, if that phrasing could exist anymore, is that he was impaled through the mouth with the bayonet of his own rifle.
Private Carver sustained fatal head injuries.
The casualties from this encounter stay at four. But whom do we blame? Where do we focus our rage? At a fog that has mostly dissipated?
I DID THIS.
EXCUSE ME, SERGEANT RUSSELL?

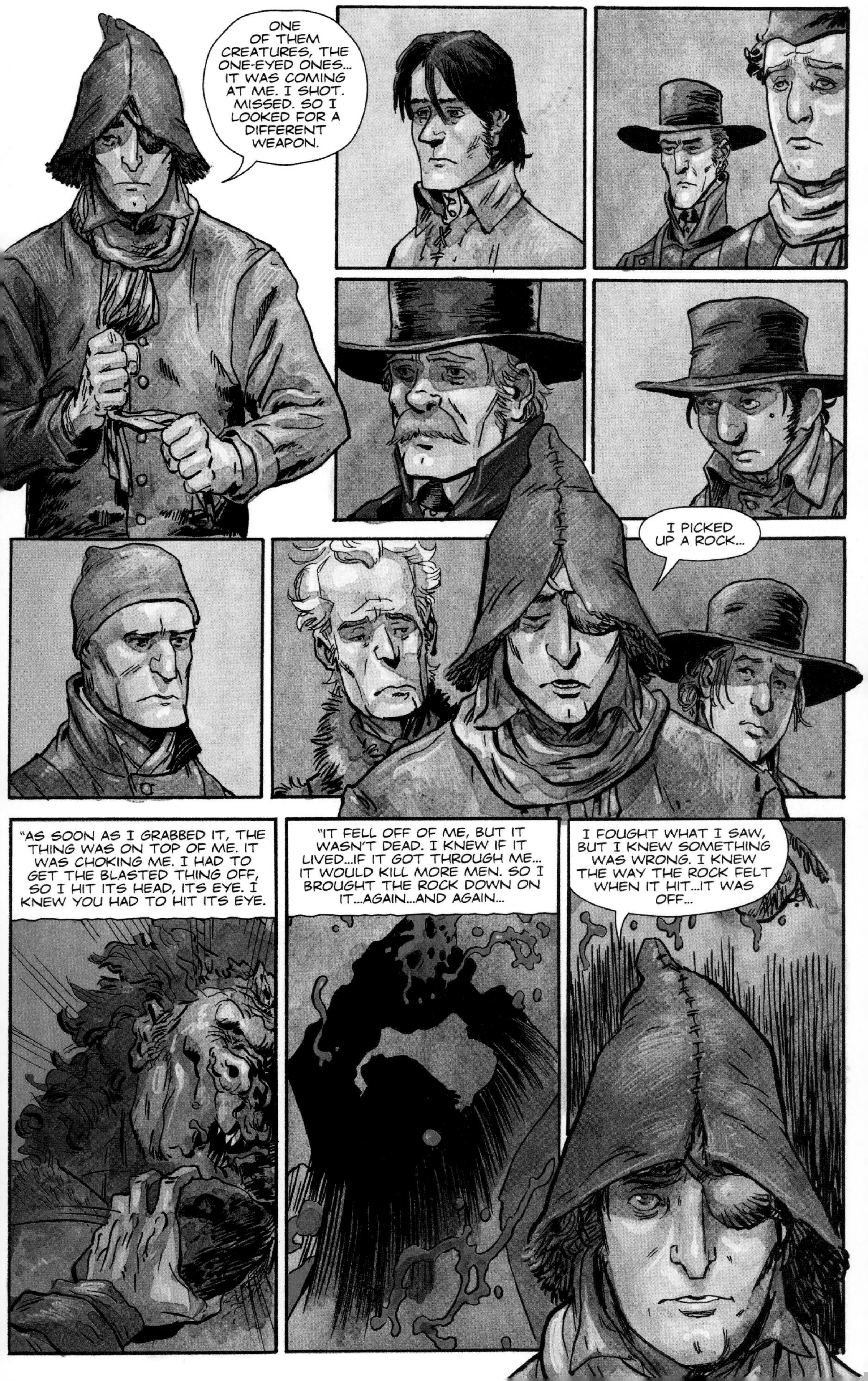
ONE OF THEM CREATURES, THE ONE-EYED ONES... IT WAS COMING AT ME. I SHOT. MISSED. SO I LOOKED FOR A DIFFERENT WEAPON.
I PICKED UP A ROCK...
"AS SOON AS I GRABBED IT, THE THING WAS ON TOP OF ME. IT WAS CHOKING ME. I HAD TO GET THE BLASTED THING OFF, SO I HIT ITS HEAD, ITS EYE. I KNEW YOU HAD TO HIT ITS EYE.
"IT FELL OFF OF ME, BUT IT WASN'T DEAD. I KNEW IF IT LIVED...IF IT GOT THROUGH ME... IT WOULD KILL MORE MEN. SO I BROUGHT THE ROCK DOWN ON IT...AGAIN...AND AGAIN...
I FOUGHT WHAT I SAW, BUT I KNEW SOMETHING WAS WRONG. I KNEW THE WAY THE ROCK FELT WHEN IT HIT...IT WAS OFF...

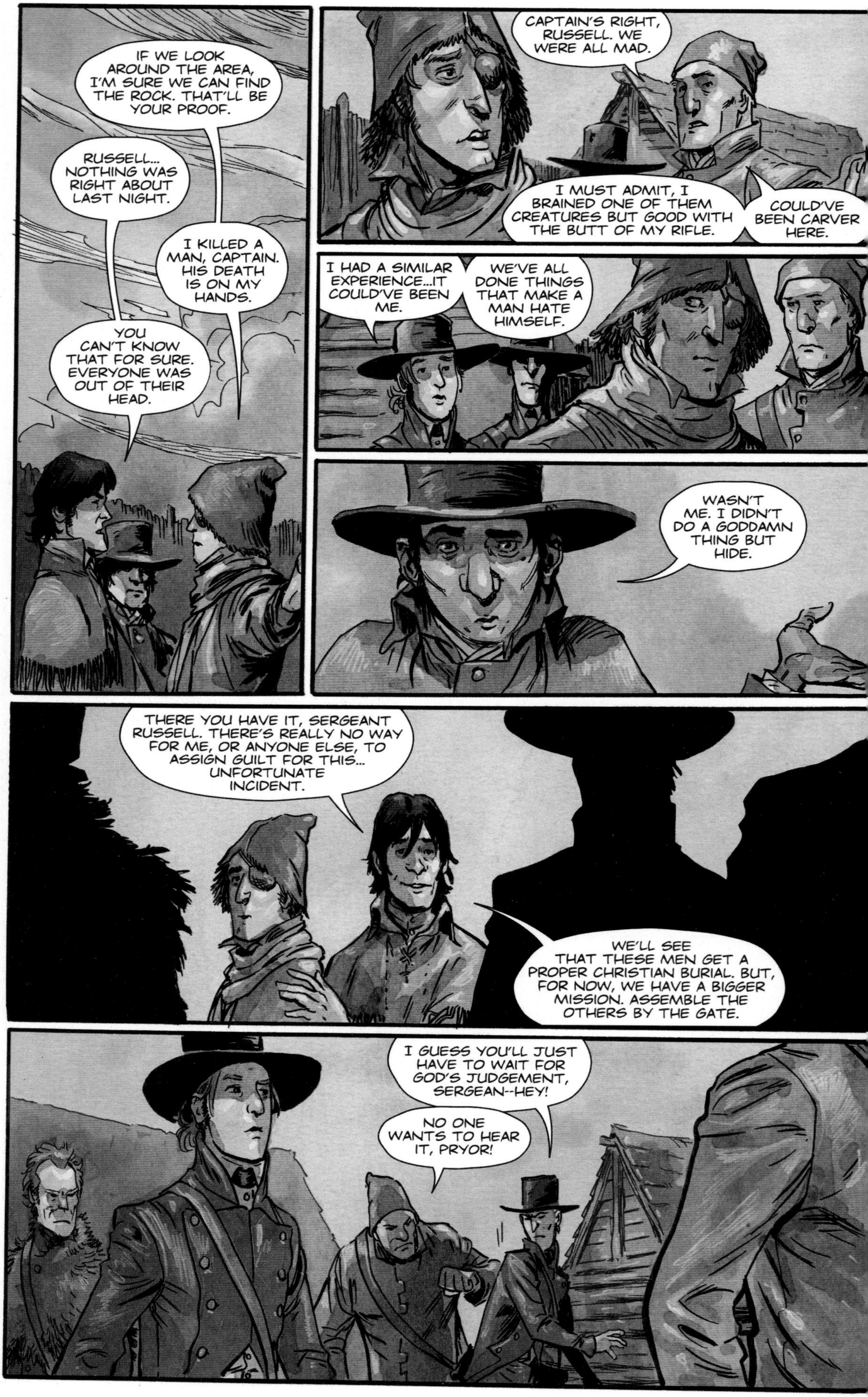
IF WE LOOK AROUND THE AREA, I'M SURE WE CAN FIND THE ROCK. THAT'LL BE YOUR PROOF.
RUSSELL... NOTHING WAS RIGHT ABOUT LAST NIGHT.
I KILLED A MAN, CAPTAIN. HIS DEATH IS ON MY HANDS.
YOU CAN'T KNOW THAT FOR SURE. EVERYONE WAS OUT OF THEIR HEAD.
CAPTAIN'S RIGHT, RUSSELL. WE WERE ALL MAD.
I MUST ADMIT, I BRAINED ONE OF THEM CREATURES BUT GOOD WITH THE BUTT OF MY RIFLE.
COULD'VE BEEN CARVER HERE.
I HAD A SIMILAR EXPERIENCE...IT COULD'VE BEEN ME.
WE'VE ALL DONE THINGS THAT MAKE A MAN HATE HIMSELF.
WASN'T ME. I DIDN'T DO A GODDAMN THING BUT HIDE.
THERE YOU HAVE IT, SERGEANT RUSSELL. THERE'S REALLY NO WAY FOR ME, OR ANYONE ELSE, TO ASSIGN GUILT FOR THIS... UNFORTUNATE INCIDENT.
WE'LL SEE THAT THESE MEN GET A PROPER CHRISTIAN BURIAL. BUT, FOR NOW, WE HAVE A BIGGER MISSION. ASSEMBLE THE OTHERS BY THE GATE.
I GUESS YOU'LL JUST HAVE TO WAIT FOR GOD'S JUDGEMENT, SERGEAN--HEY!
NO ONE WANTS TO HEAR IT, PRYOR!

*We spread out in pairs, searching for the source of the fog.*

REMEMBER. ONE SHOT FOR A STRUCTURE. TWO IF YOU COME ACROSS ANY SORT OF CREATURE.

PREFERABLY AIMED AT SAID CREATURE. LET'S TRY TO END THIS DAY WITHOUT ANOTHER CASUALTY.

I WONDER WHAT IT IS...WHERE THIS FOG CAME FROM.

YOU SHOULD PREPARE YOURSELF FOR DISAPPOINTMENT. WE'VE MADE SEVERAL SEARCHES AROUND THIS PERIMETER AND FOUND NOTHING.

WHAT ARE YOU SAYING? WE SHOULDN'T BOTHER?

OF COURSE NOT. BUT WE'VE DEVOTED MOST OF THE MEN TO THE TASK. THINGS ARE DIFFERENT NOW. WE NEED TO FOCUS ON KEEPING THE FORT SECURE. PROTECTING THE BABY. PROTECTING THE MISSION.

I'M AWARE OF THAT.

ARE YOU?

WHAT ARE YOU GETTING AT?

WHAT ARE YOU PREPARED TO DO TO PROTECT THE MISSION? TO PROTECT ITS CONFIDENTIALITY?

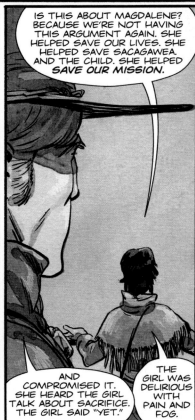

IS THIS ABOUT MAGDALENE? BECAUSE WE'RE NOT HAVING THIS ARGUMENT AGAIN. SHE HELPED SAVE OUR LIVES. SHE HELPED SAVE SACAGAWEA. AND THE CHILD. SHE HELPED *SAVE OUR MISSION.*

AND COMPROMISED IT. SHE HEARD THE GIRL TALK ABOUT SACRIFICE. THE GIRL SAID "YET."

THE GIRL WAS DELIRIOUS WITH PAIN AND FOG.

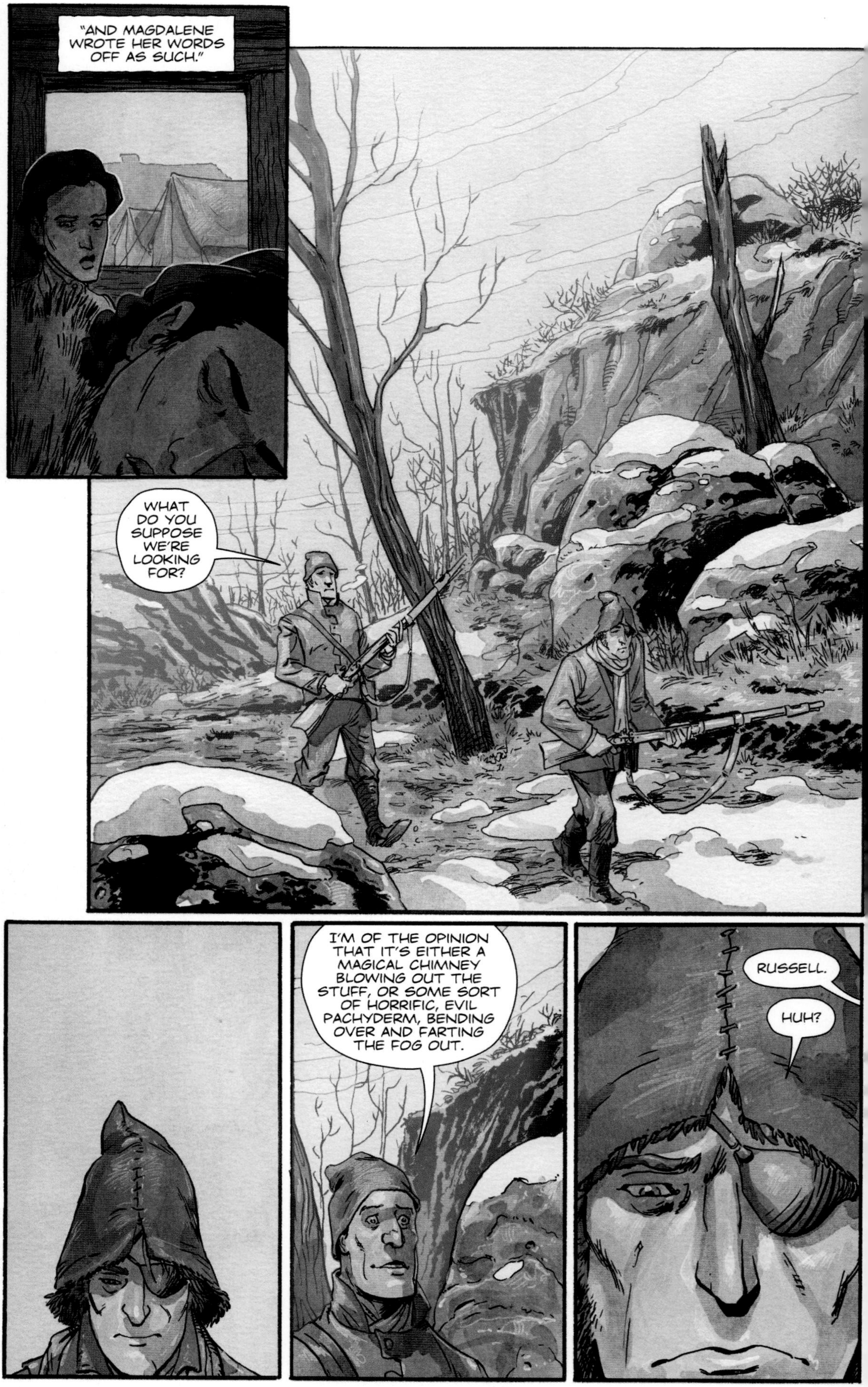
"AND MAGDALENE WROTE HER WORDS OFF AS SUCH."
WHAT DO YOU SUPPOSE WE'RE LOOKING FOR?
I'M OF THE OPINION THAT IT'S EITHER A MAGICAL CHIMNEY BLOWING OUT THE STUFF, OR SOME SORT OF HORRIFIC, EVIL PACHYDERM, BENDING OVER AND FARTING THE FOG OUT.
RUSSELL.
HUH?

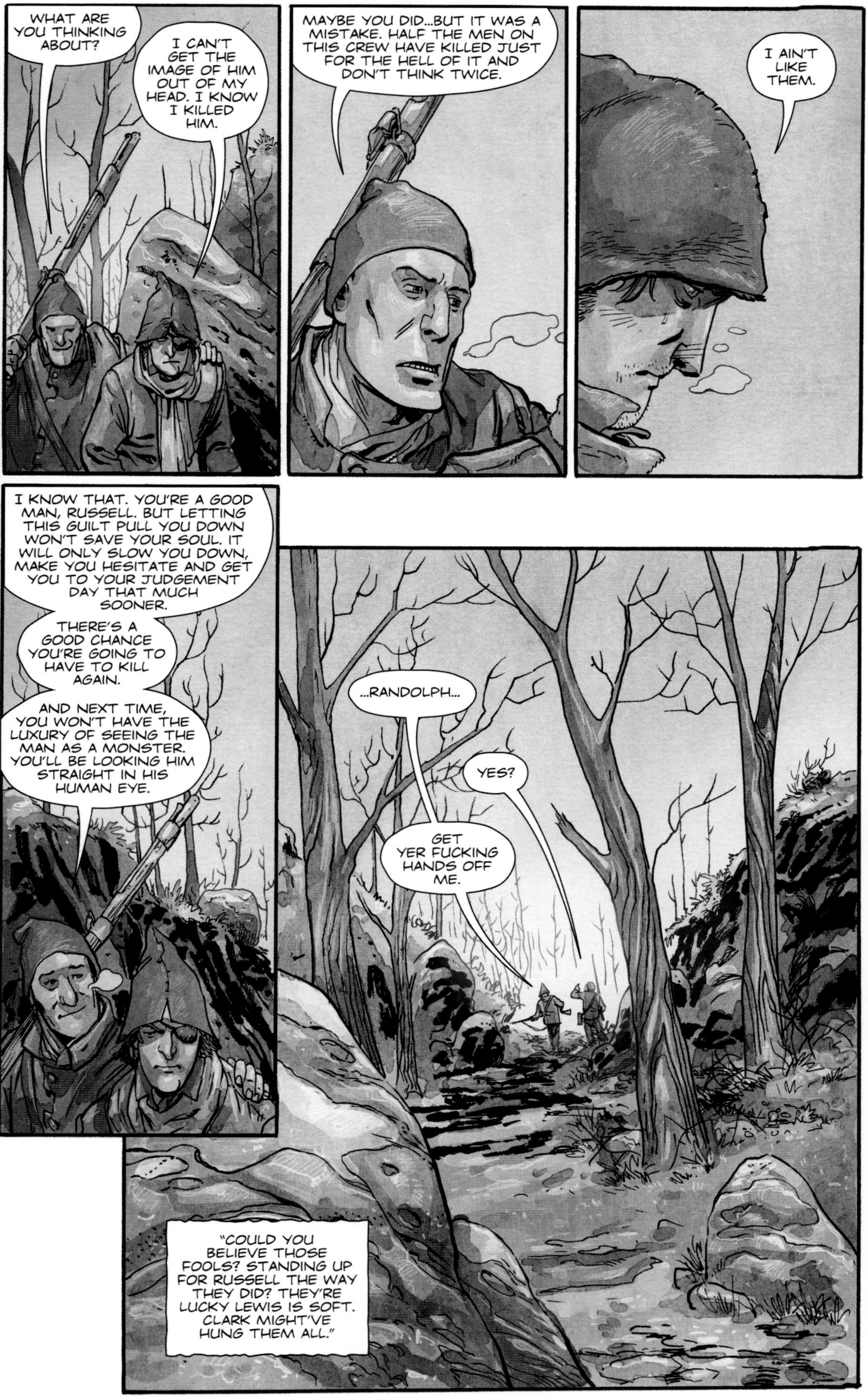
WHAT ARE YOU THINKING ABOUT?
I CAN'T GET THE IMAGE OF HIM OUT OF MY HEAD. I KNOW I KILLED HIM.
MAYBE YOU DID...BUT IT WAS A MISTAKE. HALF THE MEN ON THIS CREW HAVE KILLED JUST FOR THE HELL OF IT AND DON'T THINK TWICE.
I AIN'T LIKE THEM.
I KNOW THAT. YOU'RE A GOOD MAN, RUSSELL. BUT LETTING THIS GUILT PULL YOU DOWN WON'T SAVE YOUR SOUL. IT WILL ONLY SLOW YOU DOWN, MAKE YOU HESITATE AND GET YOU TO YOUR JUDGEMENT DAY THAT MUCH SOONER.
THERE'S A GOOD CHANCE YOU'RE GOING TO HAVE TO KILL AGAIN.
AND NEXT TIME, YOU WON'T HAVE THE LUXURY OF SEEING THE MAN AS A MONSTER. YOU'LL BE LOOKING HIM STRAIGHT IN HIS HUMAN EYE.
...RANDOLPH...
YES?
GET YER FUCKING HANDS OFF ME.
"COULD YOU BELIEVE THOSE FOOLS? STANDING UP FOR RUSSELL THE WAY THEY DID? THEY'RE LUCKY LEWIS IS SOFT. CLARK MIGHT'VE HUNG THEM ALL."

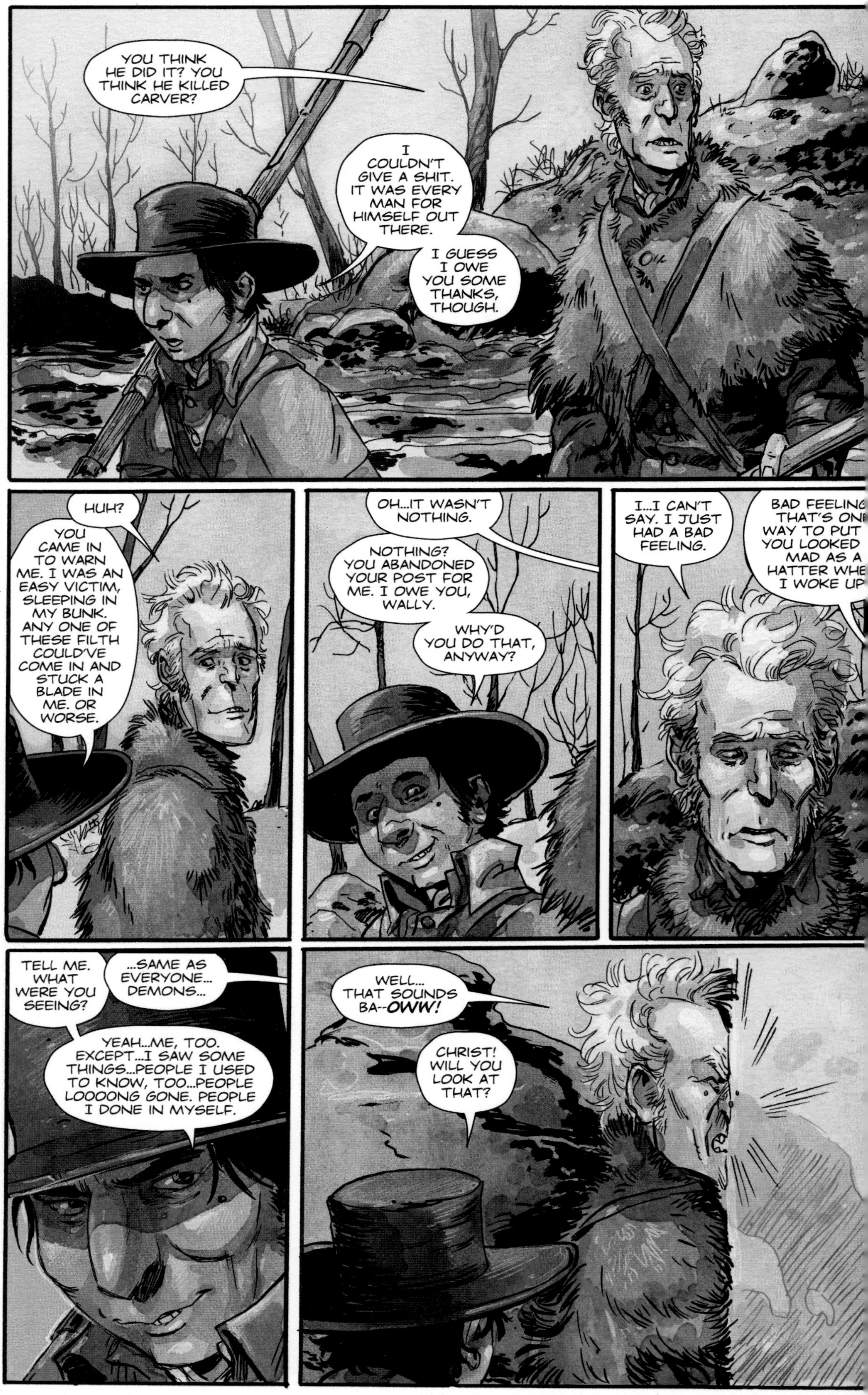

YOU THINK HE DID IT? YOU THINK HE KILLED CARVER?
I COULDN'T GIVE A SHIT. IT WAS EVERY MAN FOR HIMSELF OUT THERE.
I GUESS I OWE YOU SOME THANKS, THOUGH.
HUH?
YOU CAME IN TO WARN ME. I WAS AN EASY VICTIM, SLEEPING IN MY BUNK. ANY ONE OF THESE FILTH COULD'VE COME IN AND STUCK A BLADE IN ME. OR WORSE.
OH...IT WASN'T NOTHING.
NOTHING? YOU ABANDONED YOUR POST FOR ME. I OWE YOU, WALLY.
WHY'D YOU DO THAT, ANYWAY?
I...I CAN'T SAY. I JUST HAD A BAD FEELING.
BAD FEELIN THAT'S ON WAY TO PUT YOU LOOKED MAD AS A HATTER WHE I WOKE UP
TELL ME. WHAT WERE YOU SEEING?
...SAME AS EVERYONE... DEMONS...
YEAH...ME, TOO. EXCEPT...I SAW SOME THINGS...PEOPLE I USED TO KNOW, TOO...PEOPLE LOOOONG GONE. PEOPLE I DONE IN MYSELF.
WELL... THAT SOUNDS BA--*OWW!*
CHRIST! WILL YOU LOOK AT THAT?

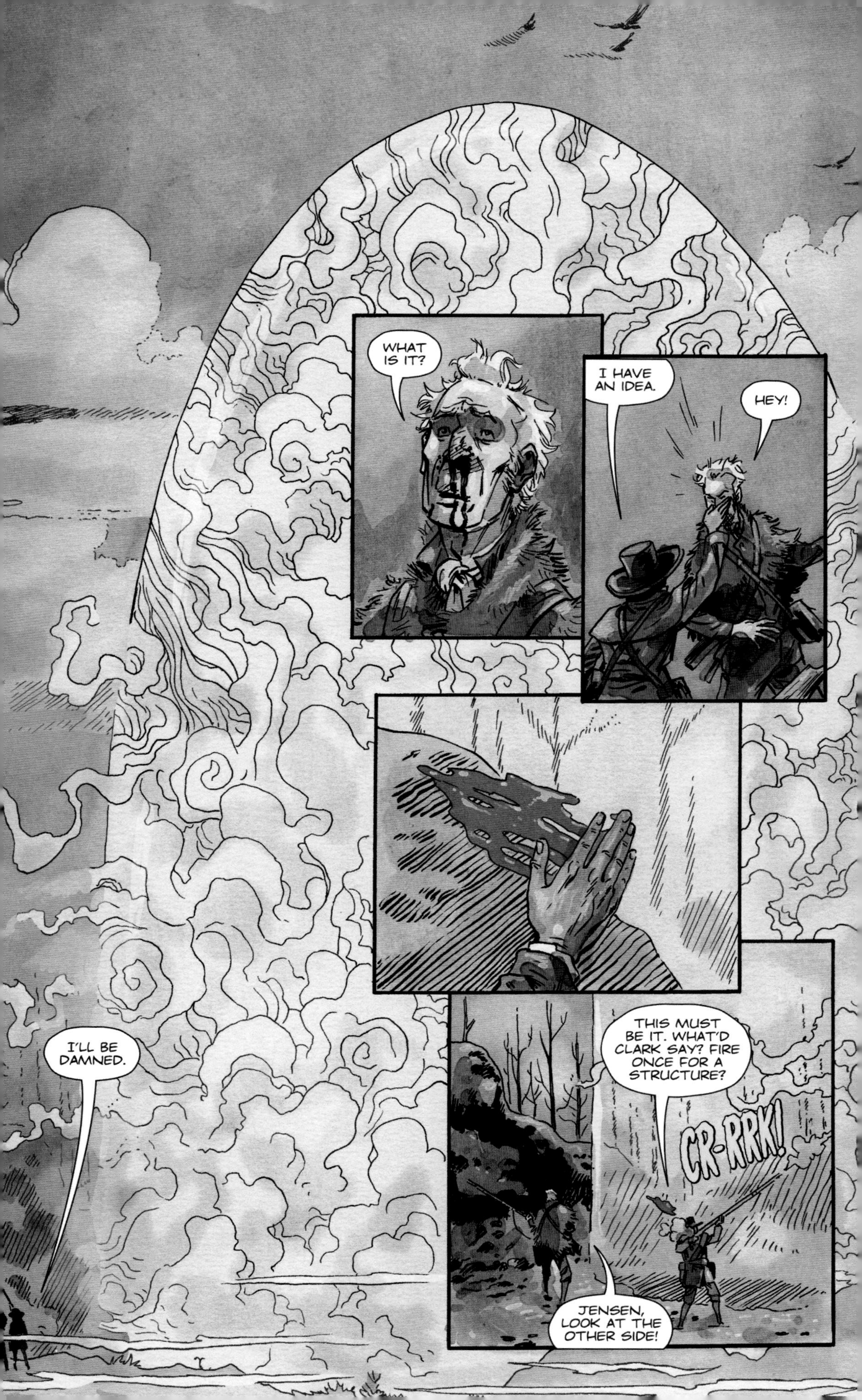
WHAT IS IT?
I HAVE AN IDEA.
HEY!
I'LL BE DAMNED.
THIS MUST BE IT. WHAT'D CLARK SAY? FIRE ONCE FOR A STRUCTURE?
CR-RRK!
JENSEN, LOOK AT THE OTHER SIDE!

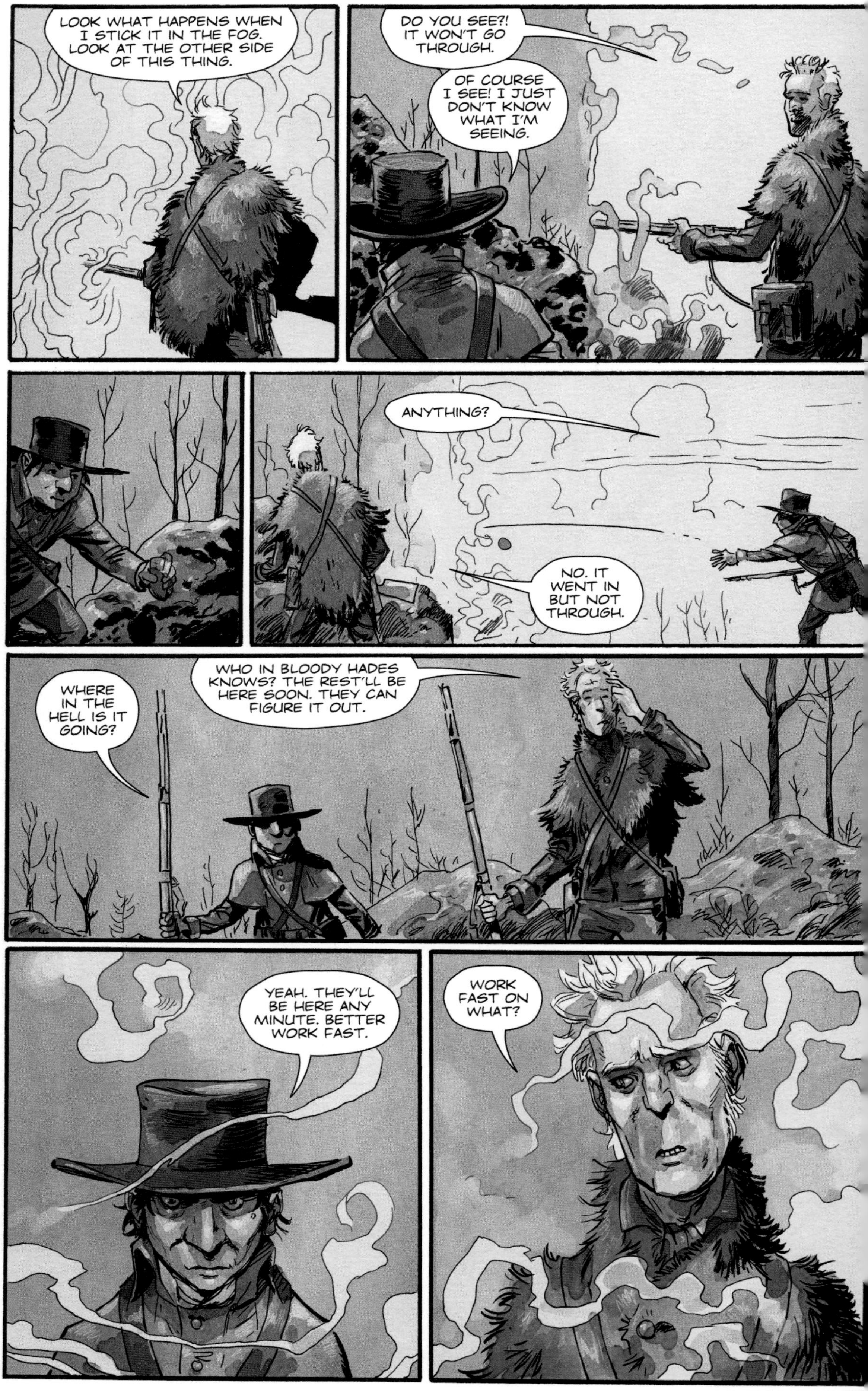
LOOK WHAT HAPPENS WHEN I STICK IT IN THE FOG. LOOK AT THE OTHER SIDE OF THIS THING.
DO YOU SEE?! IT WON'T GO THROUGH.
OF COURSE I SEE! I JUST DON'T KNOW WHAT I'M SEEING.
ANYTHING?
NO. IT WENT IN BUT NOT THROUGH.
WHERE IN THE HELL IS IT GOING?
WHO IN BLOODY HADES KNOWS? THE REST'LL BE HERE SOON. THEY CAN FIGURE IT OUT.
YEAH. THEY'LL BE HERE ANY MINUTE. BETTER WORK FAST.
WORK FAST ON WHAT?

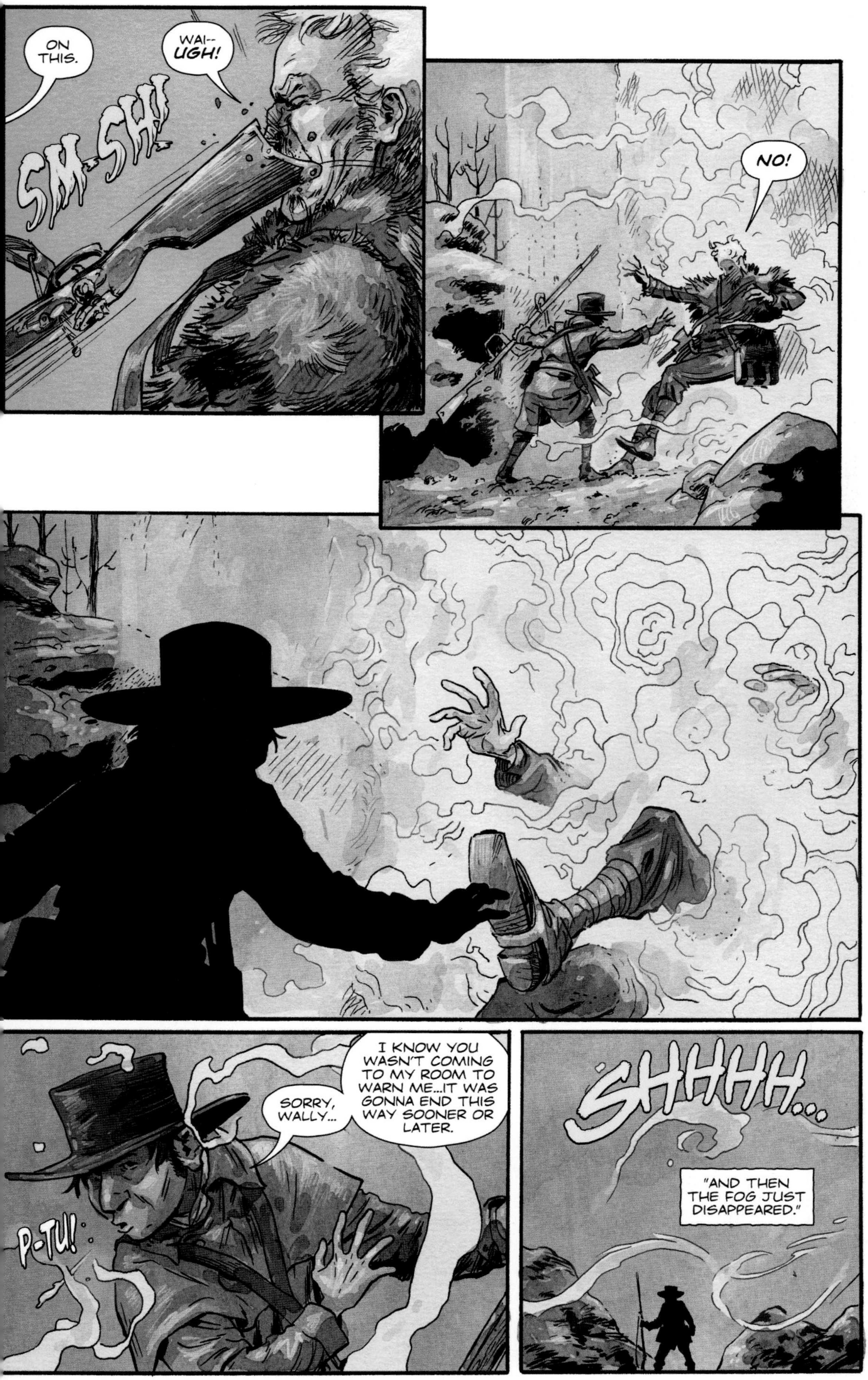
ON THIS.
WAI-- UGH!
SM-SH!
NO!
SORRY, WALLY...
I KNOW YOU WASN'T COMING TO MY ROOM TO WARN ME...IT WAS GONNA END THIS WAY SOONER OR LATER.
P-TU!
SHHHH...
"AND THEN THE FOG JUST DISAPPEARED."

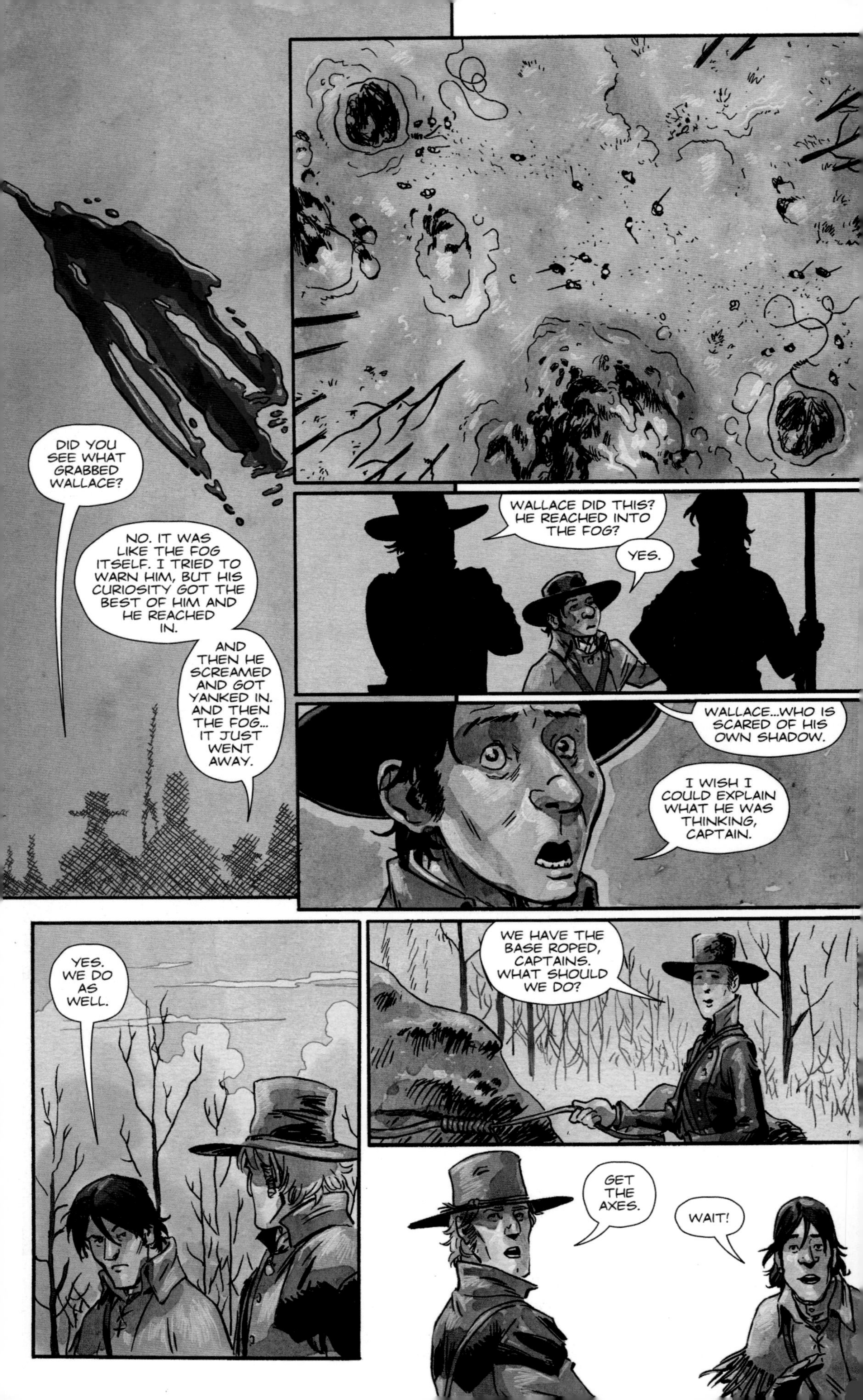
DID YOU SEE WHAT GRABBED WALLACE?
NO. IT WAS LIKE THE FOG ITSELF. I TRIED TO WARN HIM, BUT HIS CURIOSITY GOT THE BEST OF HIM AND HE REACHED IN.
AND THEN HE SCREAMED AND GOT YANKED IN. AND THEN THE FOG... IT JUST WENT AWAY.
WALLACE DID THIS? HE REACHED INTO THE FOG?
YES.
WALLACE...WHO IS SCARED OF HIS OWN SHADOW.
I WISH I COULD EXPLAIN WHAT HE WAS THINKING, CAPTAIN.
YES. WE DO AS WELL.
WE HAVE THE BASE ROPED, CAPTAINS. WHAT SHOULD WE DO?
GET THE AXES.
WAIT!

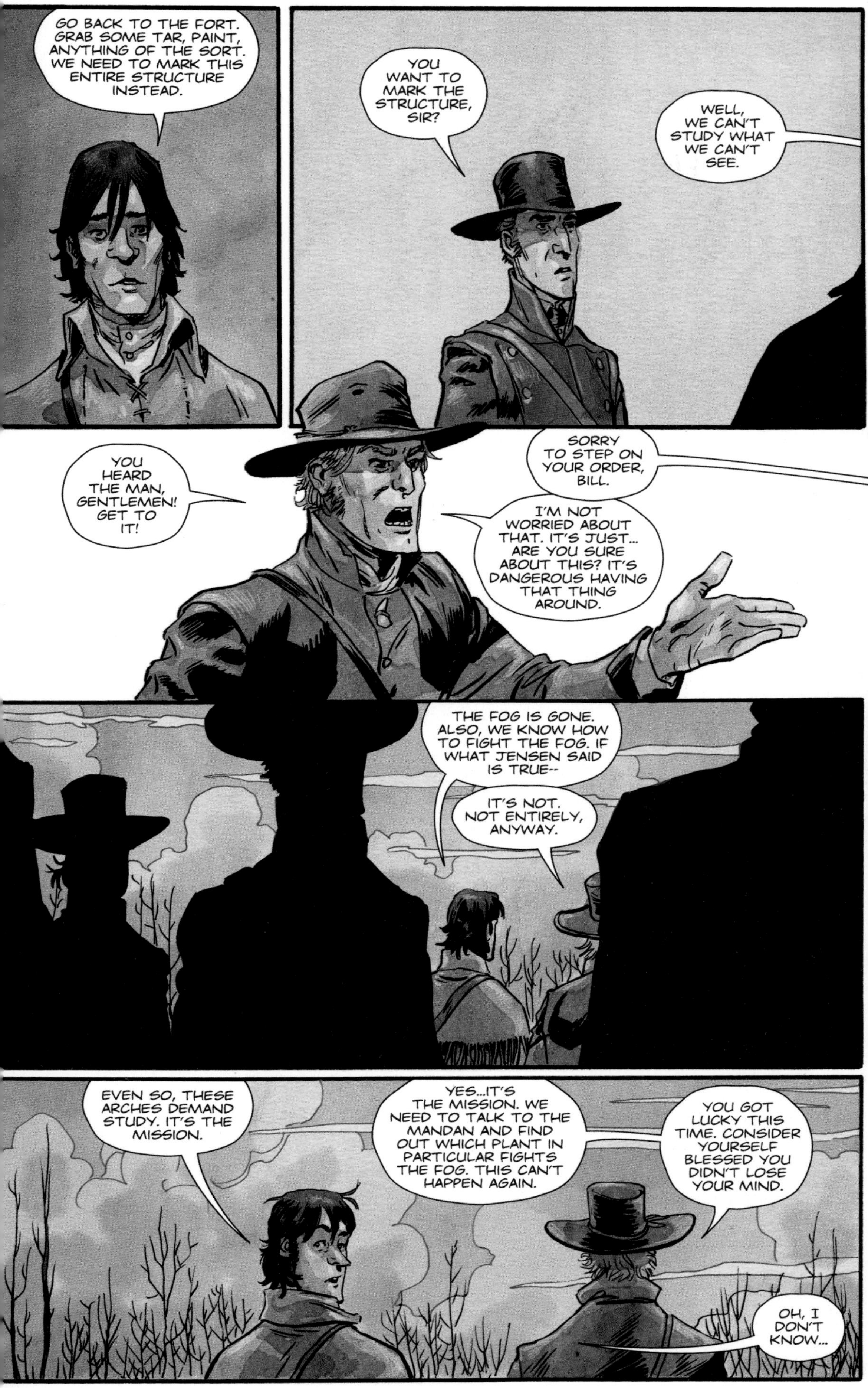
GO BACK TO THE FORT. GRAB SOME TAR, PAINT, ANYTHING OF THE SORT. WE NEED TO MARK THIS ENTIRE STRUCTURE INSTEAD.
YOU WANT TO MARK THE STRUCTURE, SIR?
WELL, WE CAN'T STUDY WHAT WE CAN'T SEE.
YOU HEARD THE MAN, GENTLEMEN! GET TO IT!
SORRY TO STEP ON YOUR ORDER, BILL.
I'M NOT WORRIED ABOUT THAT. IT'S JUST... ARE YOU SURE ABOUT THIS? IT'S DANGEROUS HAVING THAT THING AROUND.
THE FOG IS GONE. ALSO, WE KNOW HOW TO FIGHT THE FOG. IF WHAT JENSEN SAID IS TRUE--
IT'S NOT. NOT ENTIRELY, ANYWAY.
EVEN SO, THESE ARCHES DEMAND STUDY. IT'S THE MISSION.
YES...IT'S THE MISSION. WE NEED TO TALK TO THE MANDAN AND FIND OUT WHICH PLANT IN PARTICULAR FIGHTS THE FOG. THIS CAN'T HAPPEN AGAIN.
YOU GOT LUCKY THIS TIME. CONSIDER YOURSELF BLESSED YOU DIDN'T LOSE YOUR MIND.
OH, I DON'T KNOW...

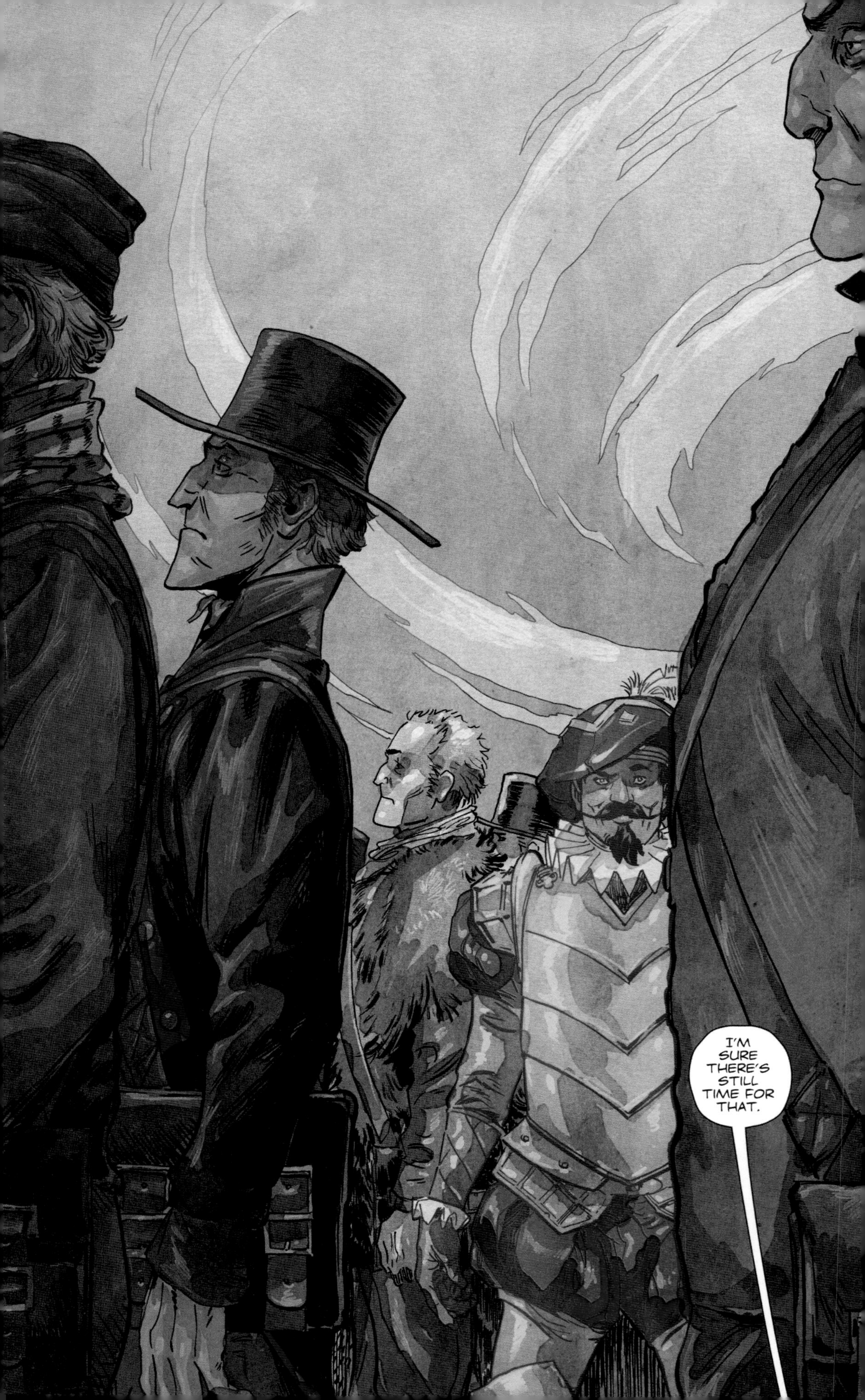
I'M SURE THERE'S STILL TIME FOR THAT.

*To be continued...*

# For more tales from Robert Kirkman and Skybound

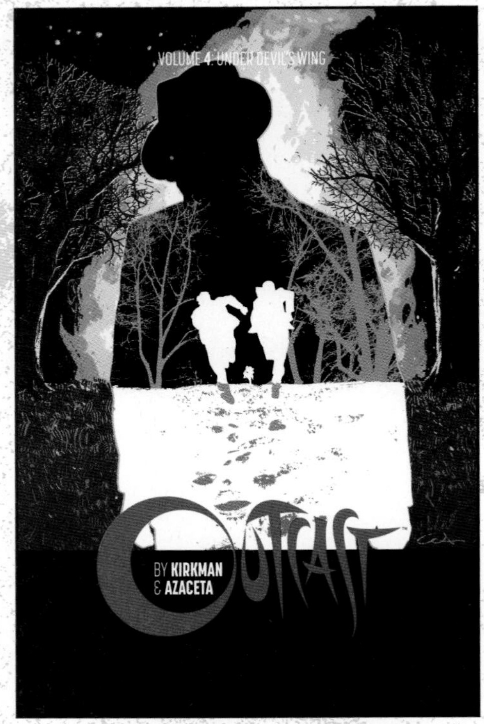
VOLUME 4: UNDER DEVIL'S WING
BY KIRKMAN & AZACETA
OUTCAST

**VOL. 1: A DARKNESS SURROUNDS HIM TP**
ISBN: 978-1-63215-053-0
$9.99

**VOL. 2: A VAST AND UNENDING RUIN TP**
ISBN: 978-1-63215-448-4
$14.99

**VOL. 3: THIS LITTLE LIGHT TP**
ISBN: 978-1-63215-693-8
$14.99

**VOL. 4: UNDER DEVIL'S WING TP**
ISBN: 978-1-5343-0050-7
$14.99

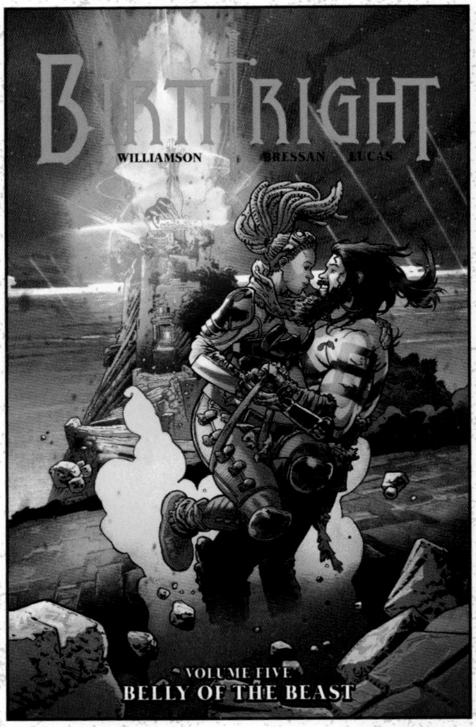
BIRTHRIGHT
WILLIAMSON BRESSAN LUCAS
VOLUME FIVE
BELLY OF THE BEAST

**VOL. 1: HOMECOMING TP**
ISBN: 978-1-63215-231-2
$9.99

**VOL. 2: CALL TO ADVENTURE TP**
ISBN: 978-1-63215-446-0
$12.99

**VOL. 3: ALLIES AND ENEMIES TP**
ISBN: 978-1-63215-683-9
$12.99

**VOL. 4: FAMILY HISTORY TP**
ISBN: 978-1-63215-871-0
$12.99

**VOL. 5: BELLY OF THE BEAST TP**
ISBN: 978-1-53430-218-1
$12.99

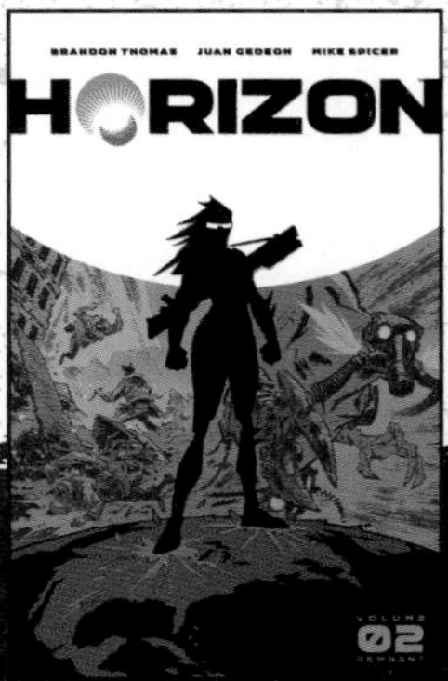
BRANDON THOMAS JUAN GEDEON MIKE SPICER
HORIZON
VOLUME 02

**VOL. 1: REPRISAL TP**
ISBN: 978-1-5343-0047-7
$9.99

**VOL. 2: REMNANT TP**
ISBN: 978-1-5343-0227-3
$12.99

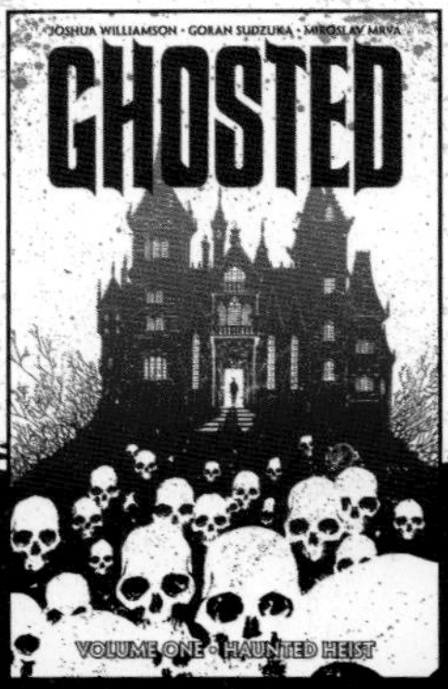
JOSHUA WILLIAMSON · GORAN SUDZUKA · MIROSLAV MRVA
GHOSTED
VOLUME ONE · HAUNTED HEIST

**VOL. 1: HAUNTED HEIST TP**
ISBN: 978-1-60706-836-5
$9.99

**VOL. 2: BOOKS OF THE DEAD TP**
ISBN: 978-1-63215-046-2
$12.99

**VOL. 3: DEATH WISH TP**
ISBN: 978-1-63215-051-6
$12.99

**VOL. 4: GHOST TOWN TP**
ISBN: 978-1-63215-317-3
$12.99

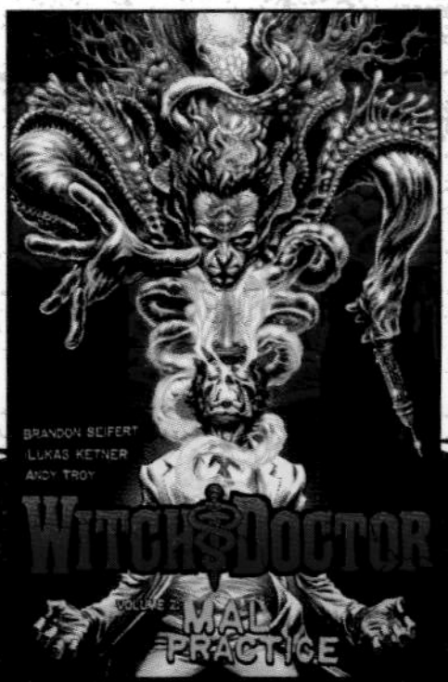
BRANDON SEIFERT
LUKAS KETNER
ANDY TROY
WITCH DOCTOR
VOLUME 2: MAL PRACTICE

**VOL. 1: UNDER THE KNIFE TP**
ISBN: 978-1-60706-441-1
$12.99

**VOL. 2: MAL PRACTICE TP**
ISBN: 978-1-60706-693-4
$14.99

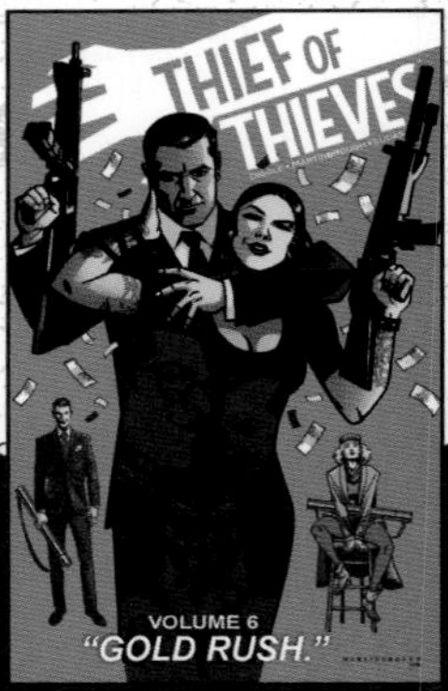
THIEF OF THIEVES
VOLUME 6
"GOLD RUSH."

**VOL. 1: "I QUIT."**
ISBN: 978-1-60706-592-0
$14.99

**VOL. 2: "HELP ME."**
ISBN: 978-1-60706-676-7
$14.99

**VOL. 3: "VENICE."**
ISBN: 978-1-60706-844-0
$14.99

**VOL. 4: "THE HIT LIST."**
ISBN: 978-1-63215-037-0
$14.99

**VOL. 5: "TAKE ME."**
ISBN: 978-1-63215-401-9
$14.99

**VOL. 6: "GOLD RUSH."**
ISBN: 978-1-53430-037-8
$14.99